POLITICAL DYNAMICS

IMPACT ON NURSES AND NURSING

POLITICAL DYNAMICS

IMPACT ON NURSES AND NURSING

Grace L. Deloughery, R.N., Ph.D.

Kristine M. Gebbie, R.N., M.N.

THE C. V. MOSBY COMPANY

Saint Louis   1975

Library of Congress Cataloging in Publication Data

Deloughery, Grace L   1933-
    Political dynamics: impact on nurses and nursing.

    Includes index.
    1. Nurses and nursing—Social aspects. 2. Political
participation. I. Gebbie, Kristine M., joint author.
II. Title. [DNLM: 1. Nursing. 2. Politics. WY100
D362p]
RT42.D44   301.24′2   74-22120
ISBN 0-8016-1245-4

CB/CB/B   9   8   7   6   5   4   3   2   1

PREFACE

Many would doubt that, in today's activist world, anyone need be challenged to action; yet that is what this book intends to do. Nurses are just beginning to become aware of the intricacies of the political world and of how the dynamics of power shifts there can ultimately affect even individual practice at the patient's bedside. There is a stage that follows awareness for many nurses in which the problems of politics are known but no behavioral change takes place. It may be due to lack of sufficient knowledge or direction to effect change. During this period, feelings of futility may consume the energy needed to become committed to political action. Feelings of futility result from identifying oneself as the weaker opponent in a number of simultaneous conflicts: doctor-nurse, man-woman, more educated—less educated, highly organized—less organized, higher paid—lower paid. The challenge to action is not a call to mimic tactics that have been used successfully by previously dominant groups. Action taken must be based on thoughtful consideration of all factors leading to success in the political realm.

All nurses are a part of political dynamics every day, and many of them are becoming aware that they understand but little of the political process in which they are involved or the ways in which they react to it. It is possible that the whole range of responses that nurses elicit as they move into new roles, into more basic research including the physical sciences, and into making a more equal share of health care decisions are an expression of political realities. In addition to the negative reactions nurses receive from others, their own responses might include a repression and denial of any feelings, a loss of self-esteem and regard for colleagues, a desire to appease those regarded as higher in the power structure, or an abandonment of sexual identity. Although nurses are not all women, nursing as a profession is identified with "femaleness" and many nurses are at a loss for ways to combine the caring, nurturing aspects of nursing with a more aggressive role in the larger world.

Any member of American society is part of many political relationships, even though an individual may not be aware of them as such. Nurses, collectively and individually, are becoming more aware of the political system and concerned with understanding and affecting it. They have been exposed to the flood of newspaper and periodical articles, radio and television broadcasts, and best-selling books that reveal a growing concern for increasing the breadth of participation in decision making throughout our social structure. This is reflected in such phrases as "grass-roots politics," "consumer participation," "community involvement," "people power," and "women's liberation." Despite the use of the terms there is a lack of understanding. A discussion of political systems should not be concerned with partisan politics or election campaigns. It refers to power relationships and decision-making forces among any group of people composing a social network or system. Political dynamics can be seen in some forms even at the level of the family, although the theories are rarely applied there, and move up through formal and informal organizations to the realm of international relations.

Although each individual nurse belongs to and has a role in many political systems, a professional group such as nursing has a role and identity beyond that of its individual members. Nursing is a profession that draws on a theoretical base to provide service to individuals. The unique activities of nursing are those that assist individuals to maintain as healthy a balance as possible in the face of physical and emotional stress. Nursing is interdependent with medicine and all the allied health sciences. The term *interdependence* is not used to smooth over an acceptance of dependency but reflects an expectation that nurses assume and will be allowed to assume a fully collaborative role as they demonstrate their readiness and capacity to do so. The central focus on meeting the needs of the individual patient that gives direction to nursing in patient care also gives direction to the role of nursing in the political realm. In any apportionment of power, the nurse has the capacity and obligation to allow and assist patients or potential patients to participate in decisions that may affect their ultimate health or illness. This capacity grows out of the knowledge gained through those close relationships with individual patients that form the heart of nursing practice. Within any political system, the role of nursing continues to be caring for and meeting the needs of those whose capacity to meet their own health needs is affected by the functioning of the system. Many people must participate if the idealized American system of decision making is to exist in fact. Simply participating enthusiastically in anything and everything is not enough. Certain lessons must be learned, and if learned in advance, they can save much crushed idealism and many hours of futile energy expenditure. If, however, the work of involving more persons in health care decisions is done and done well, this should ultimately result in more gain for nursing and nurses than vast amounts of efforts expended on promoting "the profession of nursing" as an entity.

We contend that the nature of human interaction is such that involvement in political activity is essential. This does not mean, however, that this book is a statement of our own partisan political viewpoint. We hope that the readers will represent the entire spectrum of political philosophy, from ultraconservatism to extreme liberalism, present in our American society. We are presenting a theoretical framework that should enable a nurse with any partisan conviction to be more effective in any attempts to broaden the participation of individuals in political decision making.

Some readers may doubt the feasibility of such an attempt. One fact may lend credence: after collaborating in the classroom, public forums, and professional writing on this subject for a number of years, neither of us yet knows the full range of the other's partisan political commitments. This has remained true, not because of any dramatic effort to keep secrets or because of nonparticipation in partisan issues, but simply because such knowledge is not necessary to the presentation and comprehension of the subject matter of this book. It remains the responsibility of the readers, as we have left it with our students and colleagues in the past, to utilize the materials within any political context. We believe that they will be stronger and more effective because of it. The plenitude of new material facing the practitioner of nursing who is concerned with remaining abreast of the latest advances in providing patient care might discourage the addition of this whole new world to one's scope of awareness. This may be a real factor or an excuse for avoiding an assuredly stressful encounter. Even if one accepts the potential of such study, it may seem impossible to fit it into any schedule or curriculum, especially with the abundance of basic and advanced scientific data that must be understood for the practice of the profession. If the political context of nursing is ignored, however, the number and scope of opportunities for the practice of nursing may well decrease. Thoughtful engagement in politics will lead to true interdependence of nurses with others in the health professions.

A word of acknowledgment goes to those who stimulated the preparation of this manuscript. These include graduate and undergraduate nursing students who wanted to "get involved," fellow nursing practitioners who "didn't know where to go," and graceful antagonists, nurses and others, who challenged our right and capacity to engage in constructive conflict as nurses. We hope that the material presented here will provide these individuals and others like them with a rationale for activity in political systems and encouragement to begin, as well as an understanding of the reasons for our persistence.

Grace L. Deloughery
Kristine M. Gebbie

CONTENTS

Men could learn a lesson from
The lowly turtles who crawl about;
And note they never get anyplace
Until they stick their necks out!

RUTH M. WALSH[1]

INTRODUCTION

This book is intended to enhance nurses' understanding of those political dynamics that have in the past and will continue to influence nurses as they interact among themselves and with others in the world about them. Once one begins observing life in a social system, one is observing political interactions, some complex, some simple. The movement of many people toward involvement in activities that will either improve their own lives or the overall quality of life necessitates not only their observing but also interacting with one or more aspects of some political system. Nurses, as individuals or groups, are consciously or unconsciously deeply involved in this process. Those who are only unconsciously involved are well described in the following rhyme:

Restrainer

I lead a very stainless life
And have from the beginning.
A pillar, I, of rectitude—
I never think of sinning.

Oh, not for me the wanton sins
That others may parade to.
It's not that I'm a saintly soul
It's just that I'm afraid to.

GEORGIE STARBUCK GALBRAITH[2]

Regardless of the degree of awareness, energy is expended in political interactions. This energy has the potential of contributing to the achievement, or failure to achieve, an improving condition of life, either one's own or that of others. The better understanding one has of political dynamics the greater the opportunity for effective action. In addition to understanding political dynamics it is useful to understand how one's personal and professional identity can inhibit or enhance one's actions. It is then possible to identify problems that are amenable to change by way of the political process and to work toward their resolution.

Following this brief introduction to professionals, professionalism, and politics the content is divided into four major sections:

1. Theoretical presentation of political science and organizational theory. To enhance accuracy, these will be given in the language and structure of the academic disciplines that developed them as much as possible; some accompanying illustrations are presented to facilitate "translation" into the experience of nurses.

2. Presentation of "power" as a theoretical construct and a force in everyday life. This

1

is focused around practical questions of who has power, how one recognizes powerful people, and what those people do with their power.

3. Description of those dilemmas encountered by the nurse because of issues such as "professionalism," "uniform function," and "ethics in the provision of health care" as well as personal philosophy and beliefs. We do not believe we have created new problems. Rather we hope to articulate those that have existed not just as a statement of fact but with discussion of the dynamics behind them. The sometimes subtle influence of these issues and the lack of awareness thereof have been partially causative of the current state of affairs.

4. Discussion of possible courses of action that might follow the understanding of oneself relative to power and political interaction. No one specific course of action will be prescribed. Rather it is expected that, subsequent to this discussion, each nurse will move politically in directions that seem comfortable and work successfully.

The imposition of rigid definitions is in itself a political act: an expression of power on the part of the definer, and the acceptance of that power by those who use that term as stipulated. The lack of definition is not necessarily a conscientious avoidance of the misuse of power. The conflict generated during communication that is attempted without a common understanding of terms has the potential for more harm than have the limitations of definition. The latitude between anarchy and dictatorship is sufficiently wide that the goal of making distinctions between them seems realistic. Therefore at the risk of sounding extremely pedantic and limiting the reader's scope, we will begin by introducing some basic terminology. *Webster's Seventh New Collegiate Dictionary*[3] points out that the word *politics* refers to the art and science of holding control of a governmental unit, political affairs, or business through artful and often dishonest practices. A secondary meaning given is "the total complex of relations between man and society." Although cogni-

zant of the former, it is more the latter sense of the word that we employ in this book.

The complex of relations being discussed is understood primarily as involving power, the amount of power that each individual has in relation to those around him, and the aggregation of power in a large or small number of institutions, including but not limited to governments. The corresponding adjective, *political,* may be used to refer to any other person, system, or activity that is involved in or related to this network of power relationships. It is unfortunate that for many the negative connotations of the terms *politics* and *political* come most readily to mind.

A politician is usually described as one versed in the art or science of government, engaged in party politics, or primarily interested in political offices from selfish or other narrow, short-run interests. A person will be labeled a *politician* if it is believed that his skill is being used to promote his own selfish advantage. Someone equally skilled in politics or the manipulation of power but believed to be doing so for more altruistic motives is called a *statesman.* The appearance of the individual's motives may be altruistic but, whether by design or not, also promotes some selfish or personal desires. Regardless of whether the motives are either partially or purely selfish or altruistic, the individual is a politician. There is no other word than politics, however, that conveys the necessary concept of man's attempt to deal with his fellows within organized units. The words have further utility because there is so little that occurs in contemporary society that is not related in some way to government or public affairs, and politics implies a public process.

To compound the matter these terms are commonly used in the course of everyday events to describe the activities of persons or groups who are attempting to organize one another to achieve some desired good. They are pertinent to group activities within settings such as health care organizations, and, in fact, groups such as the Medical Committee on Human Rights and the Nurses' Coalition for Action in Politics openly acknowledge their political nature.

The term *political system* refers to any group of persons and their activities as they relate to one another in an organized fashion within any given sphere of action. A speech on health matters given by a city councilman in California and the public health advisory board of a county in Georgia may both be "political" in that they are related to the governing or organization of public affairs, but they are not a political system. Within one city or county the health department, the public health advisory board, and the city or county council as they interact to affect the health of the people compose a political system. Such systems have often been masculine domains, with the inclusion of women being primarily as objects in these domains. Much of the energy expended by the women's liberation and feminist movements is directed toward opening political systems to both sexes. Not only are the politicians changing but the gender of the process seems to have changed. Weinstein[4] differentiates the Pre-Enlightenment Period from the Introspective Period on the basis of separation of emotional and abstract factors. The emotional, internal aspect is equated with the maternal (feminine) role, whereas the abstract external aspect (characterized by rationality, self-discipline, and emotional constraint) is equated with the paternal (masculine) role. The political system, as a result of the political and industrial revolutions, has undergone a differentiation. The modern political system demonstrates a more instrumental role, concerned with achievement of specific goals and exercise of control on the social or interpersonal level rather than the achievement of power over others and doing so as though they were nonhuman objects. Recognition that power may be achieved through factors other than the manipulation of external forces, mastery, rationality, and conscious control facilitated the active participation of many formerly excluded from the political system such as women, nurses, and various legal and ethnic minorities.

As already stated, it is the exercise of power over others, or in relation to others, that makes activity political. Power, meaning the ability or strength to act, in this area of political dynamics usually means not just individual power but delegated power that is present in those who represent some group or viewpoint. The more equal the distribution of power among those with conflicting viewpoints the more likely it is that the resolution or compromise will reflect portions of all the original viewpoints. As will be discussed in Unit I, the American political system is ostensibly founded on the premise that each adult has approximately equal political power, that is, the right to vote and, hence, the right to equal participation in the resolution of conflict throughout the course of public affairs.

Since politics and political systems involve groups of people who are using power, it is inherent that they involve conflict. Conflict refers to the concurrent expression of more than one viewpoint with concurrent goal-directed action. It is both universal and healthy, since little change or progress would be likely to occur without the stimulus of conflicting viewpoints. It becomes unhealthy when the choice between views is made by force or when alternate viewpoints are kept from open expression by disenfranchisement or similar measures. The resolution of conflict usually involves some degree of compromise, a process of interaction that leads to the integration of various portions of the originally conflicting viewpoints. Of course, this can only take place if all conflicting viewpoints become known to those involved in the resolution of conflict and is dependent on the distribution of power among those involved.

An understanding of political systems today is complicated by two phenomena. One phenomenon encompasses those problems in the modern world resulting from population density and the quantity of interaction in which all persons must participate in order to survive. This is stimulated by the almost universal and instantaneous communication media. No issue ever arises or is settled in isolation from ongoing events, even those half a world away. Indeed, the resolution of one problem often contributes to the conflict related to another problem. The second phenomenon is the rapidity with which change occurs. The advances of modern technology have made "instant obsolescence" a fact of life. This almost implies that teaching adaptation to *specific* changes must be replaced by teaching adaptation to the *process* of change.[5] Social institutions, including political systems, tend to change at an extremely slow rate. The increasing rapidity of change in other aspects of life has left social institutions, at least in the opinion of many, hopelessly out of date. Some critics have even questioned the ability of the political system to adapt to the complexity of problems and the rapidity of change in the modern world.[5a]   It may be hopeless to equate social systems with technological systems, and doing so may limit the capability of dealing with those issues that should be foremost in the social and political realms.

Involvement of professions in politics

Among the headings of articles that appeared in newspapers during recent years are the following: "Congressional 'Physicians' Try to Doctor Nation's Health,"[6] "AMA OK's Action on Emotionally Ill Doctors,"[7] "How a Social Worker Helps People Adjust to an 'Unjust System,' "[8] "Small M.D. Group Hit: Health Care for Poor 'Stifled,' "[9] "Surgeons Seek Curbs on Their Numbers,"[10] "State Hospital for Retarded Lack Funds: Children Silently Suffer Perils of Heat, Flies,"[11] and "The Reason Men Go Off the Deep End at 41."[12]

Public policy in the United States is the product of conflict resolution among private interests. Private interests include recipients or potential recipients of direct or indirect benefits from public policy as well as those who must either support (financially or otherwise) and those who personally provide the benefits. Conflict is inherent in the overall process. Whereas professionals as private individuals have been involved in these conflicts, professional organizations often have not. However, in recent years professional organizations more frequently have taken positions by means of formal statements or papers. This seems related to the fact that the issues were of such significance as to threaten the survival of one or more professional groups. Focus on the areas of difference or conflict that might otherwise have been of importance temporarily vanished. An article referred to earlier[10] expresses concern for control of the number of individuals to be allowed to enter the professional ranks, and another[13] sanctions the practice of procedures that, like acupuncture, might have the capacity for threatening medical practitioners.

Law, medicine, and theology are commonly listed as the classical professional groups. Law has been a traditional stepping-stone into public office. Many of the most prominent elected officials have practiced law before election to office or even between terms of office. They are expected to be "politically" knowledgeable. One needs only to read the accounts of recent major scandals associated with those holding public office at federal, state, and local levels in the United States and elsewhere to be aware of those from the field of law who were involved directly or indirectly. Individual physicians are frequently politically active. As with members of other professional groups, the opinions and judgment of physicians are sought out and respected on important issues. Articles or news releases frequently include quotations from individuals, even if in such form as "Doctors in the hospital say a serious health hazard exists." Since the advent of consumerism, various physician, insurance, and health advocate groups have focused on the goal of 50% consumer participation on boards and in decision-making areas. For reasons that will be discussed later in the book the goal is, in fact, seldom or never realized. Although some physicians openly verbalize the need for accountability to the public and respect for consumers' participation, according to 1973 data of the Department of Social and Health Services in the state of Washington, only 40% of all physicians there accepted welfare patients.[14]

Although the American tradition has been one of separating church and state, individual clergymen have played active roles in public life. Recently, for example, the conflict regarding civil rights has brought many individual members of the clergy into political activity. A number of clergy serve actively in elected office. One major issue that has involved not only individuals but organized religious groups is the question as to whether public tax monies should be used to support church-sponsored educational institutions. In the state of New Hampshire a position was taken that the state should not dictate the kind of education a child receives and that all children of school age, whether in private or public schools, are entitled to identical shares of public funds available for education.[15] The number of men and women "of the cloth" in positions of responsibility for policy determination and implementation of public programs at all levels continues to increase. This varies from consultants within divisions that control health, education, and welfare in the federal government, associates of high public officials, assistants to the State Superintendent of Schools, and members of local boards of health.

As we have stated, professionals are often asked for advice regarding public issues. When those issues relate to a field like health, it is certainly possible that the health professionals might have some pertinent knowledge or data. Once they have explained such data, however, the democratic ideal would require that their voice or vote have no more weight than anyone else's. This is not always the case, even though it has been said that many with the distinction of having degrees are academic technicians but lack wisdom.[16] In practice many persons accept the *opinion* of professionals as *fact* rather than as data from which to form their own opinions. This is the heart of the objections raised against professional organizations, as organizations, making public statements concerning political issues. This same objection is raised when professionals become involved in community organization or "grass-roots" projects.

Furthermore, if professionals with conflicting sets of data and opinions participate in the same conflict, the effects may be to completely bewilder the population at large and even to paralyze the decision-making process. (A study of the fluoridation decisions in the United States[17] discusses these problems well.)

There is a related problem that arises if one does assume the appropriateness of professional organizations to participate officially in political activities. There are some issues in which the decision made may affect the role, status, or power of the professional organization or its individual members. Other issues may not affect the profession specifically but may have a bearing on the societal need that led to the development of the profession. If one accepts that a profession, by definition, only should exist as long as it fulfills a societal need, one would probably think that professional organizations should be involved only in the latter type of issue. It might be expected to follow that if they contribute to the effective political action regarding pertinent social issues, they will have contributed to the overall social position or standing of their profession. On the other hand, if they are only concerned with the standing of their profession, public support will shift to those groups showing concern for societal needs. The profession may lose its constituency or clients entirely and, in theory, cease to exist. Interesting dynamics come to mind as the number of individual social workers increase with the proliferation of societal needs. It has been labeled a "controversial profession."[17] Figures indicate that in 1940 only 45,000 social workers were employed as contrasted with 116,000 in 1960 and 170,000 in 1970. An additional 100,000 will be added in 1980. They are considered controversial in that their roles and activities in helping troubled people range from helping drug addicts to gluing together marriages that are on the rocks, to helping people get on welfare rolls, and to providing mental health service. Along with such help that provides people with an ability to cope with an "unjust" system, the middle class social worker may be also advocating certain liberal politicians by passing out literature and assisting with campaigns. This produces a dual role: (1) it goes beyond helping troubled human beings in a system that they want to make work and (2) it directs energy toward the changing of the society that they believe created the problem as they identify with those in despair with whom they deal.

The major official organization of medical practitioners, the American Medical Association (AMA), has openly and actively attempted to influence political decision making. Its endeavors to influence decisions concerning national health insurance are an excellent example. Current changes in the AMA indicate that physicians are reconsidering that involvement. To some the activity of the AMA was an attempt to preserve the profession rather than to aid society. President Wesley W. Hall, in 1971, prescribed less politics as a cure for the organization's slipping membership and ailing finances. He is quoted as telling the AMA policy-making House of Delegates that there was "a serious struggle for power in the ranks of AMA." He called for a reorganization of its entire structure. Following this challenge, former Vice-President Spiro Agnew addressed the group in praise of their interest in politics.[18]

Nursing and politics

Although organized nursing considers itself professional, and many individual nurses would say that nurses constitute a profession in the classical sense, the general public has not acknowledged nursing as such in the same manner as they would, for example, medicine or law. For this reason nurses have never been asked to participate in political activities or have they been consulted on public issues to the same degree as members of other professions. It has been rare for a nurse, for example, to be a requisite member of community advisory boards or boards of directors of worthy groups, whereas such groups almost always include physicians and lawyers. The traditional dominance of men and physicians probably has led to the assumption that nurses, as

women and followers, think like physicians and thus have their views represented. The National Commission on Manpower was created without any nurse representation, although nurses are the largest health manpower pool. The fact that most nurses are women probably deserves the most credit for this public ignorance of nursing as a force in decision making. Even in the major women's colleges, given credit for producing many articulate, active women and leading the way toward equality, men hold a majority of the teaching and administrative positions.[19] Thus the persons consulted for decisions and opinions in these "women's centers" are often male.

Hiring practices in almost all areas of the labor market have been discriminatory to women. Women have not only been undersold but also have been kept out of certain areas entirely. A new development is that of entrepreneurship among women. Women are acquiring or founding companies. Although accurate statistics are not available, *The New Woman's Survival Catalog*[20] lists more than 500 such companies. One specialist in small business predicts that this will go through an evolutionary process like that of immigrants. Like immigrants, women first will sell to their own people. It has been observed also that women are more likely to venture into businesses that are not traditionally dominated by males, perhaps indicating their cynicism about the possibility of succeeding there. Women-owned and women-operated businesses include *Ms.* magazine, which promotes jewelry and other items made by women-owned companies. The magazine and the companies have promoted one another. Strong commitments to the philosophy of women's liberation lead feminist businesses to utilize services and products of other women's businesses.

As women leave traditional positions for new opportunities in business, they seem to be venturesome and willing to experiment with new patterns of staffing and operating their organization. Work patterns, when they require attention to avoid mismanagement, are reviewed by outside specialists rather than turning to the usual organization-tightening process. A parallel seems to exist between this evolution and that of nurses going into private practice, nurse-operated clinics, and so on. This will be discussed in more detail later.

Small wonder, then, that nurses remain on the fringe of the health power system. Research reports often perpetuate this oversight. The report *U. S. Health Care: What's Wrong and What's Right*[21] discusses a study of the views of physicians and laymen but no data regarding the opinions of nurses. By contrast, nurses are frequently consulted privately by individuals for advice concerning the resolution of personal or individual problems. One nurse who recently completed a master's degree has articulately described her "back-fence" practice. Many nurses report instances in which they were approached for aid by persons stating that they were "afraid to ask the doctor" or thought the nurse would "understand better how it was." Since public issues are the aggregate and composite of individual concerns, this contrast between public and private intimacy is of interest. Perhaps nurses themselves encourage the view that they are not interested in health except as an individual thing by becoming distressed at health approached from an actively political frame of reference. An example of this reaction is the negative response a nurses' group showed when an actively campaigning national politician brought politics into his invited address, and the nurses indicated surprise and concern that theirs was to have been a "nonpartisan" meeting. Few groups have such apparently naive expectations.

Collectively, nurses have not had a long record of success influencing decisions that advanced their profession. Individual nurses have been able to influence many decisions related to health care. Nursing's favorite heroine, Florence Nightingale, was no exception, as demonstrated by her activities during and after the Crimean War. Frances Storlie[22] gives historical data on other individuals in her plea for more involvement by all nurses. The effectiveness of collective action is becoming apparent, and recent examples of group action by nurses are their successful lobbying *for* the New York State Nurse Practice Act and *against* the Massachusetts Institutional Licensure Law. Although it is not possible to determine all of the causes of this change, some factors seem obvious. The women's rights and women's liberation movements have moved many women to become more vociferous on issues of concern. Educated women who were previously silent seem to be especially open to the impact. The increasing numbers of college-educated women entering nursing, particularly as other employment opportunities narrow, adds to the pool of nurses exposed to the activism and involvement of the university campus.

The fact that health is a national, state, and local political issue of great concern, and an issue discussed not only in hospitals but in homes and on street corners, adds to the stimulus. In an approach frequently criticized in current nursing literature the nurse has traditionally utilized personal contact with individual physicians as a means of promoting her viewpoint regarding patient care or health needs. Most nurses, while laughing, acknowledged the truth in a recently published article[23] describing this so-called "doctor-nurse game." Whereas part of the game is the nonrecognition of the nurse's contribution by the physician, there are instances of public acknowledgement. In discussing the treatment of alcoholism a physician states that good nursing care, rather than drugs, seems to be the main factor in improvement.[24]

There are some possible pitfalls in the participation of nurses and nursing in political systems. One danger is that persons who have long kept silent regarding an issue may, when they finally speak, do so with such vehemence that they are not heard by others. A parallel is the sudden transition from silence to riot in some ghetto communities, which succeeded in completely alienating some members of the surrounding community. Nurses may also take on issues that appear helpful yet ultimately defeat the purpose. Nurses who only campaign when their own economic welfare is at stake may lose their constituency—those patients for whom they should be caring. There is a necessary balance because if nurses are only concerned with abstract altruisms regarding health, they may also lose the platform of a secure profession from which to speak.

Another danger relates to the understandable blurring together of the various health disciplines in the mind of the public. Many nurses have resented the fact that people have assumed nursing to be in agreement with all the formally announced positions of the American Medical Association. Few people know, for example, that the American Nurses' Association backed Medicare as formally as the American Medical Association opposed it, although not as vocally or effectively. Within a few years it will be of interest to consider a retrospective view of the positions taken by the two professional groups in relation to one another regarding the issue of national health insurance. It may be a long time before the voice of nursing is as loud or effective as that of organized American medicine appears to have been, but the potential in manpower (or womanpower) and knowledge is there.

However, in their desire to be recognized as distinct from physicians, nurses should not lose sight of the common ground between the two professions. It must be remembered that all the health disciplines are interdependent as they work to meet the societal need for health care. Nurses will receive public support for doing this and not for fighting among themselves. Although many have criticized the individual bonds with physicians that nurses utilized in the past, it would be regrettable if interprofessional conflict led to the loss of such valuable relationships. Dignified interprofessional conferences in formal settings can never accomplish some of those things for patients that can result from informal colleague contacts.

Need for theoretical understanding

Sex role stereotypes remain much alive not only within the larger society but even among those professional groups where it would be least expected. One survey[25] among specialists in psychiatry of both sexes indicated that an overwhelming and almost equal majority of the respondents indicated that a man's most fulfilling experience would be a career or profession, whereas a woman's most fulfilling experience was marriage. Implicit in achieving a successful career or professional position is the understanding of a significant body of theoretical knowledge in at least one field. The investigator who conducted this study[25] remarked, "Sure, it's a man's world, baby, but you can change it if you want to." Successful change of the status quo, however, brings mixed blessings. It may bring about a more humane society in some respects and more self-actualization for some individuals. On the other hand, a personal confrontation has been described as occurring among successful men who realize that they have reached the peak of their careers (maximized their theoretical understanding).[12] As nurses and women attain the now enviable position of those successful men, it may be expected that a similar phenomenon will confront them.

In their naiveté about politics nurses find that assumptions are easily made about moral and ethical principles being practiced if they are professed. As a result, less "watchdogging" is done to assure compliance with rules and regulations, and efforts to uncover noncompliance are directed only toward those areas with the reputation for various forms of noncompliance. Salt Lake City, a city renowned for its Mormon Church, good works, and moral zeal was found by the Securities Exchange Commission (SEC) and the National Association of Securities Dealers to be involved recently in financial manipulation and securities fraud.[26] The over-the-counter stock manipulations and other frauds were found to be so pervasive that an extensive study was initiated and "new twists to old schemes" were uncovered, including small stock offerings exempted from SEC registration as well as "blatant defrauding of brokers by shady stock promoters and even by some of the customers. The city got the reputation of being the stock-fraud center of the nation, the sewer of the securities industry."[26] It prompted proposals to undertake studies in other cities that are considered problem areas, including Los Angeles, Miami, Minneapolis, and among them a much smaller city, Spokane, the home of many speculative mining issues. There is a speculative trait among Americans that dates back to its beginnings. Speculating in "penny stocks" allows those having only a small amount of money to become involved. Specializing in such small stocks therefore encourages a great deal of business. This, in Salt Lake City, has resulted in a list of fifty-one brokerage firms for its population of 189,000.[26]

It has been said that the doctorate is a racket in American education[27] and that when Ph.D.s which are of marginal worth are granted, their value is deflated and the more competent who might have been convinced to strive for them are discouraged. How many nurses are caught up in a preconscious hope that, having the Ph.D., they will be referred to as "Doctor," and patients as well as colleagues might make the assumption that they are physicians and ascribe to them that power and status? The pressure for equal access for men and women to the halls of ivy and all the departments within them has led to the change in the stereotypes, even of women themselves who graduated from places like Vassar College, which serve as rare sanctuaries for those who study there. They are here provided protection from an awareness of job discrimination against women that they learn if they attend Yale Law School[28] in preparation for top level positions in the professional and political worlds.

With theoretical understanding, increased power, and status come an accountability and responsibility. This includes the evaluation of performance and accepting of merit awards based on the successful attainment of certain specific objectives. A sobering thought occurs to those who would accept only the "privileges" without the responsibility to produce results as an outcome of learning theory and skills. Without the separation of the emotional from the abstract, autonomy cannot be achieved. Moreover, unless this separation is made and unless there is a tolerance for the psychological and social consequences, regression results. Movement in the cycle of change is a step backward on the scale of incremental progression.

The ambivalence that must be expected is a result of a simultaneous desire for autonomy and a continued unconscious desire to maintain dependence upon that which is perceived as nurturing and protective. A current example is that of the lengthy and controversial discussions regarding the "expanded role of the nurse," equated with recent nursing legislation and legislation to increase allied professions. This new role of necessity presents a question of legal responsibility as individuals venture beyond present professional territorial boundaries and move into more independent practice. Nurses express resentment toward physicians' telling them what to do in areas in which they feel competent but are reluctant to accept in toto those areas of responsibility.

The development of progression from the early seed of the ideas leading to the expanded nurse role to actual change or action is not inevitable. The idea or fantasy thought (in freudian terms) may be considered as originating in response to deprivation. The idea is conceived at the emotional level, taking the form of wish fulfillment. Before it can be operationalized it must be consciously thought out and modified. Logic and causality then refine the conscious idea. The refined idea must be congruent with two worlds: (1) the internal structure of morality in the individual's unconscious personality and (2) the demands and pressures of the external world. The idea of the "expanded role" may be congruent with some individual's first world, but the second world is more than those outside the nursing profession; it includes the rest of the nursing group as well.

Implementation of value change is closely related to what is held as "sacred." The more sharing of values, involvement, and responsibility for implementation of values, the greater will be the social stability and sense of reward.

This is true even though, as has been said before, no system will change unless a little conflict or disunity is present. Reward stimulates energy and perpetuates progression of change. When these conditions are not met, hostility may be turned inward and acts as a legitimizing force toward aggressive action. This may be observed at two levels: (1) within the nursing community and (2) within health-related professions.

Society should not prevent women from making free choices about their careers, and at the present time the choices available to women for obtaining the necessary theoretical knowledge and experience are broadening. This is not occurring without some opposition. Although we would not wish to present ourselves as radical women's liberationists, some of the problems we have encountered in our struggle to be wives and mothers in addition to well-educated nurses serve to validate the existence of a male-dominated society. This opposition is not new but has crushed the spirits of women throughout the centuries, although it has undergone gradual, if reluctant, change in the past 140 to 150 years. Resistance to change is a universal phenomenon, but in the case of this change men were confronted not merely with a potential loss of domination but also the loss of something that has been ego building. Without breaking through this resistance nursing will never be able to make its full contribution to society.

While this struggle continues, another simultaneous one takes place in contemporary America. This is the decreasing capacity of institutions to help individuals find a place from which to participate and make meaningful contributions. American society is frequently not perceived as stable, peaceful, and happy. The question is whether this is because of the level of tension that prevails or the inability of people generally to find fulfillment to some degree. (Obviously the two are related.) Economic achievement earlier provided man's life with some sense of meaning; in this area nurses are recently realizing a sense of meaning. However, automation and technology soon diminished the economic meaning because work contributed less to the total society. So with nurses—climbing the economic ladder and achieving more leisure in the midst of the prevailing work ethic is not all to which nurses aspire. Rather, they must find, as do all others in this society, more personal satisfaction in their work and individual fulfillment through the constructive use of leisure time to regain individual identity and finally gain or regain a vision of the future.

Geographical mobility serves as another force that diminishes the individual's potential to feel a sense of belonging. As nurses and women direct their energies toward the achievement of more theoretical knowledge and upward mobility in society and find meaning for themselves as individuals rather than being a number or object, they must be ready to deal with the consequences of the rising expectations that they must face. If not prepared for the challenge, they will be much like the young people of recent years who, searching for meaning in a world that fosters ambivalence and alienation, are unwilling or too paralyzed to act. In the same way that courts and prisons have been charged with an inability to prevent crime and health care systems charged with an inability to heal, nurses and women may be charged with abandoning the use of those abilities that they and they alone can contribute to a functioning society. The question of how this is accomplished is intended for later discussion. The grasping of theoretical materials and their application should not be seen as an alternative to functioning as a feeling and compassionate human being.

There are those who believe that the only proper place of the nurse is at the bedside of the acutely ill patient in the hospital. The scope of health care has changed rapidly during this century, and members of all health disciplines are found in homes, clinics, and communities as well as in hospitals. If health is a right rather than a privilege, if it is more than the mere absence of disease, and if health care must be provided with some equality for all, it will take many health professionals throughout the political and social system to achieve these goals. So it seems that nurses should have access to that knowledge which will facilitate their effective participation in such political dynamics. Throughout history nursing has been marked by development through trial and error, education by apprenticeship, and practice based on empirical approaches. The rapidity with which change occurs today means that such slow methods will be ineffective. As an applied science, nursing should seek theory from basic disciplines and actively apply it within the framework offered by the role and philosophy of nursing. In regard to political dynamics there is a sound theoretical base from the fields of political science and public administration. Once understood, these theoretical materials can be utilized by nurses in ways that are appropriate to the socially sanctioned goals of the profession. (Units I and II will discuss such theories.)

Before using these new theories the nurse (like any professional) should consider the impact they might have on the usual role of the profession. There are some philosophical assumptions about individuals and the social system into which individual nurses have been "professionalized" to be nurses and which have rarely been consciously considered. One of the "professional" assumptions, which will receive attention later, has to do with the right of the professional to make decisions regarding an individual's destiny without allowing that individual to participate in that decision making. This assumption is made so subtly that examples of nonparticipation in decision making, perhaps obvious to outsiders, go on unrecognized by the professionals responsible. Consider, for example, the public push to make professionals realize that not everyone wants to maintain physical life indefinitely if it must be done with multiple machines at great social and economic cost. In addition to the professional philosophy there may also be personal beliefs that lead various members of a profession to appropriately utilize the same theoretical framework in different ways to strive toward different goals

which are still congruent with that profession's socially assigned task. (Unit III covers these issues.)

Once having grasped the concept of political dynamics and considered this knowledge in relation to personal and professional issues, nurses may feel a need for some guidelines for initiating action of a political nature. Assuming that one accepts our premise that the professional nurse practicing today should be participating in the political system with and on behalf of individuals seeking health and health care, one should begin analyzing political systems and problems and actively engage in the process of change. (See Unit IV for discussion.)

Up until now nurses have often been giving nothing but a negative emotional sense and feeling of futility regarding the whole decision-making process. This feeling cannot be replaced by a positive one until nurses have a sound theoretical basis from which to plan and experience positive participation in decision making. That will facilitate the development of positive feelings which then can be shared. Translating this into economic terms, many people believe that professional nurses are an expensive luxury, and indeed, many people believe that professional nurses are not providing a level of service equal to their cost. This ratio of cost to benefit could be increased if the self-image and the role expectation promoted a higher level of nursing practice. This applies not only on an individual patient level but also on the level of the health agency or organization established to meet individual and community needs.

The need for understanding exists not only on the part of nurses but also on the part of those around them. Changes in attitude and increase in understanding on the part of others will not occur without reason to do so. It can occur as others gain respect for nurses as a community of contributing members, including a knowledge of their heritage, a recognition of their achievements to date, and some awareness of their motivations and future aspirations. For some, knowing that nurses are interested in increasing their knowledge and participation leads to changes in expectation and attitude. It is our goal to provide the reader with support for a philosophy of involvement and some of the theoretical knowledge that they will need to enable them to translate the philosophy they have into practice.

If one observes phenomena that coincide in time and seem to be related, it becomes necessary to ponder whether their simultaneous occurrence is related or coincidental. An example is that of the current moves on the part of both physicians and nurses to provide family-centered, community-based health care. Either of the professions could be striving for a larger sphere of interest and power, each could be responding independently to requests for improved care, or both factors could be operating. Only thorough research, well grounded in the theories of social change, would reveal the casual agents operant in the change.

In contemporary mythology nurses are kind, understanding workers of mercy and mother figures like Florence Nightingale and Clara Barton. Most people forget that the people like Florence Nightingale and Clara Barton did in fact go on to activities far removed from the mother-role stereotype. Nurses are otherwise seen as gruff, insensitive, money hungry, and uncaring. Nurses are not alone in receiving the criticism when people in society think of life, death, and the dollars they spend to obtain the best that is available in health care. In response to criticism and demands on them physicians have enlisted the aid of assistants such as Medex trainees and former military medics. With a few months of on-the-job training these assistants are expected to take the overload off physicians under their supervision, often in rural areas where the physician is not readily at hand to supervise. Charges have been made that training programs to prepare such physician assistants are a waste of taxpayer money because nurses could perform the same tasks but have been neglected or ignored. Whether spoken or written, feelings prevail that the duplication is perpetuated because nursing consists largely of women and is being cast aside as a discriminatory move in favor of men. (Note that physicians' assistants begin at salaries which may overlap with those of nurses only at the highest administrative levels.) As nurses and their professional organizations become more fluent with knowledge and concepts related to political dynamics, they are seeking recognition for their work and articulating their role, that is, pointing out that physicians and physician assistants are oriented to crisis care, whereas nurses' activities center on health promotion, education, and maintenance. They insist on legitimizing the decisions they make independently in everyday practice through changes in the nurse practice acts in the respective states. It has been said that nurses wait for physicians to tell them what to do except when the physicians are absent and patients are dying. Nurses make diagnoses and will do so in the future but will depend more on the physicians to care for the acute phase of illness, which is their major interest. This will not only address the physicians' interests but will also utilize the nurses' skills to the utmost. The old mythologies about roles are no longer acceptable. Nurses and others must be guided by newer models of practice.

Awareness of the existence and impact of minorities, prominority programs, and antiminority feelings is also necessary. The National Association of Social Workers established a fund to assist members who require legal defense to fight against being fired in social service cutbacks or to serve as client advocates in courts of law to protect agency policies.[29] Liability insurance becomes more commonly carried by professionals as lawsuits against them increase. Social workers are sued for alleged negligence in preventing suicides, removing a child from an adoptive home, or encouraging a spouse to break up a marriage by divorce. Some social workers perceive the increase in legal problems as a reflection of increasing government and public dissatisfaction with social service programs.[30] Unemployment rates are higher among college graduates than other groups for the period from 1969 to 1972.[31] The demand for professional workers is slowing. According to the United States Bureau of Labor Statistics, the unemployment rate among workers with only an elementary education is lower than their better educated counterparts, yet the total number of nonhigh-school graduates in the work force has declined greatly in recent years. What are persons to do? Their elders encouraged an education as assuring them better employment opportunities. They often pointed out that education was something like an insurance policy, "something nobody can ever take away." Now in some cases it becomes a liability because fields are closed because of surplus of workers or because the educated person is considered "overqualified" and is excluded from jobs in other areas.

The minority group issue has increased professional involvement in politics. Although some minority and ethnic groups still have inadequate numbers of professionals in proportion to the population, the difficult controversy of "reverse discrimination" arises when nonminority persons who have better qualifications are denied admission to schools or jobs. The De-Funis case, against the University of Washington, is still before the United States Supreme Court and may help to establish future directions.[32] The Constitution and American tradition supports the view that special efforts should be made to overcome the historical effect produced by slavery. However, as the DeFunis case points out, other minorities also can make claims, and the question arises regarding real standards. When standards of merit and equality of opportunity are abandoned, quotas are the natural outcome. The boundaries of what are considered minorities are certain to create hard feelings on the part of some. Granting preference in proportion to the seriousness of past discrimination is an equally impossible undertaking. (Black slavery, to the Japanese-American, is no worse than concentration camps during the Second World War were to them.) Target minority groups have been referred to by the United States Department of Health, Education and Welfare and the Equal Employment Opportunities Commission, but the wording in statutes, the intent of legislation, and Supreme Court decisions all support the position that racial quotas are out of order in America. Equality of opportunity and selection based on merit are congruent with traditions of justice. Additional recruitment efforts in areas where additional minority students or workers are needed would better ensure equality of opportunity and neither lower standards nor give preferential treatment to minorities with lower qualifications. Not least among the results would be increased self-esteem and self-confidence of individuals from minority groups.

Nursing literature has for several years included many statements about the need for change, and individual authors have pleaded with nurses about the absolute necessity of their involvement in the process of change. The question to be raised, then, is why no more nurse participation and *real* change have, in fact, occurred. In our experience with students and nurse practitioners, there is one major factor in common among nurses as a group of professionals that affects and limits them in this area; until nurses individually achieve an understanding of the dynamics and impact these factors have on them, they will continue to act in congruence with traditional ways. This is evidenced in the inability of the nursing profession as a whole to implement the changes that are presently necessary to improve health services. It should result in an increase of public support for incorporating professional nurses as essential members into the health care team.

The size and diversity of the nursing profession and its vocational assistants contribute to the slow rate of change and the problem others have identifying with the newly stated ideal stereotype of the interdependent, decision-making, community-leading, caring nurse. Until most persons coming into contact with a nurse can identify practices that are consistent with that image, blocks will exist. As long as expatients say, "I never *saw* a nurse" or "They just gave pills," the nurse will not be acknowledged as a change-inducing professional.

Individuals who perceive a cause have risen through the years among various groups and have fought lonely battles to right what they saw as wrong. Meanwhile they are thought of by their fellows as altruists or "nuts"; some cheer them on while others jeer at them. Some question the motives even to the extent of charging selfish motives with statements like, "If it wasn't for his own livelihood, he wouldn't give a hoot." Many hours are devoted to lobbying and waging the war. As one searches for reasons for the commitment, it is often because there has been first-hand involvement that brought personal significance to the issue. Some such "causes" for which people devote their energies are of such a nature that their correction or resolution would seemingly affect few people. Such causes as health care, too, may be seen as affecting few if one looks at society only in segments of those who are absolutely indigent and find care of any kind inaccessible to them. In addition, one must add to their number those persons, along with their families and communities, who receive care only when a major crisis occurs. In the city of Seattle, seven hospitals and many private physicians' offices sit on what is known as "Pill Hill." Only a few miles away a free clinic study of one neighborhood found that 65% of the people had no insurance and no private physician and relied only on the hospital emergency room for care.[33] Added are those who receive crisis care and some additional care of such marginal quality as to lead them into a false sense of "being healthy." Much of the latter care may be covered by some type of prepaid health plan through the employer or public assistance. Yet people know little about how the health care system works, except that it does not work well. Much of the care they receive is designed to fill gaps between hospital and home. Nursing home care, subsidized by government funds, may be cheaper but is by no means "free." The next group of people to be added are those who pay cash from the pocket and look for those health providers who charge the least, a process that might be either wise "shopping" or foolish. Getting

sick, for these people, can be really frightening. Worrying about how they will pay the bill may be the worst part because everyone has heard shocking stories about families hit by a catastrophic illness that left them with thousands of dollars in unpaid medical bills. As one continues to add to the numbers affected by the health system, one goes up the socioeconomic ladder, and by the time one reaches the top, one encounters persons who may be able to afford care but may have reached their position under such physical and emotional stress that they require large amounts of health care from those having various areas of expertise. Even these persons tend to receive only care for episodes of identifiable illness, and not continuously, in the effort to promote or maintain health.

Health professionals join the public at some point in that they, too, require care from their colleagues with various other kinds of expertise. Whether they receive that care depends on the availability of time, the kind of expertise needed, and their financial resources. Traditionally, physicians have had an exchange policy with their physician friends so they "trade" their expertise with those having other specialties to receive what they need of health care for themselves and their families. When needed, nursing care has been purchased relatively cheaply, but this is beginning to change. Nurses have usually paid full or a partially reduced fee for service from their physician colleagues. To bring all this back into focus the readers are reminded that health care as an issue or "cause" does in some way affect all of us. Those few who have been crusaders for improved health care and a better system of delivery are those who for some reason found it hit them below the belt. Nurses have been among the lonely crusaders but have also been found suspect and have won few friends. Perhaps because nurses are primarily women, related and hidden issues have contributed to the suspicion and loneliness.

For those nurses who believe they are carrying out an unrewarding crusade they might take some mixed consolation in the fact that they are not alone in their being held in suspicion. Private insurance companies are suspected of graft, proprietary hospitals are considered unsuitable, public hospitals are criticized as inadequate, private physicians are charged with ordering unreasonable numbers of diagnostic tests to increase their fees, and nurses are questioned about wage increases in light of their "doing" less. Examples of accusations are numerous. One person, George Coffee, incurred bills of $110 for 110 days of attention, $8 for two bottles of brandy and six bottles of whiskey, and $25 for burial expenses in 1860. There was little a hospital could do for him then; treatment was simple, billing was simple, and paying the bill was not all that difficult. "Nowadays, the hospital can keep you alive . . . but it's the cost of those 'medical miracles' that catches attention. In the old days there were some patients who died with certain diseases . . . today, they live to stomp their feet and scream about the bill."[32] Indeed, costs have skyrocketed. Only part of the addition (nobody really knows how much) is due to advances in medical technology.

Inequities in billing have also been blamed. Although hospitals charge everyone the same rate, not everyone pays the same amount. Blue Cross, Medicare, Medicaid, and private insurance companies each have their own formula for what they will pay, based on what the hospital claims are its "actual costs" as determined by negotiation. One hospital, for example, reported that Medicare paid 83% of its patients' total bills, Blue Cross paid 90%, and Medicaid paid 85%. Meanwhile, the private patient paid 100% and allegedly subsidized some of the bad bills as well. The result was that the person who pays out of his own pocket shells out more for exactly the same service than the amount that persons on other payment programs pay.[33] One state legislator claimed that $400 million in excess Medicare claims were paid to hospitals in 1967 and that the overpayments were the fault of administration of the program and lack of prescribed and simple regulation by the Department of Health, Education and Welfare

rather than the fault of the hospitals. Because of ineffectiveness on the part of the federal administration, he charged that federal funds were used to pay for "private-duty nurses, TV sets and telephone service to Medicare patients," all of which are illegal under the mandate.[33] Health care is considered an enterprise, and funding for health is often based on a method of cost analysis that is applied to any other enterprise. The rationale is given that if 60% to 65% of hospital costs are for labor, to cut cost one must cut the number of personnel and design cheaper hospitals as well as ones which can be more efficiently operated. This is one approach, but to date, it has not satisfied many.

Comprehensive health councils were established with consumer majorities on their boards dictated by law. But who are the "consumers" making up the majority, and what power do they have? Hospitals seeking accountability to the public must have clear signals and priorities from administrators of governmental programs that do not change from day to day. In discussions of large public programs, growing population, and the anonymity that accompanies urbanization, cries are faintly heard that the individual must receive more focus. Early childhood programs are geared toward later individual achievement. Teaching the "fundamental skills" of reading, communication, and mathematics to the underachiever is challenging the creativity of educators through funds available under federal programs. The cause of underachievement may be related to a complex web of health-related circumstances. The amount of learning can be more easily evaluated, however, than can the actual impact of efforts directed toward alleviation of the underlying causes. When funds are allocated, it is easier to justify the classroom program than the supportive health services provided. When only modest or no significant improvement is shown as a result of special education programs, the blame is often placed with the pupils, the teachers, or the school system rather than with the lack of emphasis on the actual root of the problem.

Various approaches to coordinating needs with resources have been taken; one recent development is that of private nonprofit corporations such as the East Los Angeles Health System, Inc.,[34] and the Western Medical Group.[35] The intent of such organizations is to bring about communication among numerous individual providers and/or agencies, thereby cutting costs and improving services. No less important than communication at that level is the need on the part of the citizenry to be concerned and interested in the improvement of their health care. Even though the service is available, it is of no value and the money is wasted if it is not utilized. Health officials often refer to a need to "educate" people so that they will take an interest in their health. Will "spreading the good word" educate people to use a wide range of services, especially preventive services, when their previous orientation was on their obtaining health care during a crisis?

In an effort to reach their publics, health professionals have challenged colleges and universities with the development not only of their clinical skills and healing arts but also their ability to communicate with one another and their clients. As a result, instead of completely eliminating the journalism department in 1972, the administration of the University of California at Los Angeles moved ahead with a plan to open a professional journalism graduate school.[36] It was considered not necessarily to be sensible university politics but, rather, a wise educational policy.

Although government charges the health providers and consumers with abuses, it also charges state and local governments with being recalcitrant and failing to carry out mandates. One example is pollution. Compliance with exhaust emission standards and enforcement, surveillance of industrial waste, and control of litter depends on state and local government. Dissatisfaction with court orders to bus children for purposes of achieving racial balance and concern about the taxpayers' bitter disenchantment with state and local school systems are pervasive and mounting.

Unionism and strikes have been one response of professionals who feel caught among the levels of government and societal pressures. Quarrels over wages, work loads, hours, and services expected contribute to the loss of certain images and intangibles that once had great value—the quiet atmosphere, dedicated workers, "neighborhood" facilities, and confidence which people had that their needs would be met. Are these old ideals and values no longer tangible and must people conceal their bitterness about the fact? For many the search for a sense of identity, recognition, and happy times continues. When will those times come again? Is the community college movement today an indication that people are seeking some understanding and meaning in an otherwise meaningless existence? School and job phobias are present-day diagnoses that are treated by specialists in psychiatry. Is the solution to be found in understanding why one reacts negatively to a school or job situation? Must this society look for alternatives such as medications* to ameliorate the adverse effects of emotion and stress in everyday life?[37] All these issues, not superficially tied to traditional nursing, may jar the reader as being out of place. One goal of this book is to aid nurses in realizing that almost *no* issue is irrelevant to the practice of a health care profession.

Nurses are challenged to provide assistance to many others seeking answers to the same social questions. We would individually and together say what Thomas Jefferson wrote to a black, self-educated scholar and friend[38]: "I can add with truth that nobody wishes more ardently to see a good system commenced for raising the condition both of their mind and body to what it ought to be."

---

*An example is the drug oxyprenolol, used in the treatment of heart disease and being researched in England because it was found to suppress rapid heartbeat among race-car drivers.

References

1. Wall Street Journal, Nov. 2, 1971.
2. Galbraith, G. S.: Restrainer, Wall Street Journal, Oct. 5, 1971.
3. Webster's seventh new collegiate dictionary, Springfield, Mass., 1971, C. & C. Merriam Co.

4. Weinstein, F., and Platt, G. M.: The wish to be free, Berkeley, Calif., 1969, University of California Press.

5. Toffler, A.: Future shock, New York, 1971, Random House, Inc.

5a. Reich, C.: The greening of America, New York, 1971, Random House, Inc.

6. Congressional "physicians" try to doctor nation's health, San Diego Union, Sept. 14, 1973.

7. AMA OK's action on emotionally ill doctors, Los Angeles Times, Nov. 29, 1972.

8. How a social worker helps people adjust to an "unjust system," Wall Street Journal, Dec. 21, 1972.

9. Small M.D. group hit: health care for poor "stifled," Long Beach Independent, Feb. 2, 1973.

10. Surgeons seek curbs on their numbers, The Register, Oct. 6, 1972.

11. State hospital for retarded lacks funds: children silently suffer perils of heat, flies, Los Angeles Times, Dec. 15, 1972.

12. The reason men go off the deep end at 41, Los Angeles Times, Aug. 5, 1973.

13. Acupuncturist faces N. Y. licensing charge, Los Angeles Times, Nov. 29, 1972.

14. Somebody else paying bills, Spokane Chronicle, May 21, 1973.

15. In New Hampshire, a financial experiment, Los Angeles Times, May 30, 1973.

16. University degrees do not a scholar make, San Diego Union, May 23, 1973.

17. Crain, R. L., Katz, E. and Rosenthal, D. B.: The politics of community conflict, New York, 1969, The Bobbs-Merrill Co., Inc.

18. Less politics was prescribed, Wall Street Journal, Nov. 29, 1971.

19. Carter, S.: New mission for women's colleges, Los Angeles Times, Nov. 26, 1972.

20. Rennie, S., and Pjrimstead, K.: The new woman's survival catalog, New York, 1973, Coward, McCann & Geoghagan, Inc.

21. Strickland, S. P.: U.S. health care: what's wrong and what's right, New York, 1972, Universe Books, Inc.

22. Storlie, F.: Nursing and the social conscience, New York, 1970, Appleton-Century-Crofts.

23. Stein, L.: The doctor-nurse game, American Journal of Nursing **68:**101-105, Jan., 1968.

24. Viamontes, J. A.: Review of drug effectiveness in the treatment of alcoholism, American Journal of Psychiatry **128:**1570-1571, 1972.

25. Her advice to therapists—heal thyself, Los Angeles Times, Aug. 1, 1973.

26. Salt Lake City gains reputation for being a stock-fraud center, Wall Street Journal, Feb. 25, 1974.

27. Education doctorate racket, Long Beach Independent, Jan. 26, 1973.

28. College is severing socialite traditions, San Diego Union, Sept. 6, 1973.

29. Social workers face increased legal problems on the job, Wall Street Journal, March 26, 1974.

30. Judging racial quotas, Wall Street Journal, March 26, 1974.

31. Rising costs add to fear of illness, Spokane Daily Chronicle, May 19, 1973.

32. Hospitals financial system complex, Spokane Daily Chronicle, May 23, 1973.

33. Aspin blasts big Medicare overpayments, Long Beach Independent, Aug. 16, 1972.

34. Health systems group established in east L.A., Los Angeles Times, Nov. 29, 1972.

35. S & L to finance medical facility, San Diego Union, Aug. 7, 1972.

36. Editorial: Journalism at UCLA, Long Beach Independent, Oct. 18, 1972.

37. Medicine and you, Long Beach Independent, Sept. 11, 1972.

38. Bedini, S.: The life of Benjamin Banneker, New York, 1972, Charles Scribner's Sons.

UNIT ONE

THE AMERICAN POLITICAL SYSTEM

When great-grandfather cast his vote
Things took more time to be done—
And often a month went by before
It was known which man had won.

Later, when grandpa went to the polls,
In one week the newspapers stated
(With reasonable certainty)
Who'd be inaugurated.

In father's era the radio came,
And then the voting machine,
So a waiting nation knew the next day
Results on the political scene.

Today there are modern research polls
Which, by scientific detection,
Predict the winner on TV screens
The night before the election.

Such technology is impressive,
But I'd like to have it noted
That I don't like to be counted out—
Before I've even voted!

G. O. Ludcke[1]

1

ORIGINAL INTENT

Government is "the complex of political institutions, laws and customs through which the function of governing is carried out in a specific political unit."[2] It is also "the executive branch of the U. S. Federal Government including the political officials and usually the permanent civil service employees."[2] The second definition is incomplete because it excludes the legislative and judicial branches that are basic to the government as defined in the Constitution. From an initial discussion of the content of the various levels of government in the American system this unit will proceed to look at the changes that have occurred, especially in the metropolis, and at some current issues and problems.

Original intent of American government

The Constitution, which is the document by which the American system of government was formally established, was signed by the required nine states in 1788. It recognizes only two levels of government in the United States, federal and state, and does not consider the distribution of power among the political subdivisions of states. It is necessary to reflect on earlier events and statements and the writers themselves to understand what other provisions were intended in the document that now has stood, often misunderstood and misused, in the United States for almost 190 years. Much about these three factors (preceding events, documents, and people) is reflected in the words the writers used to express the principles and ideas in which they believed.

The idea of a democracy was a move against government. Government, for example, during Rousseau's time, consisted of feudal monarchies and feudal aristocracies. An early democrat, Rousseau expressed the desire to abolish kings and lords so that government could be simple. The history of the American people is largely a desire to have as little government as possible. As people fled Europe, detesting the governments from which they came, they brought with them an antigovernment philosophy that pervades American

21

society even today. These early immigrant and religious minorities fostered a notion that in this new land they would be able to mind their own business and not be bothered by the outside world (whatever that was). It seems that the framers were aware that they could not achieve a utopia but that they could establish self-government through a deliberative process.

The development of legislative and executive power in decision making grew out of the deep distrust that the colonists had of strong executive power in addition to the earlier experiences with rulers in England. It was considered such a basic need to curb the powers of the executive that provision for the separation of powers is a feature of not only national and state governments but carries into local government as well.

This American tradition begins with the Mayflower Compact, which contains a clear commitment to enacting laws that are *thought to be* just and equal and that, furthermore, are thought to be *meet and convenient* for the general good. However, Lincoln, as indicated by words contained in his Gettysburg address, looked on the Declaration of Independence as the document to which Americans must look for guidance in identifying their ultimate commitments. He spoke of "four score and seven years ago" when "a new nation" was established, and that would be the date of the Declaration of Independence. This discussion of intent will focus on concepts which grew out of that Declaration and which continue to influence the development of programs such as health care services today.

The Declaration of Independence sets forth the doctrine of "unalienable rights" (life, liberty, and the pursuit of happiness). It then continues: "that to secure these rights, Governments are instituted among men, deriving their just powers from the consent of the governed, that whenever any Form of Government becomes destructive to these ends, it is the Right of the People to alter or to abolish it, and to institute a new Government, laying its foundations on such principles and organizing

its powers in such form, as to them shall seem most likely to effect their Safety and Happiness." One of the provisions which was clearly established, then, is that of altering or abolishing a government which rides roughshod over its citizenry. The Constitution was the document that followed, establishing such a form of government as was seen congruent with the achievement of the goals of safety and happiness. In defining a democratic system the Constitution provided for the process of changing the government peacefully, should the people consider that it no longer allowed them to work toward their safety and happiness. That process, amending the Constitution as spelled out in Article V, could change the basic commitments binding the nation and its people. If amendments are adopted, however, they then become the new commitments that must be honored as were those commitments that they replaced. For those dissenting with the policies in question there would appear to be three possible alternatives: (1) consent and live up to the policies as they are defined by society at that point, (2) leave the territorial boundary in search of a society whose basic commitments are more compatible with theirs, or (3) continue to work toward policy change. As did the Declaration of Independence, the Virginia Bill of Rights stated: "That government is, or ought to be, instituted for the common benefit, protection and security of the people, nation or community; . . . and that, when any government shall be found inadequate or contrary to these purposes, a majority of the community shall have an indubitable right to reform, alter, or abolish, in such a manner as shall be judged most conducive to the public will."

Documents preceding the writing of the Constitution that help to make a reasonable interpretation of the Constitution's intent include the policies advanced in the Northwest Ordinance in 1785 and 1787. The Continental Congress, under the Articles of Confederation, passed these laws. They were to serve as a pattern of government in the western territories included under the ordinance. The first, the ordinance of 1785, was commonly known as the Land Ordinance and contained provisions for the surveying and sale of the land. The ordinance of 1787 provided a system of participatory government for the Northwest territory, including various units of local government such as townships and counties. It made some provision for the protection of human rights, provided for the legal guarantee of personal contracts, abolished the ancient primogeniture laws, and forbade any form of involuntary servitude.[3] Phrases such as these were also added to state constitutions, no doubt because they were so deeply cherished that no practice thereof would be left to chance. To define what is meant by "due process of law" is no easy matter; yet it is possible to reflect on the intent to provide as a safeguard to each person charged with an offense a sequence of procedural steps throughout which he is considered innocent until proved guilty. The Declaration of Independence, signed in 1776, speaks of "natural" rights with which all men are endowed by their Creator: the right, or rights, to life, to liberty, and to the pursuit of happiness. It further proclaims that governments are instituted to protect men (presumably all men) so that they might enjoy these natural rights. The Constitution, ratified in 1788, and the Bill of Rights, adopted in 1789 (but seriously opposed by many of those who composed the Constitution), together make no references to the laws as the will of God and avoid the term *rights*. The Constitution, in its Preamble, states that the new government was created not to *protect the rights of men* but rather for a *number of purposes* (not mentioned in the Declaration of Independence): of establishing a more perfect union, justice, the blessings of liberty, and the general welfare.

A review of literature [4,4a] does not explain clearly why the incongruence exists, but some explanations have been proposed. They include the fact that different men wrote the different documents and the possibility that a shift in the religious sentiment occurred between 1776 and 1787. The question has been

raised as to whether the framers of the Constitution and the Bill of Rights did, in fact, betray the spirit, the intent if you will, of the principles of 1776 when independence was won from England.

However, Lincoln reemphasized the basic commitment of the Declaration of Independence in the proposition "that all men are created equal." If the Declaration indeed has the status granted it by Lincoln, one is faced with whether the scope of the phrase "all men are equal" is understood. What did the writers really mean by all men and what was equal? From all that can be gleaned, what was meant was something short of what modern equalitarians believe. State constitutions which were adopted about that point in time qualified the statement significantly. South Carolina qualified as equal voters those who were free and white, who acknowledged the existence of God, and who owned a specific amount of land. Other states specifically excluded women and slaves. The Constitution and the Bill of Rights say nothing about equality, and it is these latter documents by which Americans are governed. The word *equality* was seemingly not spoken of again in public political documents until Lincoln did so. What he meant when he used the word is also not altogether clear; subsequent generations did not interpret it as simple equality and still do not practice it, despite the United States Supreme Court support several generations later. The question is whether it is, then, a central principle or original intent of the American government, and American life and experience or whether the tradition by which Americans live is one of inequality. This is a crucial question when we consider health care in the discussion that follows. Is it the intent that every American has the right to "equal" care with his fellow citizens, or is the purpose of the American government, health care system, and health professions, to "provide for the general welfare" for which equality is not necessary?

To understand the concept of equality it is necessary to go back further in history. The idea of democracy was not born with the Declaration of Independence or the Constitution. It is instead a by-product of many factors originating over the course of centuries of history, encompassing the Judeo-Christian teachings, Greek philosophy, common law, and the hopes of those held in bondage by feudalism. Democracy is an outlook, an attitude, a climate. So the evolvement of democracy was like a change in climate. It would not make sense unless one believes that people should have any say about how they are to be governed. Democracy is an attitude toward people and a moral system that guides any attempts to encourage people to participate in government and decisions that affect their own destiny. Democracy has been said to go even further, to the expression of love toward one's fellow man, more than lip service to liberty, justice, or equality but, in addition, a search for ways that will enhance each man's happiness and work toward the actualization of all that each man is capable of being. One often-cited freedom is that of free exercise of religion, according to the dictates of conscience. Only by twisting these words out of context can atheists and agnostics be said to have free exercise of religion (or irreligion), since American culture has continued to affirm and expect the Judeo-Christian beliefs.

Although the real world of medieval days was cruel, men of the church held to the concept that another world existed. Carvings dating from the medieval period depict peasants, carpenters, and those of low worldly status as ascending in eternity to the status of kings and those of high status here on earth. It is not difficult to follow the idea of equality in the eyes of God to the words "all men are created equal," as contained in the Declaration of Independence. Being equal in the eyes of God does not, of course, mean that all men are equally intelligent, talented, or upright and good or that they are all the same size or have the same amount of physical strength. It does mean, however, that men are equal in that each is a human being and therefore equally valuable because of his human qual-

ity. Aside from that, everything else is unimportant because it is not the external aspect which counts but the internal person. Only if all men have internalized this moral code and are capable of being compassionate can basic democracy work. Democracy as an intent and ideal of a society otherwise fails and is possibly destructive to man in the hands of those whose lives are not guided by that philosophy.

Another apparent intent of the founding fathers was that of individualism. This seemingly implies the freedom to use oneself in pursuit of a better life, using courage, taking risks, and aiming at the achievement of all that one is capable of becoming. If individualism was, indeed, the intent, there arises a question as to the congruence of those who support a "teamism" philosophy. John F. Kennedy is often quoted: "Ask not what your country can do for you but what you can do for your country." The focus is away from the self, or submerging of the self, and toward the good of society or contribution to the team (equating other citizens with members of a team).

The conflict between the elected individual and the mandated office filled has existed throughout American history. Individuals have been admired and trusted public officials, their accomplishments have been acknowledged, although the general public, if questioned, would be unable to outline the responsibility that the official's job entailed. One individual concurrently admired and distrusted equally is Secretary of State Henry Kissinger. A certain uneasiness is commingled with the recognized position he holds and his brilliance. Apprehension surrounds the spectacular manner in which he performs his duties, although his duties are not clearly understood or his performance identifiable. Some wonder if this statesman is to be trusted or if he is, in fact, leading the nation internationally to the point of disaster. Traditionally the United States foreign policy has been intervention oriented or isolation oriented. Those with either orientation have suspicions of the Secretary of State. With neither public consensus nor polarization on foreign policy he must construct an American policy in which the country declines to assume its position as a world power and yet adheres to policies that traditionally are incongruent with that position. Kissinger is the man who stands between those who hold to the belief that the United States should be a "light unto all nations" and those who hold a more or less Machiavellian view. Now is the time for liberal democracy, with policies that value international stability and balance of power. This, among unfriendly nations, will require compromise unpalatable to many purist citizens. If the United States is to be a responsible great nation, it must do more than follow the slogans "make the world safe for democracy" and create an "enduring world order." As a still relatively young nation, the United States is presently confronted with a challenge that requires more maturity. The public burden of responsibility may fall on one controversial character, but it challenges every citizen of the nation at this point in its history.

Experience in recent years with an increasing emphasis on law and order, judicial conservatism, and rules raises an interesting dilemma. Is such an orientation congruent with the ideal of individualism? One might say that it is if the concern is on providing every individual with increased freedom for self-actualization. If, however, its greatest concern is for "protection of society" (team), the price paid (exemplified in law, courts, and throughout society) by all individuals (whether accused of wrong or not) is the necessary submerging of personal goals. The Reign of Terror in France provides a good example of this conflict. When people were freed by the Revolution to seek individual goals, the founders of that free state became so concerned with enforcing the freedom that they rigidly required and forced conformity which was more demanding than that which existed prior to the period of supposed individualism.[5] Writing during this Reign of Terror, Saint-Just saw the need for people to sacrifice self-interest in favor of the public good. The tie that binds humankind and the thing worth the

sacrifice of all good, as he saw it, was love of one's nation, and love of oneself was the root of all evil. He recommended the punishment of not only the guilty but also those who were passive in what they did for their country. To him liberty was impossible without virtue, and virtue was grounded in enforced laws and institutions that formed the framework for an orderly world. The first responsibility for a political leader was to maintain equality, even if by force and terror.[5]

In contrast to this the early documents and statements made by writers like Thoreau supported the thought that the founding fathers wished to employ as little force in the internal management of government as possible. Provision was made for militia to defend the government from outside threats, but there was no preparation for a compliance system to govern its own people or to make the components of government to work together. Almost implied is a belief that because the citizenry is dedicated to the principles of freedom and religious ideals people will be internally "good" and compliance provisions need not be considered. The governmental components have worked together, and some sense of community exists among even those members of the society who strongly disagree. It has the effect of providing a climate in which resolution of conflict or compromise is a tolerable outcome and tempers the extremes.

Along with the avoidance of force, economy has also been an ideal. Big government does not readily allow such an ideal in practice. Since economy has been equated by the American ancestors of a religious orientation with goodness and virtue, whereas spending has been seen as sinful, there has resulted an uneasiness about the growth of government and large programs of all kinds. To many they exemplify spendthriftiness, socialism, communism, and an open invitation to thievery.

Federalism, it has been stated,[6] can only exist and function in a democratic environment. It is a contractual arrangement that links the government and its people in such a way as to preserve the diversity of interests while ensuring their unity. It is perhaps the ability to cope with diversity and conflicting interests that is its greatest attribute and stability-producing factor in the midst of rapid change and turbulence. The traditional theory of American federalism contained within it an inherent supposition that the federal government had no direct concern with local governments. The concept of state sovereignty that is the essence of federalism made it the responsibility and prerogative of each state to establish its individual state constitution and be responsible for units of government within its boundaries. The rationale for this local control is the belief that many problems are unique to a given area rather than universal so that the most appropriate program to meet the local needs can be developed at the local level. It is this rationale that, as late as the 1900s, led to home rule, whereby states relinquished some control for the affairs of a local unit of government, mainly counties, with the intent of eliminating some organizational complexities and overlapping of funds and programs. Revenue sharing originates in the same set of beliefs. President Coolidge is quoted in his 1925 message to Congress as saying, "The functions which the Congress are to discharge are not those of local government but of national government. The greatest solicitude should be exercised to prevent encroachment upon the rights of states or their various political subdivisions. Local self-government is one of our most precious possessions. It is the greatest contributing factor to the stability, strength, liberty and progress of the nation. It ought not to abdicate power through weakness or resign its authority through favor. It does not at all follow that because abuses exist it is the concern of the Federal Government to attempt their reform."

By contrast, in a message to Congress in 1961 President Kennedy said, "Our communities are what we make them. We as a nation have before us the opportunity—and the responsibility—to remold our cities, to improve our patterns of community development. . . .

An equal challenge is the tremendous urban growth that lies ahead. . . . We must do more than concern ourselves with bad housing—we must reshape our cities into effective nerve centers for expanding metropolitan areas." In this continuing balance between federal and local governmental control the town meeting has been cherished as an example of real democracy in action. It is said that in the town meeting all men were considered equal and the views of all were heard. There are an increasing number of present-day historians who are challenging that image. They say that the New England town meeting was, indeed, not a model of democracy. Many now point out that in the New England town meetings only *men* who were heads of households voted. In Virginia it was the gentry *(men)* who made the decisions. Historians cited many of the devices which the powerful used to control the town meeting and point out that "political, ideological and social deviants and dissenters, as well as many of the poor . . . were exited from the town so that . . . the apparent consensus with the town meeting reflects the exclusion from the town of those who didn't fit the consensus."[7] It is our goal to support a philosophy of democracy in which town meetings and other decision-making processes can work without the need for exclusion of large groups of the populace.

The place of health and health care

Any federal health programs legally have their root in the constitutional phrase "to promote the general welfare." The vague nature of these words may be taken to mean that health as a specific was held to be a local concern if it were a governmental function at all. The various state constitutions accept this responsibility, since most specifically mandate provision for public health services. The proliferation of federal programs in various areas of health may be interpreted as a failure of local governments to meet this mandated responsibility to its citizen. Despite this, local government continues to carry a heavy responsibility in health care delivery. City hospitals, for example, are the only source of care for 20% or more of people in large urban areas.[10] Federal programs, Medicaid and Medicare, were expected to change that situation, providing a source of dollars with which patients could purchase health care from any of the range of health care providers. Current public concerns indicate that this has not been effective, and further federal involvement appears inevitable.

The underlying distrust of government had a profound influence on the development of health care services. The Jeffersonian principles of local control won out over Hamiltonian federalism in the establishment of statements in the Constitution protecting states' rights and the protection of private interests and property. It is of great significance that "community needs," "local programs," and "citizen participation" (the Jeffersonian model) are slogans of the day, whereas the means set forth for funding and enforcing of programs that serve the individuals in the local community are federal (the Hamiltonian model).

In the colonial communities of the 1600s to 1700s physicians were few, and people to a great extent relied on folk medicine. The physicians were potentially powerful political persons because they were handed responsibility for all that related to health, including not only diagnosis and treatment of illness but also sanitation, communicable disease control, medical care for the indigent, and caring for people in their own homes. The local town (or county in the South) government began early to support medical relief to the poor. Sometimes churches provided such services. At first care of the sick poor was usually at home or in the home of a relative or friend. Physicians were paid by the case, and gradually one physician assumed the care of all persons considered indigent and was paid an annual salary.

By about 1730 large colonial communities were building almshouses (general hospitals for the poor) with a physician employed on a salary basis. Since the doctor who asked the least salary was usually employed, the quality of care was certainly less than the best. Some-

times transients were cared for by the local facility, but one might speculate that the rationale was that of isolating the individual for the protection of the local residents. The chronic mentally disordered were housed in the local poorhouse as well. Medical care, then, was only an extension of local poor relief patterned after the Elizabethan poor law of 1601.

Care of the sick in hospitals in the United States developed from the tradition of Christian charity practiced in the Middle Ages so that the early hospitals in the United States were closely related to almshouses and intended primarily for those considered as the sick poor. The Pennsylvania Hospital, said to be the first such institution and built with voluntary funds, opened in 1751. It was much later that individuals with financial means were willing to be hospitalized during illness and to build hospitals that were not labeled as charity or government supported. In the present century private support of hospitals has declined, and governmental funds have provided proportionately much more support.

The asylums for the insane in the early 1800s were the first of so-called health facilities that were government supported. The first such hospital was the present Eastern State Hospital, Williamsburg, Virginia, established in 1773. Tuberculosis sanitoria comprised the other type of institution that were predominately government supported. There was probably a twofold reason: (1) tuberculosis was considered a major public enemy and was among the leading causes of death and (2) treatment for tuberculosis in the 1800s was so expensive and long term that people could not supply their own financial resources. Even today, with antibiotics and revolutionary medical interventions, most tuberculosis hospitals remain government supported. Mental disorders (psychoses) and tuberculosis together remain so much government supported that they account for over half of all hospital beds in the country that are tax supported.

Contagious disease control plans increasingly developed into government programs with urbanization. Before that, in rural settings persons with diseases such as small-pox, cholera, and plague were cared for in the home without the need for additional isolation and quarantine measures. As cities grew up, institutions to provide more adequate isolation were considered necessary, and local "pesthouses" were established. The plague epidemic in New York in 1794 was an impetus for the development of such special isolation hospitals, one of the earliest being Bellevue Hospital. There was not much distinction between the pesthouse, poorhouse, or mental hospital. They were usually outside the community and did not experience much change until after pathogenic microorganisms were discovered as causative agents of communicable diseases. Today both hospital and community care of communicable diseases is provided chiefly with local (municipal or county) monies. The larger cities had boards of health by 1860 to deal basically with the problem of communicable disease control through environmental sanitation measures. From the beginning public health services were concerned primarily with environmental sanitation and were divorced from the medical care of the indigent, which was then placed under welfare services or relief to the poor. (Many speculate that this avoided violating the economic prerogatives of the private physician.) A somewhat different pattern of medical care existed in the southern colonies. Free medical care was provided to slaves by plantation physicians and paid for by plantation owners rather than by the government. After the Civil War the heavy burden of the medically indigent black fell on the community. It was this extraordinary burden that provided the impetus for development of full-time county public health departments.

Aside from local governmental involvement in programs dealing with diseases considered as public menaces, the philosophy of individualism prevailed, and medical care was the exclusive work of private physicians. Governmental involvement was kept to a minimum, health departments were given little credit for decreased mortality and morbidity from the contagious diseases, and they were

usually called on only in the event of epidemics. Health officers were not salaried or full-time employees of health departments until after the Civil War.

Resulting from the intent of state sovereignty, the federal government was delegated only powers granted by the states. States, however, were slow in acting on mounting data collected by others, such as the American Medical Association, which described health conditions of the nation. Massachusetts was the first state to establish a permanent state board of health of 1869. The federal government first became involved with health matters when the United States Public Health Service was established to provide hospital care for merchant seamen, neither a public health service nor preventive in nature. In 1798 Congress passed legislation to provide funds for this care through compulsory insurance policies maintained by the seamen. Until the twentieth century, health functions of a federal nature were restricted to protecting the nation through quarantine measures for communicable diseases, medical care of certain persons such as military personnel and dependents, and a limited amount of research. An attempt was made to establish a national department of health during the period about 1880, when yellow fever was prevalent. It was dissolved after four years of operation. The clause "provide for the general welfare" was not interpreted as including activities for the promotion of the general health of the public.

Throughout the history of this nation it is usually voluntary or private groups that demonstrate needs. Gradually the functions are assumed by governmental agencies. For example, the role of the nurse in the health department originated from the role developed by the visiting nurse, who was supported by private funds and who gave care to the poor in the home. Private or voluntary agencies do not necessarily give up their efforts when the functions become governmental responsibility. What results are overlapping and duplication of services or artificially strict rules about boundaries. In some areas a public health nurse (public employee) may be reprimanded for washing a patient's hair because that is considered the domain of the visiting nurse (a private employee).

It was with the Social Security Act of 1935 and the New Deal that the national contribution to state and local funds for public health and medical services increased significantly, although it was still pitifully small. Grants-in-aid were provided by the United States Public Health Service and the Children's Bureau for the first time for preventive services, and many new full-time county health departments were set up. Health insurance plans that presaged Medicare and Medicaid were considered and rejected during this period.

The development of laws governing medical practice and licensure of health professionals follows the same pattern as that of laws and protective measures in other areas. They were the responsibility and right of the states. Only when the public welfare is endangered can the confidential material from medical records be brought before a public court. The deeply rooted concern for freedom from governmental restraints fostered irregular medical practices and a proliferation of marginally prepared medical practitioners. New York, in 1760, was the first state to require examination and licensure to practice medicine. Other areas of federal involvement include medical research and education, stimulated by circumstances related to disease and manpower shortages during wartime. In addition, private commercial interests were permitted to sell anything they chose until the Pure Food and Drug Law was passed in 1906. It took until the Tulfanilamide incident for Congress to pass laws prohibiting interstate sale of any new drug without federal stamp of approval for safety.

As discussed earlier, medical care of the poor was early recognized as a responsibility of local government, particularly towns and counties, and the states. The town physician who cares for the poor is still in practice today in some areas. Articulation of health services of a preventive nature as separate from therapeutic medical care still presents an administrative division that hampers implementation of comprehensive health care of the population. One change is that the town physician has been replaced by the public clinic. Those in rural areas who are able to pay have a family physician. In urban areas private clinics (comprising a group of physicians) to a large extent have replaced the family physician to provide more efficient, less costly service to larger numbers of people.

Medical care as a human right, in contrast to privilege of those with means, developed during the years of the great depression. Unemployment and illness were recognized as being related, and provision of medical care was often a necessary aspect of getting an unemployed person back on the job. In 1933, under the Federal Emergency Relief Administration, the federal government provided funds to local communities through the states for payment to physicians for services rendered to such patients. It was expensive, and care was limited to acute illnesses. In 1935 the Social Security Act ended that program and returned medical care for the indigent to the states and local communities. Federal funds continued for medical service to special categories of cases such as the aged, the blind, and dependent children. Still allocated by welfare departments and fragmented, the total expenditure is estimated to far exceed that for preventive services provided by public health agencies.

At least one administrator and writer in the field of public health[8] expresses the view that it is useless to continue discussing how local government has failed to live up to the traditional ideals. He states that local governments and health departments, instead, can meet the challenges and that they are "the logical, the best-equipped, and the most effective instrument to meet these challenges." He goes so far as to say, "Reorganization must not only permit, but in essence must *force* the interplay between units, between professionals, and with recipients of service." It is not readily clear how congruent this is with the intent of the founding fathers. There is no specific constitutional support for use of federal support in local programs, nor is there a prohibition. The administrator just quoted does not discourage support of local programs from federal sources, but he is more concerned that local governments must take political action as necessary to reorganize public health organizations so that the environment (including leadership, personnel, philosophy, and programs) are flexible and responsive to community needs and pressures. This would, indeed, be local demonstration of the participatory democracy apparently intended.

Those who are concerned by the current unrest and demands for change should reflect on the earlier discussion of the democratic principle. The Constitution did allow for change, and it is to be expected that this will happen as the cultural, technological world changes and the level of education changes the people. Koestler[8a] presents the degree of appropriate participation in democracy as being a function of the understanding the average member of the group has of the total social structure. The growth of such knowledge is not continuous, and a jump of technical progress leads to a drop in political maturity, with a concomitant drop in the capacity for self-government. The correction comes gradually; only when the level of mass consciousness catches up with the objective state of affairs will democracy be asserted. This conquest may be peaceable or by force. The current unrest among American young people may not be caused by wars, poverty, racial discrimination, or poor health care but, rather, insecurity necessary during one of the gaps between the gradual wearing away of old values and the alteration of the political mechanism to accommodate them. Democracy tomorrow will differ from democracy yesterday, and today people are somewhere in between.

An example of a somewhat far shift is that of changes in interpretation of "maintenance of the national health, safety and interest." A case is reported of a 26-year-old conscientious objector who was drafted by the Selective Service System but objected. He had then the option of putting in two years of alternative service doing anything that the draft board considered to be a contribution to the maintenance of national health, safety, and interest. When assigned to carry bed pans at a Veterans Administration hospital, he refused on the grounds that it did not utilize his talent. He offered to give musical performances instead. This offer was accepted as meeting the criteria.[9] The responsibility to be assumed by government in advancing the concept and pursuing policies that do indeed lead to the social, political, and economic equality of all men is a tremendous one. The most input and participation in decision making from the largest number of citizens are certainly two means of moving in the direction of the original "intent." Unfortunately Americans have inherited two apparently incompatible traditions: one that holds to equality in a broad sense, the other that qualifies it because of communal needs. This dichotomy is a serious one and results in contemporary problems such as those related to provision of health care. In an administrative state such as has been developed in the United States, laws are no longer neutral. Laws carry forth standards, and it is virtuous to be law abiding. However, if the law becomes immoral and antihuman toward the individual, it violates each person's inalienable right to the pursuit of happiness. In this form of government one has an obligation to hear all people, to be aware that one is not necessarily right, and to think of others as not necessarily bad because they disagree. This establishes the climate that is necessary for health professionals to provide services that do, in fact, meet people's needs. Following these threads through the current upheavals in the governments within the United States is a challenge that we hope will be met in the following pages.

References

1. Wall Street Journal, Jan. 1, 1972.
2. Webster's seventh new collegiate dictionary, Springfield, Mass., 1971, G. & C. Merriam Co.
3. The constitution of South Carolina of 1778, II, 1623.
4. Bozell L. B.: The death of the constitution, Triumph III, no. 2, Feb., 1968.
4a. Kendall, W., and Carey, G. W.: The basic symbols of

the American political tradition, Baton Rouge, 1970, Louisiana State University Press.

5. Weinstein, F., and Platt, G.: The wish to be free, Berkeley and Los Angeles, University of California Press.

6. Elazar, D. J.: Continuity and change in American federalism, Public Education Papers no. 2, Philadelphia, 1967, Temple University.

7. MacDougall, S.: Radical historians get growing following, dispute "myths" of past, Wall Street Journal, Oct. 19, 1971.

8. Cowen, D. L.: Community health—A local government responsibility, American Journal of Public Health 61:2005-2006, 1971.

8a. Koestler, A. (trans. by Daphne Hardy): Darkness at noon, New York, 1958, The Macmillan Co.

9. Salerno, G.: Alternative service: more young men have nonmenial "C.O." jobs, Wall Street Journal, Oct. 11, 1971.

It is not strange . . . that such an exuberance
of enterprise should cause some individuals
to mistake change for progress.

MILLARD FILLMORE

2

CHANGING ROLES
AND RELATIONSHIPS

Without political ideas government would be impossible. What people think determines how people are governed. As the thoughts and ideas of men change, so does government change. To make changes in government it is more important to know what is going on in the minds of men than it is to gain physical control over their bodies. Changes in the thought patterns of people are likely to be so slight as to be almost imperceptible at first, but as people do begin to see things with a different perspective, their laws, constitutions, courts, and allegiances all become modified with relative force or position.

One evidence of shifts in people's thinking is changes in everyday speech. Words are invented, twisted in meaning, or stretched to describe broader ideas. If one wishes to learn about the hopes, insights, prejudices, and foolishness of generations past, one may do so by the study of old words. To really get a fair review of the meaning of the intent of the American government it was necessary to review words that were used by the founding

fathers as they described the governmental structure that they wished to build in the context of their world. Books written during the early part of American history were written by those who were literate—the upper classes—and reflect their biases. The poor common people did not contribute to the literature. "We, the people of the United States," as written in the Constitution did not include the poor and ordinary folk and has not always been construed to include women. As one discusses *changing* roles and relationships therefore one must be aware of at least two possibilities: (1) that people's ideas are the same but the words used to describe them are different or (2) that people's ideas are now different but the words used to describe them are the same.

The language of government and politics reflects the evolving scope and depth of changes in the way people think. Some words are familiar, but their definition and use have changed. In other instances the political terminology of today would have been completely incomprehensible a century ago. Study of a dictionary reveals the concerns and issues of the culture or period of time at which the work was produced. In review of changing political and social concerns it is helpful to study the Westchester *Dictionary of the English Language* (1859).[1] Such study reveals that the vocabulary was devoid of words dealing with race relations, the labor movement, urbanism, modern technology, or involvement in world affairs. The words *cost accounting, business cycle, assembly line, manpower, raw materials, power politics, sabotage,* and *syndicates* which were often related to political issues as well as economic aspects, also were unknown. *Population explosion, birth control,* and *contraception* were words not in use; *hormones* and *vitamins* had not been heard of. A more complete list[2] of absent words includes the following:

absentee voting	fair housing
administrative	fluoridation
adult education	free enterprise
Anti-Saloon League	gangster
antitrust law	gerrymander
apportionment	grants-in-aid
(of representation)	grass roots
backlash	health insurance
balanced budget	home rule
big business	juvenile delinquency
birth control	kindergarten
bipartisan	labor union
black power	life expectancy
bossism	local government
centralization	mass behavior
child labor	mass man
city manager	mass production
city planning	megalopolis
closed shop	MIAs
consumer goods	middle class
cost of living	old age pension
cultural anthropology	parking meter
culture complex	plain clothesman
demography	public health
disadvantaged	public housing
division of labor	public school
elitism	racism
energy crisis	senior citizen
entrepeneur	skylab
environment	social mobility
equal opportunity	social science
escapism	take-home pay
ethnic group	traffic jam
fair employment	traffic light

unemployment	vital statistics
unemployment compensation	wage slave
	Watergate affair
urban renewal	wetback
urban sociology	zoning

In addition to the conceptual differences reflected by the previously unknown vocabulary, the basic data sources without which the current system would fail have undergone massive change.

Statistics regarding literacy and college or school attendance at all levels were not available 100 years ago. In 1870 there were perhaps less than a dozen professors of history in the entire country and no professional students of political science.[3] To many, any change is a good change: to the critical student of government any change and no change must be regarded with an equally questioning gaze until value becomes evident. As Will Rogers said, "Lord, the money we do spend on government, and it's not one bit better than the government we got for one third the money 20 years ago."[4]

Consistencies

Before beginning to review the changes that have occurred, the reader should also be reminded that there are some consistencies with the earliest forms and functions. Elazar's excellent discussion[5] of the overriding continuity of American federalism may indeed be a beginning to a discussion of changes. For purposes of his discussion he presents three political principles: contractual noncentralization, territorial democracy, and multifaceted democracy.

Contractual noncentralization is power that is diffused or dispersed among many centers, which are guaranteed their legitimate authority by the central power, in relation to the powers dispersed among many governmental units and guaranteed by the United States and state constitutions. Noncentralization is only possible when there is no legitimate means of either centralizing or decentralizing the power. This applies to the American system, which can move far in either direction without breaking the structure or spirit of the Constitution. It is to be distinguished from decentralized (by the central government). In having overriding power the states in the federal system do not derive their power from the federal government but from the people. In structure therefore they are protected from federal intervention, although in function they may carry on many activities in which the federal government also engages. They do so, however, without jeopardizing their role or power in decision making.

As the national government has become more involved in programs dealing with health, little can be generalized about the relative power of various centers (or levels) in decision making. Noncentralization, unlike decentralization, describes a diffusion of power so that a simple rank order cannot be made of power in various programs or endeavors at the various levels as it might be in a decentralized or pyramidal system. For example, whereas the national government has primary power in international trade, the states have primary power in education. The fact is that operationally, however, all levels of government are involved in each of these and all activities of government. This applies to the local government as well.

Although local units of government are theoretically created by the states, they obtain some political power by virtue of this noncentralization. They may develop programs and policies within their respective areas but require outside assistance to implement them. An example is a large county that has its own highly complex mental health program, which it may operate independently from the state or federal government if it wishes, or that may develop funding to provide the mental health services through private sources.

This partnership between public and private sectors and among levels of government has been possible because of the flexibility with which the Constitution may be construed. Noncentralization historically has also been termed by some as territorial democracy. It is an approach proposed to accommodate the gamut of national and local interests and to maintain the basic integrity of the various levels of government while making possible public programs for which otherwise there would be no means of operation.

Attention has been given to the importance and relevancy of the state level of government to the people of the United States. Certain services and policies of the states are specific and meaningful to residents within the states. As more programs that were previously state responsibility receive federal emphasis and support, the state seems to be less a vital institution in the minds of men. Even though the lives of people within a state are affected by various state government activities, they may not perceive the impact or become particularly interested and involved. An individual's interest is drawn by activities at the local, state, national, and international levels. Issues may touch all levels but be more prominent at one or another level.

Two types of cognitive mapping have been proposed[6] to describe where and on what people place importance. One type of mapping is in terms of issues. Some may place more importance on foreign affairs issues, others may place more importance on civil rights issues, whereas still others may place greatest importance on tax and economic issues. The second type of mapping suggested is according to geopolitical units. The national government of the United States, as well as the governments of all other nations, encounters difficulties that have their origin at least partially in some subnational loyalties. A charismatic, highly personable governor or specific issues such as disagreement over a state tax program may increase the importance that people place on state politics. To the extent that interest among citizens of a state overlap around such forces will the two types of mapping also overlap.

The states do not stand out as prominent for various reasons. The states of this nation are as large or larger than many nations of the world, and in reality they are too large to facilitate any meaningful civic participation. Local governments are immediate to the lives of residents; national and international governmental systems are seemingly more important and associated with grandeur. Somehow state governments are caught between.

A study by Dahl* ranked what importance respondents placed on governmental affairs at the local, state, national, and international levels. As Dahl predicted, the majority gave greater emphasis to local and national affairs (including international affairs as an extension of national affairs). State governmental affairs, although they are not uppermost in the minds of people, held a secure position. Results also indicated that the individuals who pay the most attention to state affairs are residents on farms or in small towns, and in states of the southern and western regions of the United States. The attention they give to state affairs was inversely related to the person's highest educational level completed. State affairs were given greater importance by the working class and increased proportionately to the length of time during which the person resided in the state, with lifelong residents paying the most attention to state affairs. The conclusions drawn were that the states still are important entities in the eyes of the public.

New interrelationships

The beginning reader of the federal Constitution and the other documents outlining government in the United States might well believe that the lines of demarcation between them are clear. Although it may have been the intent to have tidy divisions, there have developed multiple crossings of both levels of government and the public-private sector line. Beginning with this latter point, there has been a growing linkage between government, especially the federal government, and private sectors. The result is the identification of great national associations or corporations that, in their own right, have power to influence congressional decisions that traditionally belonged only to state and local governments. The recent oil shortage and scrutiny of American business abroad led some to say that

*Referred to by Jennings.[6] First appeared in Dahl, R. A.: The city in the future of democracy, The American Political Science Review **61**:953-970, 1967.

private business also makes international policy—a clear violation of constitutional intent. The involvement has potential as a means of encouraging noncentralized government. An older example might be the Job Corps. More recently the health maintenance organizations have been labeled as a way to develop private medical industries under federal contract to provide health care. Although planners hoped this would lead to health care for people in area that greatly lack comprehensive health services, the legislation does not require it. Even if it had, there is question of the realistic potential for compliance with intended purpose that is raised when one combines federal and private sectors. Are there state and local powers that are readily mobilized to force compliance with intended purposes, especially of a nationwide private sector?

Pluralism theoretically requires representation of interests. It implies that conflicting views can exist side by side. The views and interests are, in reality, organized ones. For example, the views and interests of "labor" are, in fact, those of large labor organizations that may not represent individuals. Decisions may be made by experts or professionals on the basis of their perception of what is best for each individual. What is built, in the process, is a bureaucracy where decisions are not identified with one person; therefore no one can be accountable.

It was with industrialization and technology that metropolitan development and problems began. A growing margin between American culture and its social structure continues. Much has been written about life of the assembly plan worker by sociologists, many of whom have never been inside such a plant. Theoretical knowledge not necessarily based on experience drives the present postindustrial revolution. Dissension between capitalist and worker has faded somewhat and has given way to increasing tensions resulting from professional and intellectual class. This new group claims recognition based on expertise and knowledge rather than capital. Theoretical planning of the future is their dream; the computer is the tool to be used with decision-making theory being the master of the process. Whether one is an industrial worker or a professional intellectual, one is caught up in a conflict between a culture that nurtures measures of self-indulgence and an economy that demands increasing specialization after self-denial through long costly training. The latter conflicts with the self-fulfillment, personal human development ideal.

Innovations of the nineteenth and twentieth centuries, such as railroads, telephone and telegraph, electricity, automobiles, airplanes, and motion pictures have had great impact on life today. However, a more significant impact has come about from a social framework that brought isolated areas and peoples into the mainstream of society through various forms of communication and transportation. Before television, uprising and violence such as occurred in coal-mining areas received less visibility and so was more easily dissipated. In contrast the riots of the 1960s in the ghettos and on university and college campuses received widespread and immediate visibility. There was little insulation from the shocks of these upheavals, since it is likely that few people were unaware of them because of television, radio, and the printed word.

An advantage of the past existed in that the character structure, with emphasis on self-control, thrift, and deferred gratification, was more congruent with the need of the economy for rational behavior and accumulation of capital. In the postindustrial period young people are encouraged to seek self-fulfillment in work that is meaningful to them and to resist conformity to specialization, although specialization will continue to increase. Conflict between hedonistic philosophy and stark economic reality creates the nature of American society. What the future will hold is dependent on working out the dynamics between culture and political powers that control American economy.

The expression of powerlessness through "tuning out" the establishment may be the younger generation's response to the depersonalized nature of such a bureaucracy. Many organizations such as Common Cause or the Ralph Nader consumer groups have been organized to harness this machine. Even if appropriate measures to keep the public-private relationships within the bounds of constitutionality were developed, the current programs and relationships will linger. There is always perpetuation of a program or organization for some time after that program or organization has discontinued performing the function for which it was created and that organization will continue to struggle to survive.

As a further point regarding the historical continuity of governments, Elazar* maintains that the development of public-private relationships for providing services and programs at all levels is reviving the whole notion of federalism to a level of operation never before contemplated. This is based on two fundamental points: (1) rather than being in conflict, activities of government must be shared by all levels of government for maximum effectiveness and responsiveness to public needs and (2) it is possible for all levels of government to gain power at the same time; that is, one level need not gain power at the expense of another. In the 1800s there were evidences of cooperative ventures among the levels of government involving the development of schools, roads, railroads, and early public welfare institutions, to name only a few. Such programs were financed through federal and state land grants and even cash grants-in-aid. In 1932 the word *municipalities* first appeared in an act of Congress, making available loans to cities for self-liquidating public works projects.[7] This might be considered the beginning of a new kind of federalism, sometimes referred to as a marble-cake theory of federalism.[8] By 1960 the federal government was involved in providing assistance to local governments in the areas of hospital construction, mental health, training programs for local health personnel, health

---

*Elazar's views are questioned by some political scientists who have held that the federal system functioned best when the various levels were functionally and structurally separate.

grants for the study and control of cancer, heart disease, and venereal disease, as well as indirect health programs such as school lunches and air pollution control.

Currently, with the immense volume of dollars passing through federal-local and federal-state programs, it has become apparent that the federal government cannot easily manage and coordinate funds and programs. At least two procedures have evolved: (1) state departments dealing exclusively with federal affairs and (2) state and local coordination efforts for dealing with federally funded programs. As government at all levels—federal, state, and local—has grown throughout the years, there are no indicators that a reversal trend is in sight, either in terms of size, activities, or funds involved. Sharing will no doubt continue, but there may be shifting of functions due to the noncentralization phenomenon. Regional programs are likely to become more prevalent as a means of dealing with problems that cross local and state boundaries. There are issues surrounding regional governments, programs, or planning that are too vast to present here.

Despite problems, sharing seems necessary, and the question of how sharing can be encouraged is a real one. Coercion as a means to bring about sharing and participation in decision making is without a doubt an unrealistic approach, under which intended goals of the sharing will most likely remain unrealized by the public for whom they were planned.

In all of the changes if the states are to maintain their position of unique power in the American governmental system, they will need to contribute to the facilitation of federal-local relations that have become so widely prevalent and accepted by much of American citizenry. It is already apparent that many of the states' problems evolve from federal-local relations which have already been established. The local government, particularly small cities and towns, has difficulty confronting the great federal government bureaucracy in Washington to meet needs. At the same time "Washington" is aware that it

cannot make successful policy for all localities across the country. This is the states' challenge. As it frequently appears at this time, the states are merely a formal route through which federal funds flow to local areas. They can no longer continue to make themselves as much like local government as possible to get in on the communication act. They are beginning to resume acting as central governments in their own right and developing policies and plans related to the subdivisions for which they are responsible. Alterations in channeling federal funds, giving state units control over the monies they process, are increasing at present. One example is the channeling of federal funds for maternal and child health through state health departments rather than directly to local health units.

Local and state financial crises

State and local expenditures continue to expand, and it is frequently repeated among the citizenry that state and local services are in a sad state of affairs because of lack of funds. An alternative to the continuation of the present state of things is the concept of revenue sharing. It calls for distribution of a certain percentage of federal income tax revenue to the states to be used by the respective states as they see fit. It was proposed by those who operated on the assumption that the states, including their cities, had exhausted financial resources to the extent that they could not possibly raise taxes further to meet their obligations. The idea of revenue sharing was proposed[9] by Melvin Laird in 1958 when he was a congressman from Wisconsin; he called it the "Great Republican Alternative to the Great Planned Society." It was supported by former President Nixon in his Budget Message of the President, January, 1971, where he referred to it as a way of "returning government to the people," that is, of transferring some of the functions of the federal government (determining needs and allocating funds to programs) back to the states and cities. The question has been raised concerning whether the state and local governments are, in fact, in such disastrous straits or whether there is real need for making better utilization of financial resources now at their command. Some express a need to reexamine the alleged and evident inadequacies of state and local services for other signs of causation, such as unwillingness to meet social obligation rather than lack of financial resources. Furthermore, revenue sharing may not assure that the social and economic problems would be eliminated, since funds can well have a way of being utilized at any level in such a manner as not to be addressing the public's expressed need any better than before the funds existed. Many have proposed that direct action by federalization of welfare is the only method of assuring that social problems of local citizens are really addressed. This, of course, was the underlying basis for the various local-federal programs and grants-in-aid to local communities that are now being eliminated or drastically reduced.

One previously prevalent myth was that the central government could disburse funds without necessarily needing to exercise controls on the recipients of the funds. In discussing the increasing emphasis on revenue-sharing as a means of support for local programs, for example, schools, there are those who maintain that local control need not be reduced and centralization of power will not be the inevitable result. The argument has been that it is possible to expect federal monies for local programs and that local government will automatically provide for compliance with intent. If that were the case, it seems that federal programs would not have originated to solve problems of inequities and major legislation would not be continually rewritten or abandoned, if noncompliance had not invalidated the original intent. The compliance measures utilized by the funding agency may extend beyond the original terms of the contract with the federal government (an unanticipated consequence of change).

An example is cited[9] of a private institution, Columbia University, receiving federal payment for contract work. A threat of cutting off funds has been made by the government apparently because of inadequate proof that the university is providing employment opportunities to women and minority groups. In this instance the original intent was to discourage discriminatory hiring practices among government contractors, but ultimately the compliance measures have pushed for what appears to be reverse discrimination beyond the original intent of the contract with the federal government, and perhaps beyond the intent of the original law. The maintenance of power and control has often proved to be an illusion when there is control of the purse strings.

As health programs become increasingly tax supported, the question of assuring compliance comes to the forefront. Who is to be responsible for reviewing dentists and physicians to see that they are doing their jobs and how much they are charging the local Medicaid program for medical care provided to the needy? Provisions for professional standards review organizations have been passed as an amendment to the Social Security Act, after proposal by Senator Wallace F. Bennett of Utah. Other approaches are under consideration. The possibility of strict reviews of services provides reason for concern to physicians and fear of undue intervention into professional practice. The American Hospital Association is quoted[10] as stating that the legislative amendment providing review procedures was "the most extreme invasion of the private practice of medicine in history."

Surveillance procedures seem necessary, as illustrated in the following example.[10] A team of physicians examined a child with an inflammation of the ear and referred him to their ear, nose, and throat specialist. They billed Medicaid $20 for the visit. The case was reviewed by Deputy Commissioner of the New York Department of Public Health and his staff. The conclusion reached was that one shot of penicillin was all the child needed and that the referral to a specialist was highly unusual. The local Medicaid office refused to pay the physicians' bill.

The American Medical Association has proposed an alternative to pressures for government intervention in the form of "peer review." Their argument is that physicians are the only ones qualified to judge whether proper treatment was given. With the power and control from outside review, it is argued, medical practice has lost part of what makes it a profession. Argument in favor of the Bennett legislative amendment was that "He who pays the fiddler calls the tune. Those who are paying the dollars want the assurance, an assurance predicated on more than faith, that they are getting their money's worth."[11]

The trend in the revenue-sharing approach now used is an attempt to mandate the disbursement of funds to be spent at local option. The maintenance of this system is not guaranteed if local decision makers do not use funds with sophistication and expertise and once again encourage the growth of more centralized governmental units. One other influence is that just as metropolitan areas have learned to negotiate more effectively with the central government, increasingly larger proportions of people are moving away from the center of the relatively few metropolitan areas. The power of those cities to deal individually with the federal government will consequently diminish as a result of decreased self-sufficiency and local expertise. They will need to rely more on their respective states for assistance in the process of dealing for the dollar. This will probably add to the forces supporting the revival of power at the level of state government. States do take action both to preserve power and to prevent its development elsewhere.

Growth of nationalized programs extends to many areas. One is that of workmen's compensation. The program, modeled after the nineteenth century European industrial insurance plans, incorporates the notion that accidents on the job are a cost of production and should be paid for by the employer and not society. However, a great variation exists among the states with regard to benefits and how the programs are administered. Some states began programs in the early 1900s when work-related accidents and deaths increased with industrial expansion. The programs remain totally state operated. Fearing

federal take-over of the program in 1975, states are rapidly enacting changes to upgrade their laws to prevent the federal government from imposing standards. Some of the problems are that state benefit levels have not been keeping up with inflation and rising wage levels. As a result, in twenty-three of the fifty states the maximum amount disabled workers receive for a family of four is below the official United States poverty level of $82.69 per week. In some states the maximum is even as low as $50 per week. More than 12 million of the 85 million American workers are not covered at all by this form of insurance because of gaps in state laws. These include domestic and farm workers, who are least able to carry the burden of disability. One bill being considered in Congress would guarantee disability benefits to at least two thirds of the employee's average wage, obviously increasing the cost of the program considerably but eliminating present fragmentation and weaknesses.

Although revenue sharing was intended to ease the burden of local taxpayers in terms of developing certain programs, it has not entirely done so. It has been considered by some officials as a godsend, whereas other town officials have flatly rejected it. Many of the towns refusing the assistance are small and may not have had experience dealing with federal government before. However, reasons they give include not wanting the federal officials breathing down their necks, not needing the money, or inability to use the funds for the particular project the community needs most. Some local officials regard revenue sharing as unneeded, unpalatable, and having too many strings attached.[12]

The source of the money is also in question. The issue of increasing sales and property taxes at state and local levels has met with increasing resistance from voters. The support for their negative vote is that it takes proportionately more from the incomes of the lower income individual and his family. Consequently bond issues have been repeatedly turned down, and local services are cut to levels never dreamed possible after the golden era of the 1960s, when state and local expenditures were increasing by leaps. The proposed alternative to the use of sales and property taxes for the support of local services (and schools) is increased federal taxes, presumably income tax. Income tax has, to date, been judged as perhaps the better way of distributing the tax burden among individuals according to their ability to pay. This, however, is a generalization that does not account for the tax loopholes and ways of evading the tax regulations by individuals of high income levels. These are reported in news media daily; one has difficulty measuring the presumed fairness against such unfairness, since dollar amounts so lost to the general federal resource are only speculative.

Local areas vary tremendously in their cultures and needs. In New York City, for example, subway car cleaners will soon be making $11,472, or $1,600 more than the average Ohio school teacher earned in 1973.[12] New York's and other cities' politicians are fighting in Washington, D. C., for all the federal mass transit operating subsidies they can get to keep fares from increasing while paying the transit car cleaners the increased wages. The Ohio teachers and other citizens will therefore be paying federal taxes so that New York citizens can ride buses without increased fare and so the transit car cleaners can receive the $11,472 salary. While this was happening, the United States Internal Revenue Service found that former President Nixon owed over $475,000 in unpaid taxes.

Federal changes

Although it has not yet commanded its potential to be realized, one political scientist has proposed that the "House of Representatives should be the most vigorous institution of the federal government."[13] This is because its biennial elections offer greatest representativeness, its authority to raise revenues provides means to be responsive to needs, and with its responsibility for determining national objectives it can also test for legality or illegality. From this it would appear that the House of Representatives thus replaces the old town meetings. The committee structure of the House began in 1800 with the establishment of four standing committees and multiplied into twenty-one standing committees by 1958. The intent of the committees was to provide careful study of matters and division of the work load among the representatives.

The current functioning of the committees and consequently of the House is so complex, with 435 representatives functioning on the numerous committees, that it cannot be as dynamic an institution as it might be. The Speaker is hindered in providing the leadership necessary; information on which decisions must be made is not always received or utilized. The committees do not have the overall view of economics that is necessary to establish priorities, nor is coordination facilitated. Changes are possible because no rules and few customs prohibit them. Seniority, now discarded, earlier determined that representatives newly elected had little opportunity to influence decisions because their seniors were assigned to those positions and committees in which they had power to control the activities and ultimate decisions.

The House Speaker's power presently is more personal than inherent in the institution of his office. He cannot establish agenda, discipline, or reward. He makes appointments to committees but is unable to favor the senior members, and he does not have the necessary control over establishment of committees. The individual who can fulfill the role under such circumstances certainly is a rare gem.

In 1961 a change of the House Rules Committee, supported by the then Speaker Rayburn, added two Democrats and one Republican. This was done to create a majority in the committee of eight to seven members so that the Democrats or liberals had a better chance for passage of liberal legislation. Such legislation had previously been blocked because the committee was divided eight to four with regard to party affiliation but six to six with regard to ideology (Southern Democrats and Republicans versus liberal Democrats).

As compared with the executive branch,

the House lacks resources for receiving information, processing it, and planning and developing priorities. The executive branch, the President and his advisors, prepares the national budget, despite the fact that it was the House which was charged with fiscal responsibilities. From this has developed the extraordinary executive impoundment of funds that the House had deemed necessary. To counteract this development a joint Study Committee on Budget Control, comprising House and Senate members, was established in 1972. The budget committee structure must have access to more data and be created with more participation from the House leader (Speaker) so that the House can regain the powers which have been usurped by the executive branch.

Legislative committees have evolved as a system of numerous standing committees. The political parties gradually developed procedures so that the committees were systematically controlled by the majority party with representation from the minority party. Then the seniority system came about. In 1921 the number of committees was cut drastically, and in 1946 seniority control was eliminated and subcommittees were increased. More recently, since 1970, reforms resulted by way of the Subcommittee Bill of Rights, which outlined the selection of subcommittee chairmen and the powers and duties of subcommittees.

The standing committees are currently not serving the House as well as they might because of their boundaries of jurisdiction being unclear; duplication of effort is the obvious result. Often bills are drafted in such a manner that they will reach a specific committee, but because of several committees with differing points of view interested in the issue they vie for control. Although study from different points of view may be desirable, the intent of the original proposal may be diverted. Instead of finding a committee with which an issue or proposal naturally is identified and in which it might receive fair consideration, it may in fact become something like a football being fought over by committees that are foes for purposes of winning something, usually power, similar to a game to be won. There is a parallel of this in the area of professional organizations, committees, and institutions. Senators depend on their peers who serve on Senate Committees to consider what is Senate business. Committees are essential, but problems of organization, procedure, responsibilities, and functions have seemingly become confused so that the balance among the branches of government designed and outlined in the Constitution has gone out of alignment. In recent years the executive branch has gained extraordinary authority from Congress, and some areas that demand attention in behalf of the society are now being neglected by all of government.

Conflicts at the committee structure level are not to be considered minor. The Armed Services Committee has responsibility for maintaining and operating the Panama Canal. The Commerce Committee also has some jurisdiction over the Panama Canal. The Committee of Veterans Affairs handles soldiers' and sailors' civic relief; yet the Armed Services Committee deals with housing of soldiers and sailors. The Committee on Agriculture and the Committee on Interior and Insular Affairs both deal with forestry and forest reserves. These are only a few examples to illustrate the problem with the present committee structure. Is it any small wonder that conflicts exist and create inefficiency?

In considering realignment of the committee structure, Brock[13] has suggested four alternatives, consisting of organization by function, by parallel action with the executive branch, by clientele served (special interest), and by geographical area (regional government). To better respond to the constitutional mandate Brock prefers to reorganize Congress along functional lines and to reorganize the executive branch so that its activities would be subject to the same efficiency and scrutiny.

The amount of business that must be addressed by present-day government as compared with the early days of America has greatly proliferated. As an example, whereas most of the seventeen Senate standing committees during the first session of the Ninety-third Congress were referred fewer than 100 bills (as of July 1, 1973), four of them were referred more than 200 bills. The heaviest work loads were handled by the Commerce, Finance, Interior and Insular Affairs, and Labor and Public Welfare Committees.[13]

Some reforms contained in the 1970 Legislative Reorganization Act provided for extended closure of committee meetings, proxy voting permissible in a limited way, and more fund guarantees for the minority party. From the standpoint of democracy in action two significant changes occurred: Roll calls were made public, and committee hearings were permitted to be broadcast on radio and television. Prior to 1973 the committee chairman, whether conservative or liberal, had autocratic power and assumed almost total power over his committees. Chairmen were henceforth prevented from "stacking" their committees. For example, now when variances in assignment occur no member, can retain more than two of his old subcommittee assignments until every member had made his one choice. In addition, under the Subcommittee Bill of Rights, power was distributed from committee chairmen to subcommittee chairmen. Subcommittees now must have ratios in compliance with party ratio in committees.

The conservative faction of the Democratic party, in its alliance with the Republican congressmen, previously blocked any more liberal legislation. Rather than reforms coming about from the floor of the House of Representatives, the Democratic Caucus has recently been used to a larger extent. This is particularly important to Democratic liberals in providing them with an opportunity to exercise their power, binding Democrats together and giving them stronger influence.

It is through committees that Congress outlines national problems and molds policies. Committees are not, however, an accurate reflection of the entire spectrum of interests within the political system or in the two houses of Congress. Congressmen tend to seek committee assignments for personal satisfaction and reasons of promotion. This includes

wanting reelection, wanting increased influence over policy making, and exerting increased influence in Congress. This understandably makes them vulnerable to the interests of those who most are affected by their decisions. General interests are therefore poorly represented. Committees are slow to respond to shifts in societal viewpoints because of shifts in membership that take time and thus lag behind social and political changes.

Legislators' personal goals with regard to committee assignments are not always congruent with the reasons why they were elected. Their most important responsibility is that of serving their constituencies in whatever manner that is achieved. It might be accomplished by personality characteristics and reputation but also may relate directly to the committees on which the legislators serve. Those being elected for the first term(s) therefore would be expected to seek committees that hold forth the greatest promise of paying off in obtaining something for the constituency. There is a pecking order that relates to congressmen's seniority. This is seen in a review of the committees and the observation that the more senior prestigious committees comprise elder congressional members, and "first-termers" seldom achieve assignment to these committees. It then holds conversely that there are committee assignments which are shunned because their work neither holds glamor nor pays off. To illustrate this point several senior committees are the Standards of Official Conduct (which adjudicates ethics cases), Ways and Means, Appropriations, and Rules. The least sought are the District of Columbia committees, which have limited relevance to those outside the Washington, D. C., area, and Senate Rules and Administration and House Administration, which are housekeeping groups.

Congressmen's liberal or conservative orientation and ideology have greatly influenced the committee assignments they seek. Some committees have historically embraced liberalism, the House Education and Labor Committee being a prime example. It is a committee that has for years brought to confrontation ideological issues dividing liberals and conservatives. Liberals with zeal to frame legislation in the area of education and labor and in behalf of the lower socioeconomic constituencies seek out this committee. Having the blessing of the labor union alliance, the AFL-CIO is influential backing to a congressman wishing an assignment to those committees with a liberal orientation. On the other hand, the members of the House Armed Services Committee and Internal Security Committee tend to be conservative and conduct business more conservatively than the House of Representatives as a whole.

Other examples of malrepresentation in Congress exist. Coastal areas congressmen control the merchant marine and fisheries committees, those west of the Mississippi are overrepresented on committees of the interior, little urban representation is seen on agriculture committees. The importance of the work of these groups to almost all constituencies makes "irrelevancy" a difficult assertion. Some scrutiny by those concerned but not directly involved would seem to be appropriate.

Strategies have been under consideration to make committees more representative of their parent group, Senate or House. Some balance seems to be developing but must undoubtedly be brought about with caution so as not to jeopardize committee effectiveness and morale and increase useless, heated confrontations in committee meetings. Committees might be left to attract members who have intense interests, but if the committees ceased to serve as an arena for airing diverse views, the House and Senate would then have to undertake the deliberation aspect and be responsible for moderating proposals that were presented from the committees. If a regular membership rotation became mandatory, it would allow enthusiastic new blood to break the closely knit alliances that develop on some committees but would also eliminate the expertise that comes with experience and seniority. Determining the period of optimum efficiency is a haunting question, however. Over recent decades control that committees

held over the ultimate vote outcome has been lessened through such developments as the counting, recording, and reporting to constituencies of votes, which resulted in better attendance and voting records of congressmen.

(Major changes in the present system and its functioning should be directed at controlling the powerful specialty-oriented pressures that inhibit the voice of the public and prohibit that which is for the general good. More will be said about this later.)

Although both houses of Congress were created equal in power, they differ greatly in size, responsibilities, the way in which they function, and those that constitute their membership. Difference has advantages, but the existent jeolousies and conflict cannot be allowed to make it impossible for the houses to cooperate for the benefit of the common good of the nation. Joint committees and conference committees have been used to bring the two houses together. This must be balanced against the advantages of each house presenting and defending differing viewpoints on issues. Ways might be encouraged to increase contact of members of the two houses along party lines or to create parallel committee structures. The latter trend seems to be exemplified in the recent creation of the Senate Committee on Veterans Affairs to parallel the previously existing House Veterans Committee. Alterations of the present system must be cautiously undertaken so that cooperation does not stifle careful interhouse debate and study of any matters that will become national law.

In the course of carrying out their duties, these men and women in Congress who represent American society must act and react on controversial issues; they need to do so in a somewhat structured manner so as not to risk the releasing of too much conflict through mass arousal of outsiders, which would awaken unexpressed conflict that could be uncontrollable. Congress has been referred to as serving the function of keeping societal conflict under control, serving as a place where competing interests are adjusted through the battles fought there. It is the members of Congress who determine outcomes of societal conflicts; society does not make the determination. The committee system is directly involved in the controlling of conflict over issues and determination of the outcomes. Deliberate mechanisms are utilized. By having fewer individuals involved, fewer positions must be dealt with, and when the parent house acts, the members of the committee present the recommendation and facilitate expedient movement toward a vote. The process in which members engage has parallels elsewhere. With increased inflation, energy shortage, price and wage controls, and the resultant shortage of raw materials many companies have turned to bartering as a way to get materials that are vital to their business. By using the system of bartering, it is possible to keep prices down and limit black-market activity. Professionals have undoubtedly used this technique for many years and in many ways. Perhaps seldom have they thought of beneficial effects outside of a personal "in the pocket" reward. Such trading is frowned on by many, but one might question how few have thought out the effects, be they negative or positive.

One result of the increasing of size of committees would be that of representing a greater spectrum of difference and generating greater open expression of conflict. Closed hearings serve as one means of keeping out those who might create a conflict. If an individual who has potential interest in entering into conflict is unaware of the occurrence of conflict or what is involved, a fight is less likely to occur. Members similarly might be specifically asked to join in a conflict, but when brought to the floor, members who were involved in the committee hearings and are knowledgeable maintain control of debate, keeping others ignorant of that which they wish to be kept unknown. Because committees are relatively small, the members interact closely, and intense conflict is avoided to maintain cordial feelings among friends. If committees were larger and if members were rotated more frequently, this close interaction

would be diminished. The seniority of committee chairmen deters conflict and leaves the group with a degree of freedom from outsiders so that they can deal with internal business in a way which might be paralleled to family privilege. Seniors also proclaim knowledge gained with experience when in debate special expertise settles conflict. When policy-making capacity is threatened by entrance of the public into the deliberations at hand, there will be increased emphasis on the consequences of such public intrusion over and above the day-to-day aspects of harmony and efficiency internal to the houses of Congress.

For the public to learn what goes on in Congress the press must receive the information. The press utilizes criticism as a tactic by pointing out alliances, the costs of bills under consideration, inaction, or chairman ineffectiveness. If a press reporter makes it evident that he cannot be silenced or used to advantage by a committee or its members, his access to information will be abruptly limited to what he could get in a meeting open to the general public. However, disgruntled members of the minority party or staff may quietly provide tidbits of data, taking great care, however, to protect their positions. Reporters use the strategy of quoting "unnamed sources," although the strength of their statements may be less. Two patterns of press coverage have developed—one to rotate assignments, the other to maintain the same assignment. Each has positive and negative aspects explained simply in the advisability of retracing steps where previous stories were obtained. Knowing that reporters change, a committee member might be more likely to provide inaccurate information, or having been provided with inaccurate data, a reporter who stays on the same "beat" would remember and not return to that information source. Without going into further detail, the interdependence of Congress and the press is a safe assumption to make. The relationship depends on trust, fairness, and responsibility —all values that are individual but determine the quality of information available to the public. It is difficult for the press when it is under attack from many directions by judges and lawyers, legislators, and even the President as they develop ways to keep newsmen from getting data. In Chicago a court recently ruled that any federal employee caught criticizing his employer or making harmful statements concerning governmental efficiency would be fired.[14]

Two perspectives have been taken in articulating research into the American political system. One is that Congress is the only worthy focus of study. The other is a focus on the committees and political parties. In the United States there is a significant enough lack of party solidarity and concurrent strength within the structure of the committee system to perform as a protection for Congress against an unusually assertive President and diffused partisan parties. This seems to make the executive and legislative branches function in a manner which differs from that of other nations.[13] In Great Britain, Parliament has been said to function more like one machine of which committees form a vital component but one in which one committee has little utility except as it fits in its place. In the United States the committees, on the other hand, operate independently as self-contained machines within Congress.

Leadership in the American legislative system is formally and informally divided into several categories. The Speaker of the House and the President Pro Tempore of the Senate are designated leaders. Party leaders, the majority and minority leaders, and whips are formal leaders of their respective political parties. Chairmen and ranking minority members in particular provide leadership within committees. Those men and women with special attributes of intelligence, respect, demonstrated ability, or diligence attain informal leadership status.

The executive branch has undergone the most visible growth and change since the beginning of the government. Patronage and various forms of alleged corruption led to the reorganization of the United States Post Office Department, making it a Civil Service System. Under this system it was presumed that equal opportunity existed for jobs and that the best qualified individuals would pass the Civil Service exams and become responsible for mail service in the United States. Postage rates continued to rise and yet the department was neither able to operate "in the black" nor to satisfy the public with the quality of service. This facet of history is one component of a larger area of change in orientation within the political arena. The pendulum has swung, as it has done in the past from time to time, between the expectation and demand for government to increase its involvement and responsibility in welfare programs and public services, and the increasing expectations and demands that government encourage and support the meeting of societal needs through free enterprise.

The Postal Reorganization Act of 1970 exemplifies this change. It established a semi-independent body with more autonomy than the old federal post office department ever enjoyed. When the postal service was reorganized in 1970, Congress directed that henceforth all classes of mail were to pay their own way rather than allow the previous discounting of postage on second class mail (newspapers and periodicals). One historian, Arthur Schlesinger, Jr., is quoted as describing it as an American tradition "to transmit second-class mail at cheap rates because the circulation of newspapers and magazines has been deemed essential to the enlightenment of the Republic and to the strengthening of American democracy."[15] Publishers are expected to go bankrupt and readership to take a drastic loss if rates on such materials go to the expected increase of 242% in 1976 as compared to 1971. Increased advertising may create some revenue to compensate for the postage costs increase. Publishers argue that it was the publications which were heavy with advertisements which caused the steep postage rate hikes. The extra advertisements required more paper, while prices of paper climbed simultaneously. This continues to the point where one does, indeed, ask the question "Where does the cycle end?" or "Where did the cycle begin?" One solution proposed is to maximize the sales of publications on newsstands, thereby cutting down on mailing. An alternate proposal was proposed to Congress by Senator Edward Kennedy (Democrat from Massachusetts) and Senator Barry Goldwater (Republican from Arizona), who otherwise see eye to eye on few issues. Their proposal would spread postal increases out over a ten-year period and decrease the number of postal increases on second class mail for the first 250,000 copies of a publication. Action on this proposal was, at least temporarily, postponed in the wake of Congressional involvement with Watergate and related matters.

Issues such as these touch the profession of nursing in numerous ways. Issues create alliances among those who often are bitter political enemies. Nurses have continued to urge continued education through subscribing to and reading of the literature. As a help to becoming a profession in its own right, nursing uses research as an everyday idiom, and "publish or perish" still remains the criterion for upward mobility in universities where many nurses carry out their duties as educators. As Senators Kennedy and Goldwater joined forces, so will perhaps the traditionally conflicting professional groups, publishers of cultist and scientific materials, as well as many others.

Administrative action in the name of the President's executive privilege caused reverberations in the congressional halls and found legislators stunned as budget proposals and impoundment of funds proposed under legislative responsibility caused regular clashes between the executive and legislative branches. Possible responses to such a crisis are to reduce the power of the President and to increase the power of Congress in decision making. Either creates problems from both immediate and long-term viewpoints. Cutting down the President's privileges would affect future presidents as well as the present one and has no effect on past chief-executives. Strengthening Congress's power requires an extensive study of the effects on all aspects of the internal and external components and dynamics related to a complex network.

With the increased role of the federal government in meeting the needs and demands of American society comes a substantially greater volume and complexity in the making of decisions. Obtaining and evaluating data necessary for formulating and overseeing public policies have become an increasing problem. The civil servants who number several millions, in addition to thousands of computers, make up an overwhelming bureaucracy over which a total of 535 legislators must maintain a watchful eye. Changes in both the House and Senate seem inevitable, but political scientists in general do not predict them to occur soon. Discussions and proposals for change are encouraged so that all aspects may be carefully researched prior to the implementation of modifications.

The government in the United States at all levels has traditionally been built on the concept of checks and balances. In the past the executive, legislative, and judicial systems at the federal level functioned in that manner. From a naive viewpoint it would seem that the present situation would be optimal in that the Republican executive and predominantly Democratic Congress would balance one another. The balance is a delicate one, however, and the effect on actual governmental workings may not always be to the good.

A search for escalating accountability of government to the electorate seems appropriate to many at the present time. The seemingly easy approach in the absence of party solidarity would be to turn to congressional committees. With already overworked committees and the large numbers of them, that can hardly be expected. Party reform may be the answer, brought about by increasing leader visibility and authority, permitting especially the Speaker of the House and minority floor leader more power in making appointments and clearing all privileged reports. Use of modern technological advances might be increased to promote communication, awareness, and accountability of elected officials to one another and to the public. Needless to say, cautions must be taken in any reform to prevent tyranny on the part of the House Speaker, minority floor leader, and committee chairmen. Committee consolidation around subjects that are contemporary and meaningful is one possible step toward reform.

Despite the formal arrangement personality factors of the men in the office appear to be among the major forces shaping what happens while they are in office. If this is true, the responsibility of the electorate is either simplified or complicated. It would be simplified in not having to understand the extremely complex system of branches of government, political parties, and committee structures. It would become complicated by having to know the person himself—no small undertaking since previous experiences, physical features, and speech content do not serve as totally reliable data. Even if all voters were psychiatric specialists, there undoubtedly would be disagreement among them as to data and their meaning.

Considering the puritanical orientation of the founding fathers, moderation and a lack of ostentation would scarcely have been considered mediocrity. In the current culture, however, the two concepts are often confused. As a note on changing philosophies within the United States, this discussion should include attention to the concern expressed by former President Nixon in speeches which warned that the moral strength of America has included the competitive spirit that made Americans strive to be "number one" in the world in the various aspects of its existence. Certainly competition was not labeled by the founding fathers as an essential ingredient. One might question whether the growth of competition is, indeed, an indication of disintegration and degeneration. Many citizens, accepting competition yet afraid of being overwhelmed, are looking carefully at what areas deserve priority and in which the United States should be number one. Eighty percent of respondents in one study[16] indicated that the United States should be first in the world in medical science, manufacturing technology, social reform, general military preparedness, and world political leadership, but only about half the respondents indicated that Americans need to be first in sports. (Contrast this ranking with the relative amount of interest given public affairs broadcasts and sports shows on Sunday afternoons!) There are those who believe that being number one is an important part of one's American heritage which they want to relay to their children. They also believe that spending money flying to the moon should not be paramount over feeding hungry people in the United States.

Youth in the 1950s and 1960s took the view that it was their responsibility to set the world straight and bring sense out of absurdity. In recent election campaigns they have provided significant power. In their frustrations with the complexities of understanding and changing government, they have returned to behavior more like that of their elders, who with the return of the birds in the spring, engaged in pranks such as panty raids and swallowing goldfish as a means of expressing their feelings. In the midst of the Watergate scandal, runaway inflation, the initial energy crises and then gasoline shortage, labor strikes, and worldwide upheavals of numerous kinds, some pursued the spirit of "streaking" rather than sneaking about in response to it all. To some professors it presented a challenge to continue lecturing as a streaker entered the room. Administrators of some colleges and universities took a hardnosed attitude and considered streaking a serious offense, whereas others observed streakers as annoyances or a welcome merit in comparison with the bloody riots of five years before. With some sense of absurdity these youth seem to be including a laugh at themselves. For what can top the sight of a person wearing sneakers to provide speed and a scarf about the neck to protect the streaker's flesh against the 20-degree weather of some campuses in the colder areas of the country? Editorials everywhere addressed the fad. Some called it decadent, immoral, and deplorable behavior, resulting from lack of parental or educators' discipline. Others viewed it as a reaction against loose morals and coed nudity as practiced in the days of hippiedom and as a return of nudity to its rightful role. Others defended the streakers for providing refreshing opportunity for all to laugh together at a harmless fad during a time when the nation had nothing to laugh about.

Just as this section began with a survey of language as evidence of past changes in the philosophy of politics in the United States, it will close with a review of some more recent vocabulary shifts.

Among recent additions to our language are "hardtop convertibles" that are incapable of converting, the destruction of property through "trashing," and "pacification" by elimination of opposition. One eliminates prisons and crimes by adding "correctional facilities" and "car-borrowing" or "inventory leakage."[17] What was once "poverty" has become "low income level" by order of a federal interagency committee.[18] More political language will undoubtedly change.

References

1. Schattschneider, E. E.: Two hundred million Americans in search of a government, New York, 1969, Holt, Rinehart & Winston, Inc., p. 108.
2. Op. cit., pp. 123-130.
3. Op. cit., pp. 110-111.
4. Ketchum, R.: Will Rogers, the man and his times, Boston, 1973, American Heritage Publishing Co.
5. Elazar, D. J.: Continuity and change in American federalism, Public Education Papers no. 2, Philadelphia, 1967, Temple University.
6. Jennings, M. K., and Zeigler, H.: The salience of American state politics, American Political Science Review 64:523-535, 1970.
7. Short, R. S.: Municipalities and the local government, Annals of the American Academy of Political and Social Science 207:44-53, Jan., 1970.
8. Grodzins, M.: The federal system, Goals of Americans, Report of the President's Commission on National Goals, Englewood Cliffs, N. J., 1960, Prentice-Hall, Inc., p. 265.
9. With strings attached, Wall Street Journal, Nov. 15, 1971.
10. Morgenthaler, E.: Local panels to review doctors' work and bills are urged by critics, Wall Street Journal, Dec. 16, 1970.
11. Shafer, R. G.: No thanks, respond some towns offered Uncle Sam's largesse, Wall Street Journal, April 4, 1974.
12. Review and outlook: needy New York, Wall Street Journal, April 4, 1974.
13. Brock, B.: Committees of the Senate, Annals of the American Academy of Political and Social Science 4:15-26, Jan., 1974.
14. Pankratz, H.: Assaults on free press described, Denver Post, April 22, 1974.
15. Bradshaw, K., and Pring, D.: Parliament and Congress, London, 1972, Constable & Co., Ltd.
16. Hughes, E. J.: The living presidency, New York, 1973, Coward, McCann & Geoghegan, Inc.
17. Hechinger, G.: The insidious pollution of language, Wall Street Journal, Oct. 27, 1971.
18. News roundup, Wall Street Journal, p. 1, Nov. 16, 1971.

A sudden solid traffic wall
Impossible to flout
Is always triggered by the fact
That I am backing out.

E. B. de Vito[1]

3

THE METROPOLIS

Although not all nurses practice or live in metropolitan centers, the social and political issues highlighted by a review of the current urban condition is useful. Discussion of metropolitan affairs here is not specifically confined to standard metropolitan statistical areas, as defined by the United States Bureau of the Census, or to the interstate megalopolis rapidly encroaching on the entire eastern seaboard. The growing and shifting population, the percentage of the population living in intimate proximity, and the struggle of living healthily under such conditions provide a rich source of study.

The growth of American cities followed the establishment of the United States as a major national power, and they have not the centuries of history written about them as do those of Europe, which generally evolved together with national power. They have, in general, demonstrated what might be considered a surplus of problems, as compared with rural communities, in terms of social,

health, police and legal, housing, employment, economic, and various other aspects. Max Weber[2] believed that there are still not enough comprehensive, verified research data to allow a suitable sociological definition of a city. Those based, for example, on ecological institutions, are inadequate, and one must not confuse physical aggregation with growth of the city in a sociological sense.

Life in the city is an interhuman struggle for gain, compared with the earlier struggle of man against the forces of nature. It may be thought of as a state of mind, a body of customs, traditions, organized attitudes, and sentiments, and a resultant kind of personality. The city, in its relationship to agricultural or rural life, is not clear cut. However, it was early established as the marketplace, around which major activities centered. In the Middle Ages and in antiquity it was also a fortress or garrison. Only occidental cities in the Middle Ages fully qualified as a "community," having their own courts and autonomous law, at least partial autonomy and autocephaly (with election and administration by authorities), along with a market and fortification. A new set of norms developed that Weber called the Protestant ethic, characterized by a desire for worldly and financial success. It emphasized hard work, thrift, and asceticism—reinvesting one's surplus income rather than spending it on luxuries or nonproductive prestige symbols. Thus the behavior approved and encouraged by the rise of Protestantism and that required by capitalism are seen to be similar. Weber also saw a religious change that was supportive of rationality that later takes form in science and bureaucracy. This all might be summed up in a statement on the transition from seeking "sacred" to "secular" rewards. Rather ironically therefore, Christianity gave birth to a secular organism. Another significant point is that at the time when the laboring classes were forced into conscious protective institutions, they were not prevented from this by magical or religious barriers. This is not to say that the same values are not held to in other religions and secular belief systems, although in different manners; moreover, it might be more accurate to say that the values of worldliness and asceticism rather than a particular religion, pehaps, have provided the catalyst for the growth of industrialization and the modern city.

Los Angeles has been described[3] in several oversimplified ways—on one hand in negative terms as a *non-city* and on the other hand in positive terms such as the *city of the future*. Each city has its unique features; for Los Angeles there are such factors as its having no clear center of gravity, since although Hollywood and Vine is said to be the center, it is merely marked by a few one- and two-story banks, a Howard Johnson's restaurant, and some parking lots. It certainly does not stand out in the minds of all as the heart of the city. Its 70-mile development along the Pacific Ocean, the foothill of Beverly Hills, Baldwin Hills, BelAir, and similar areas, the flat land of the infamous Watts area, and the heavily congested freeway network per-

haps more accurately portray the image of Los Angeles to most who know it and/or live there.

Alternately there remain areas within the United States that are still virtually cut off from the rest of the society and whose needs are essentially unknown, not to mention being addressed. Residents of a 500-square-mile area in northwest North Dakota called Squaw Gap in December, 1971, received phone service after a twenty-year struggle to do so.[4] The residents, however, came to wonder how to stop the phones from ringing as calls and congratulations came in from all parts of the country to interview the folks living in Squaw Gap.[4a] Typical of many other modern conveniences, services, and programs, not all the aspects are desirable or easily reversible. In terms of understanding the delay in providing a telephone line for Squaw Gap, principles with impact on the metropolis also have relevance.

Along with the various other changes comes one that is easily overlooked—the change in the predominant sounds in this country. The quiet sounds of meadowlarks and wind and raindrops of a rural society have been replaced by the large machines, constructing large office buildings, the rumble of large produce trucks passing along the freeway, and the hammers striking nails as signs of all kinds are posted almost anywhere. Noise pollution, this is called. In addition to the high noise level, today's teen-agers rock and bop to music from their blaring tape recorders and pocket and automobile radios. Is it because they have become so accustomed to noise that their music must be several levels greater for them to appreciate the difference? Is it a form of security blanket to them to be constantly surrounded by noise? Is there a permanent hearing impairment that will be present throughout their lives? Will they not be cognizant of even their own heartbeat? What will be the result as they age and their earlier ability to hear decreases? Will their fellows be required to use a microphone to carry on conversations with them?

Certainly poverty as an aspect of American

life has been forced into the national consciousness as a result of urban growth. The rural poor are not obvious to other than their immediate neighbors; the urban poor, and the conditions under which they live, are painfully obvious to many. A skid row exists in small and large cities alike. Programs have been designed that address skid row as a social welfare problem that is amenable to correction through social casework and rehabilitation techniques. Regardless, political dynamics underly the disgraceful phenomenon. Housing in cubicle hotels, rooming houses, bar hotels, and missions are examples of exploitation, perhaps mutual exploitation in the case of some. Many of the residents are single, alone. Others in similar circumstances do not live on the so-called skid row but are "lower class" families who live in the central city. These families have been described in both popular and scholarly literature on immigrants and in contemporary works about the black and white poor. Predominant themes are immorality, disorganization, and brutality. Certainly part of what is described is pure reality. The poor are disproportionately reflected in divorce figures, illegitimate birth rates, and juvenile delinquency incidence as compared with their nonpoor counterparts. Two fallacies in interpretation of data have been defined.[5] First, through focus on the obviously multitudinous problems, obscured is the fact that the majority caught up in such situations cope somehow with their poverty and stigma or rise above them in many ways. Second, controversy over the cause of the disorganization remains. Some argue that the poor are perpetuated through a subculture which will make it impossible for them ever to participate in the mainstream of society, whereas others argue that the only difference between the poor and nonpoor is money. Findings of a study[5] of lower class young families, undoubtedly surprising to some, show that the majority of them functioned adequately, that is with regard to coping with job, child rearing, and love relationships within and outside the family. Findings suggest that the malfunctioning of the poor results more from inadequate facilities and opportunities than from subcultural traits.

Crime of the grossest order has become prevalent. Whether the criminal is classified as mentally sane or insane poses another issue; however, the crime of man against man is no more or less than madness of some kind. Recent news are chockfull of gross crimes in which mercy, morality, and concern about punishment were of little consideration. The murder and burial of some twenty-five or thirty-five young males in Texas and a similar discovery earlier in the harvest fields of California are only two examples. Although questions affecting the criminal do not restore the lives of the victims, they must be asked. "Is the prisoner fit to be tried?" "Is he to be blamed for what he did?" "Is he too insane to punish?" "Are penal or psychiatric measures more suitable?" "How does one compare the crime of car theft with that of murder?" Crime, or awareness of crime, increases as people live in greater proximity to one another.

Psychiatric treatment facilities and approaches have been drastically changed in most areas of the United States and other western cultures. This has had a significant impact, since the emotionally marginal members of this society are no longer confined to institutions. Until there is significant evidence that persons are dangerous to themselves or others, they may not be confined involuntarily. The fear of having inadequate evidence has made professionals and courts unwilling to risk charges and suits based on illegal violation of human rights. Many of those not being treated gravitate to a marginal existence in urban centers.

Urban riots and struggles for civil rights in the past decades have challenged cities in America, bringing under attack their political systems and administration of justice. Many writings appeared that describe the conflicts and ways in which they were handled by public officials and the courts. Jacob[6] extended a survey of urban judicial systems to consider the organization of urban courts at city, county, state, and federal levels. The focus is on the informal organization of the system, that is, the politics of police, judges, prosecutors, lawyers, and other judicial personnel. Conclusions presented are that urban courts do not function so much to dispense justice as to dispose of cases. Through techniques such as negotiation and bargaining, defendants are encouraged by prosecutors, lawyers, with knowledge of the judges, to plead guilty to lesser charges to avoid court trials. This is cited as especially true in the case of criminal charges. Because the courts are overloaded, they are able thereby to save time and expense, although the judicial officers realize the value of hearings in court to learn the facts. Police are cited as playing a central role in involving persons in the criminal process through various mechanisms. They exercise considerable freedom in making decisions, making arrests, collecting evidence, and giving testimony in court. More broadly, police departments make such determinations as what laws they wish to enforce or not enforce, and the degree of their professionalism varies. Even when found innocent after police arrests, persons do not escape without some form of penalty (records of arrests are maintained; questions are asked on all kinds of applications).

One frequently made observation is that justice, like health care, is dispensed along socioeconomic class lines. Defendants (patients) who are wealthy upper class citizens (as individuals or corporations) have the advantage over defendants (patients) who are poor, since the former are able to employ the shrewdest lawyers (health professionals) to defend (care for) them, negotiate settlements (treatments), and use the law (health system) to their advantage. Despite this, police, prosecutors, and courts are culturally expected to administer justice in spite of the increasing number and kinds of crime and violence. In response police have their own unions and exhibit increasingly political activism to protect themselves amidst proliferating allegations and crimes against them. Their ranks are being closed to recruits of whom they do

not approve and who do not support their own governing organization and will resist civilian control boards. A challenge to society, theorists, and officers of justice is that of what best serves as a deterrent to crime. The question that was raised many years ago and still is not satisfactorily answered is whether or not punishment does, in fact, have a deterrent effect.

Organization and reorganization

Community organization has been advanced as an effective means of dealing with citizen noninvolvement that is designed to increase pride and quality of life in communities through extensive, expensive programs. One is hard put to set forth examples of significant successes attributable to community organization projects. A provocative discussion[7] of a large program involving the South Shore Area in Chicago's inner city raises a question concerning the actual good accomplished by gaining involvement of many community citizens. Questioned also is whether residential integration of black and white residents is worth fighting for, even if it is achievable, when status-power differences exist among them that will determine black-white integration. Before this can be realized, disparities and inequalities between the races must be eliminated.

A contrasting type of organization occurs at the governmental level. With the growth of metropolitan areas cities are often directly adjacent, with the boundaries being a street rather than distance existing between them. Innovative experiments in urban government are an expected result. One such is the Metropolitan Council model of St. Paul-Minneapolis, which was created by the state legislature.[8] Although seven years old, it is still struggling to survive. The program's purpose is having difficulty being understood by the citizens of the seven-county region, which includes two major cities, 134 municipalities, a multitude of agencies, half of the state's population, and more than half its wealth. This "supergovernment" deliberately was not empowered to make local decisions such as parking regulations or color of police cars. Rather, it was directed to develop an overall plan for the future. This includes review and critique of plans from agencies such as the airport commission, sewer board, and rapid transit commission. It has become essentially a vetoing body that only tells the proposing group to come back later with a better plan if the initial one seems inappropriate.

The Metropolitan Council has aggressively solved many of the problems for which it was created. Among its activities the council has blocked building of a jet airport in an area in which it was not considered ecologically sound, has kept additional freeways from being built through the metropolitan centers of Minneapolis-St. Paul, and has begun a land-use policy. One difficulty has been that of clear boundaries beyond which the council may not impose decisions. Another difficulty is that the state legislature does not always agree with the council's decisions and blocks them in ways visible to local residents (so that residents begin to question the council). The ultimate question is just how far a subtle and sophisticated supergovernment such as this is going to be allowed to go beyond "planning" to actual "governing." The political scientist, Charles E. Merriam, reportedly[9] recommended the establishment of city-states during the early part of the 1900s because he believed the federal system as it stood could not survive the growth of the metropolis. The question has been raised concerning what would have happened to various large cities, including New York, had they been made into city-states based on 1905 boundaries. People and communities would be surrounding them, tributary to them, but causing an interstate suburbanization.

In many urban areas there has been strong antagonism to megagovernment. St. Louis, which is said to be decaying at a pace which exceeds that of many other cities, is such an area. Located on the Mississippi River, this city with a population of about 750,000 in 1960 was then 28% black. By 1970 the population had decreased by over 100,000 and was 41% black, and the trend has continued into the middle of the decade. Some of the worst housing in the United States exists in this city's center. It is hardly unquestioned by health professionals these days that along with problems such as slums come problems of disease, malnutrition, and high population increases. It would seem that with a problem as clearly defined as that, something could be done to improve the situation. A response often heard is to "rebuild central city." This is not an easy process. The money is only one obstacle; how to rebuild is only another obstacle. People outside the slum areas are concerned that the blight will move gradually out to them. As is often the case, the mayors of St. Louis have often opposed plans such as that of George Romney, director of the federal housing program, for massive rebuilding of the central city because they fear financially the city would not receive as much federal support for all that needs attention—housing, schools, crime control, industrial incentives, and recreational facilities—as they receive from the poorly coordinated government aid type of plans. Indeed, revenue sharing has resulted in such a cut in many places. Change is also limited to whatever can be achieved, in the face of the longstanding animosities and resistance from suburbia and its leadership.

Looking at the history of St. Louis provides some understanding of how the current problems developed. The city boundaries were established in 1876, which limited growth to 61 square miles. (Statistics that in other urban areas are masked by those from more prosperous parts of town become painfully obvious here.) Large numbers of unskilled rural blacks were attracted to the city during World War II, when jobs were plentiful; nineteenth century houses developed into slums, which after the war were among the worst in the United States. These were removed with little thought of the consequences such as relocation of the population. New slums (called public housing) were created in a northwesterly direction. Encouraged by GI and FHA loans, whites built in suburbia.

Now the black migration is threatening suburbia even in the previously stable southern side, as blacks begin to attain financial means to make the exodus, and downtown is deserted. Current preferred solutions include leveling yet more poor housing, including some of the public housing, and attracting developers from suburbia to build new, middle class "towns" in the middle of the city. The large complex of health and other organizations currently serving the city population must begin facing issues such as where could and should current residents move when development arrives, how will they survive a move and adapt to new surroundings, and should the professionals move with the current clientele or stay and redevelop services for the new immigrants.

Many both within and outside government have determined that slums (a social and cultural disaster) must be eradicated. The way to do so, they propose, is similar to that of such natural disasters as hurricanes, floods, fires, tornadoes, and earthquakes. Such disasters, however, tend to cultivate among people the bonds of human sympathy. Tearing down of existing slums, however, has an opposite effect—that of dividing the inhabitants and bringing out barbaric behavior against their fellows and, in the end, destroying civilized society. Rather than looking for an easy way to get rid of slums, the emphasis must be on learning *how they are created* so that they *thus* may be eliminated. Taxes on property are currently assessed and raised every time an improvement is made on older buildings. Assessments are full or near full value on new construction so that people are personally and collectively discouraged from demolishing and replacing structures. This leads to a complete process of creating slums. At first buildings in older parts of town will not be painted and repaired. They continue to deteriorate; more buildings are left unkempt. The poorer members of society gravitate to the deteriorating area because the taxes on better homes are financially prohibitive. Here they can live as long as they do not remodel or build. They can raise a couple of generations

of offspring, each becoming more depressed than the previous one and influenced by more experienced delinquents and criminals of the previous generation(s). They have potential for destroying the society everyone wishes to enjoy. Encouraging professional speculators to buy in run-down areas furthers the problem. As buildings age, the assessed evaluation on the land also goes down, until it costs little to buy property and make a handsome income from the poor, even after the property is condemned or is threatening to collapse. When the buildings become uninhabitable and the owner chooses no longer to rent them, they are considered loss of income, and the land may be held from the sales market.

To counteract this creation of slums therefore it might be wiser to assess for tax purposes only the actual value of land and to exempt improvements from taxation. Progress in terms of constructing residences and businesses is seen, for example, in Australia, where this approach is used. Although land owners paid increased taxes, there was a resultant increase of values for land.

Many of those growing up in slum areas see a better life outside and strive to get out of their predicament, especially since the influence of slums on individuals is a slow indoctrination process. Relatively few of those immigrants to this nation at the turn of the century live there today. So for what other reasons are slums being created faster today than they are eliminated? This is no place to dissect the economics of welfare, but one point is that unless one's labor is compensated for at a rate well above the minimum wage, he must rely on society's guarantee of a marginal livelihood. Federal and state laws in a number of ways prohibit employment of those who are relatively unskilled. Slums are always depressing, but when people have hope of a way out, it is not a breeding place for modern barbarians who overthrow the society. Rome was destroyed by barbarians from outside, but American society could be destroyed from within if it continues to perpetuate slums through stupid "planning" and society's own benevolent intention of providing handouts to the "less fortunate." These dynamics are extensively described as early as 1879.[10]

Economics

For those who see the concern with changing the urban condition as more "do gooderisms," economic data may be helpful. It costs everyone money to live with society's present problems.

City governments have continued to struggle as their costs rise and tax bases decrease. As taxes are increased to support the poor, the middle class (taxpayers) leave. As they leave, the city's source of revenue also goes. Revenue sharing has been one approach, but other alternatives deserve consideration and none may be the ideal solution either totally or partially. One approach is providing public services through private enterprise. It has been a generally accepted fact that in many areas public employees are better paid and receive greater fringe benefits than their private counterparts. Examples include garbage collection and health and hospital services. In 1971 private garbage collectors in New York were making a profit of $17.50 a ton, whereas it cost the city of New York $49.50 to collect 1 ton of refuse.[11] Public hospital and outpatient services have developed into huge bureaucracies while there is considerable interest to render the service through private, smaller operations. It has even been suggested that the function of welfare investigators and office staff could be served through another procedure, perhaps tying it to the income tax system.

Whenever reorganization is undertaken, it tends toward adding additional lower levels (apparent decentralization), whereas the ultimate decision must still come from the top. The economical approach would be to keep the middle levels to a minimum both in number and staff. Evaluation is needed to determine whether the job is done or, in fact, requires the level of knowledge and skill of persons currently filling the post or performing the duties. Questions must always be raised, in government or in any organization serving society, about whether there are better ways of doing things, whether it would reduce cost, increase the quality of the product or service, and reduce the work.

Reorganization and revolution are in some ways similar. A shifting of power is part of either. Regarding revolutions, however, one author[12] predicts that a new type of revolution will mark the end of this century, that is, the dissolution of power itself rather than the passing of power from one to another, which has been part of past revolutions. First, social and national inequalities must end, and some of this seems at times to be occurring (at least in the eyes of the author Brucan). Second, classes, nations, and states must complete their missions and exhaust their potentialities. The expansion of modern states in both capitalist and socialist societies, supposedly an economic process, has increasingly hampered man's further development. However, the better educated and aware new generation questions the system and rebels against what is viewed as meaningless in terms of improving man's existence.

One of the problems today has been the ever-increasing government expenditures on social welfare programs in general, with no alleviation of the problems. If present trends continue, it has been estimated that by 1975 social welfare spending will amount to more than one fifth of the gross national product.[12] Table 1, chosen from the many available for purposes of example, summarizes the total financial outlays for various programs in 1971. Of particular interest are the expenditures for health care services in relation to other programs.

Between 1966 and 1971 total social welfare outlays have essentially doubled. Table 2 illustrates the expenditures in terms of dollars.

At the beginning of this decade it cost the city of New York nearly $8 billion to run each year. Much of this is spent in supervisory and monitoring functions to ensure that dollars going for actual services are not being misspent. One prominent citizen of New York suggested that the city could take some independent actions to solving its budgetary problems, including privatization (contracting

Table 1. Where the money goes*

	Outlays in 1971 (in billions)		
	Federal	State-local	Total
Social insurance	$53.6	$12.5	$66.1
Social security	35.2		35.2
Medicare	7.9		7.9
Public employees' retirement	6.4	3.6	10.0
Unemployment insurance and employment services	1.6	5.1	6.7
Other	2.5	3.8	6.3
Public aid	13.1	8.7	21.8
Medical programs	5.3	5.3	10.6
Veterans' benefits	10.3	0.1	10.4
Education	6.5	49.1	55.5
Housing	0.8	0.1	1.0
Other programs	2.8	2.5	5.3

*U. S. News & World Report, p. 43, Jan. 3, 1972. Copyright 1972, U. S. News & World Report, Inc.
Note: Figures may not add to total because of rounding.

Table 2. Social welfare outlays double in five years*

	1966	1971
State and local	$42.6 bil.	$ 78.3 bil.
Federal	45.4 bil.	92.4 bil.
Total	$88 bil.	$170.7 bil.

*U.S. News & World Report, March 13, 1972. Copyright 1972, U.S. News & World Report, Inc.

with specialized portions of the private sector for specific services), eliminating functions, eliminating bureaucracy (as by letting line workers make decisions), and analyzing tasks and uses of personnel.[13] Those eager for solutions to problems should bear in mind, however, that those tidy phrases, if carried out, would have the further effects of increasing the private control of public services, raising unemployment of civil servants, reducing control measures on decisions, and possibly increasing inattention to other than economic productivity measures. The metropolis brings into vivid relief the fact that each new solution creates problems, and decision making may often be selection of the lesser of several evils rather than the choice of the best options.

Planning

The issues related to planning are exemplified in every aspect of urban life today. Most urban areas were not planned, but grew "like Topsy," and planning has been called on only to correct the problems. What could be done happenstance and corrected later a century ago can now only be put into operation after many months or years of delicate negotiating. The goals of the planning are at least superficially to ensure that the best possible decision is reached, that means selected to reach the goal are the most efficient available, and that the potential for negative, unanticipated, and unintended consequences is minimized. Some who have studied planning efforts of various sorts have also observed that planning serves to support socially and economically a significant work force, to delay action occasionally until the problem vanishes or changes in nature, to give a cloak of public respectability to decisions reached in private bargaining. The creation of especially identified planning groups serves some of the same purpose identified for the congressional committees: to channel the inevitable and necessary conflict so that it remains pertinent to the issues and within reasonable bounds.

There has been much criticism of planning, and particularly of the results of social planning done within recent decades. Two types of potentially neurotic behavior are observed over and over: (1) depersonalization of the individual on the job as a result of such factors as the bureaucratic structure of many organizations and/or employees' failing to receive recognition for their personal uniqueness and (2) suburbanite living, a social situation in which individuals desiring privacy make no effort to seek it because they are made to feel guilty by their neighbors for making the attempt.

The play *The Killdeer* portrays a couple living in an attractive suburban home. Although this background is quite a contrast from the man's prison setting of the play *Short Eyes*, it becomes shockingly similar as *The Killdeer* unfolds in that the couple living in suburbia are trapped as surely as the prisoners in *Short Eyes*.* After being popular high school teenagers the couple married, raised two sons, and found after eighteen years that their marriage and lives were failures. The wife kept looking forward to better days as her husband's future flittered away through moves from job to job. She relates in a most moving manner her realization that she, like others, should have left the situation and sought a divorce or reversed the situation so that it could work. She had done neither, and she knows that she will never leave her husband and that he will never change. They are caught, as typical suburbanites, where they can neither move forward nor go back. It is not that their lives are intolerable but simply quietly hopeless and desperate. Whereas *Short Eyes* portrays one facet of life and its anguish little known to many, in both dramas the characters experience punishment that they themselves brought on. The writer pre-

sents a picture, amusing but disturbing, which may remind the individual of some people he or she knows and which points out that not only the disadvantaged or social misfits endure pains, crises, and loneliness.

Particularly humanistic individuals have decried the impact of the planning syndrome. The troubles seem to be in part related to the lack of an appropriate prescription for whom should be involved in planning for what at which point in the process. The equation of planning social problems with solving a scientific, especially a mathematical problem, led to the creation of teams of specialists who identified issues and summed them into a solution. Systems analysis may have done less to make decision making easier than it has to point out what the difficulties are in terms of problems and alternatives. With application of systematic analysis to the federal government's attempt to improve health, medical care was in essence bought for the poor. This had the effect of pouring new money into the same human and physical resources with the end result being a skyrocketing of prices. All those concerned with the improvement of health care are at least somewhat aware that underfinancing is not the major problem that must be faced. Spending more money on public needs and less on the private sector is not necessarily the answer. Conservatives and liberals alike are perplexed with questions of what to do to improve all social services, as well as health. Perhaps the government should design social programs as deliberate experiments to obtain information as to what works and what does not. The next stop is the development of "performance measures," which measure when something does or does not work. Theoretical, political, and moral issues must be acknowledged in light of such a proposal. However, it is one innovative notion worth entertaining.

Social science experiments may eventually answer some important questions, but one must be careful how the research questions are posed. One example is differing health standards and statistics between nations. In the case of often compared countries such as

---

*Both were written by Jay Broad and opened at the New York Shakespeare Festival's Public Theatre early in 1974.

Sweden and the United States there is a question of how much of the difference is based on actual differences in medical care and how much on cultural differences that affect individual habits and health. The crucial point that created disillusionment for those who put their stakes on the rational approach was that they failed to account for ultimate intuitive elements. One component of the intuitive element is what are now called rising expectations of society. "The evil which was suffered patiently as inevitable, seems unendurable as soon as the idea of escaping it crosses men's minds. All the abuses then removed call attention to those that remain, and they now appear more galling. The evil, it is true, has become less, but sensibility to it has become more acute."[14]

There is more than adequate reason to suspect that unless the planner is in some way committed to being affected by the results of the planning, a damaging plan may well be produced. In American cities, plans for the poor, the sick, the uneducated, and the black were all too often developed by the rich, well, educated whites. At the other extreme there is evidence to support the inability of someone in the midst of a problem to develop enough perspective to plan for its solution. A range of services planned exclusively by the intended recipients may be equally as bad as those planned without any recipient contribution. In developing solutions for urban problems, those who give appropriate space to the planning process do so with the goal of involving all those potentially affected by a plan *in* the plan. Several social moves discussed in other contexts recur in conjunction with planning. It has been in the metropolitan areas where women, the aged, and the racial minorities have most clearly announced their intent to participate in planning their own and the society's future. It is from these same places that education programs have developed— programs which take into account the fact that unless each planner is knowledgeable, the process may falter. Information is being disseminated on *how* planning works, on *who* has done it, on *facts* about potential solutions, and *when* and *where* to go to participate.

One concern in planning is that of how monolithic the planning group or agency should be. As is often stated, what exists now is the result of competitive interaction among many facets of the public. That has led to much of the unplanned confusion of the metropolitan areas. However, much resistance remains to any definitive steps which would alter that confusion. This seems related to the antigovernment bias discussed in relation to the founding fathers and the intent of the United States political system. There does not appear to be any reasonable way to get all necessary parties involved in planning without legislating such participation, and this appears to most voters to be too forceful an approach. John D. Rockefeller, III, reflects on this in his distinction between "planned society" and "planning society." In the former, regimentation and enforced, ordered activity could become the rule, whereas in the latter, widespread, knowledgeable involvement should come to the fore.[15]

A study[16] of various styles of participation in social policy, particularly with regard to antipoverty programs, reveals multiple approaches. The blatant failure of these programs to solve the problems of the urban poor should lead to conclusions regarding the need to devise other programs and other policy-making approaches, perhaps some synthesis of these. The typology that was identified discussed participation by elites only, non-elites only, and both, with focus on administrative concerns only and a combination of political and administrative concerns. The most hopeful paradigm (the most consistent with the political philosophy evidenced in major documents) is that of pluralist participation— elites and non-elites looking at both political and administrative concerns. Locating appropriate members of both elite and non-elite groups who are knowledgeable about both politics and administration is the difficulty.

In the discussion of changing roles and relationships in American government reference was made to the reverting of local needs and programs to state and national government. In today's metropolis many needs are met by federal and state programs, particularly for the inner city core. Some states and localities have declined participation in federal programs because of philosophical differences and concern for locally pertinent options. One example is the development of county mental health programs without involvement in the federal community mental health centers program being promoted at the same time. Only time can reveal whether such decisions have been the most useful for the municipality in question.

The Center for the Study of Democratic Institutions' publication, *The Center Magazine,* has published a program for the solution of urban crisis that focuses on migration, pollution, and transportation (note that health is omitted).[17] The heart of the proposal is the acquisition of new land surrounding metropolitan areas to build satellite communities. This would be accompanied by aggressive enforcement of antidiscrimination laws, by directing of federal housing subsidies to those with incomes of $6,000 to $12,000 per year (no limit for those going to the new satellites), by income maintenance for lowest income groups, and by the rebuilding of new housing in central cities. As with the move in St. Louis toward "new towns in town," there is little or no attention to the social consequences of these plans, neither is there indication that those involved, other than developers, should be involved in detailing goals and immediate operations.

As mentioned, in addition to the poor and the black, metropolitan areas have had to give special attention to problems of the aged. The heart of any town includes many older citizens who are left behind in a once stylish home that they cannot afford to sell, clinging to a neighborhood from which their identity has been drawn or coming in for cheap housing and some form of public transportation that can be managed on a Social Security budget. Availability of services, including health services, for a population that cannot be assured of its condition and will not out-

grow it (except by dying) and that is increasing steadily is a major challenge. As with other minority or nonpower groups, growing awareness and increased use of collective pressure (such as the American Association of Retired Persons) are aiding the elderly in their struggle. In addition to federal support programs, many states and local governments have special offices or bureaus to deal with the older citizen. Hopefully one effect will be the end of "all or nothing" thinking, which had been part of such trends as all-new housing for the elderly in "retirement villages" or modern high-rise buildings that segregate the older population. A variety of housing, health, and social solutions is indicated.

References

1. Wall Street Journal, April 6, 1971.
2. Weber, M.: The city (Translated and edited by D. Martindale and G. Neuwirth), New York, 1958, The Free Press.
3. Abercrombie, S.: Los Angeles as architecture, Wall Street Journal, Oct. 27, 1971.
4. Today it is possible to call Squaw Gap—but who'd want to, Wall Street Journal, Dec. 15, 1971.
4a. Squaw Gap line is busy; outside world says hello, Wall Street Journal, Dec. 17, 1971.
5. Geismar, D.: 555 families: a social-psychological study of young families in transition, New York, 1973, E. P. Dutton & Co., Inc.
6. Jacob, H.: Urban justice: law and order in American cities, Englewood Cliffs, N. J., 1973, Prentice-Hall, Inc.
7. Molotch, H. L.: Managed integration: dilemmas of doing good in the city, Berkeley, 1973, University of California Press.
8. Farney, D.: The Twin City experiment, Wall Street Journal, March 21, 1974.
9. Elazar, D. J.: Continuity and change in American federalism, Public Education Papers no. 2, Philadelphia, 1967, Temple University, p. 9.
10. George, H.: Progress and poverty, New York, 1974, Robert Schalkenbach Foundation.
11. Robbins, I. D.: Cutting city government costs, Wall Street Journal, May 19, 1971.
12. Runaway rise in welfare spending, U.S. News and World Report, p. 43, Jan. 3, 1972.
13. Bartley, R. L.: On the limits of rationality, Wall Street Journal, Sept. 10, 1971.
14. Brucan, S.: The dissolution of power, The Center Magazine, Santa Barbara, Calif., Center for Study of Democratic Institutions, vol. 5, Jan./Feb., 1972.
15. Discussion of Rockefeller, J. D., III: The second American revolution, New York, 1973, Harper & Row, Publishers. In Fuller, E.: A Rockefeller looks

at life in America, Wall Street Journal, April 12, 1973.

16. VanTil, J., and VanTil, S. G.: Citizen participation in social policy: the end of the cycle? Social Problems **17:**313-323, Winter, 1970.

17. Weissbourd, B.: Satellite communities, The Center Magazine, Santa Barbara, Calif., Center for Study of Democratic Institutions, vol. 5, Jan./Feb., 1972.

Stories datelined Washington
Are often quite confusing,
And official attempts to "clarify"
Are frequently amusing.

Sometimes news "leaks" are by intent,
And sometimes despite efforts to prevent;
But either way the story of course is,
"Quoted from usually reliable sources".

G. O. LUDCKE[1]

4

CURRENT ISSUES

Former American Medical Association President C. A. Hoffman, after a tour of Europe in 1972, stated that Americans are the only ones who wonder about the quality of medicine practiced in the United States because, he said, "Everywhere else the United States is recognized as Mecca."[2] He did not comment on whether the observers based those comments on accurate firsthand data or not. He pointed out that great loss is incurred in the cyclic process when money is paid to the government and then is returned to the people for so-called "free services." A Swedish lawyer was quoted as paying out 65% of his $27,000 income in direct taxes.[2]

Few people anymore hold the belief that wherever their health is concerned money is no object. Major health care programs directly result from the objects of both saving money and maintaining health. The goal of a national health insurance program is essentially the same as that of Medicaid and Medicare. They are all attempts to spread the risk of high medical costs across a broader population and to provide care to the poor without essentially any direct cost to them. Beyond this, as Medicaid and Medicare are presently run, they also funnel government monies into the private sector of health care providers. Every change or adjustment in the system has its side effects, which might be viewed in terms of gains and losses. When costs to one group of people are reduced, there is automatically a reduction in either services to other groups or payment to providers. Other effects of national health insurance, as with other such programs, include a shift in the distribution of the nation's wealth and potential restrictions on individual choices regarding where, when and from whom care can be obtained.

During the first two years (1966 to 1968) of its implementation, the federal and state governments spent a total of $14.7 billion on the Medicaid and Medicare programs. This represents about $875 per recipient household.[2a] If this sounds like a large amount, it must also be remembered that this financed medical costs of only 10% of the population. Of the $875, each of these households paid on the average of $175 in new taxes. The other $700, however, is not an accurate reflection of absolute gain in health care received, since the new Medicaid/Medicare programs, in fact, replaced care previously received from other governmental and private charity systems. Among these were Medical Assistance to the Aged and Veterans Administration, as well as an immeasurable amount of noncharged care given by individuals, including physicians, and by hospitals. These same systems exist but now charge and receive reimbursement for their services. While all of these shifts occurred, allowable federal tax deductions for medical care was reduced. This was by no means an inconsequential forfeiture of monies by Medicare recipients. The situation is compounded in that during the early years of these programs, providers of health care raised the price tags on the services now being paid by federal tax dollars. The end result was that when all factors are considered, perhaps little better than half of the $875 spent on each recipient family represents an actual gain in terms of services or care received.[2a] Similarly, those paying taxes but not receiving benefits from the programs paid increased taxes toward support of the programs as well as increased price of care for themselves out of their own pockets in one way or another.

In addition to the raising of prices for services, several other problems relate to the existing federal programs and will undoubtedly occur under any expansion of the concept. Development of an improved system for reimbursement to providers seems inescapable, such as placing a ceiling on the price of specific procedures and services. Insurers have placed such limits on their liability for years. Likewise, some system of controlled utilization must accompany any plan, possibly coercive rather than indirect, that is, limiting the number of hospital days. A shift of financial responsibility and authority must be accompanied by a change in incentive, that is, from getting the most one can from the system to preventing oneself from having to take as little as possible from the public account through use of preventive health measures. Obviously the latter necessitates the availability of preventive services on which one can draw.

In a survey of thirty-four states, the United States Department of Health, Education and Welfare[3] reported that in April, 1971, 5% of all welfare families were ineligible for payments. Although only about half of the total national welfare case load was covered by the survey, a nationwide projection of the survey figures would indicate that about $500 million a year is being dispensed to individuals who are eligible or who receive overpayments. Estimated underpayment of funds on a nationwide projected basis would amount to about $76 million, partially offsetting the $500 million figure. Of particular interest here is that about 50% of the blame was considered as "honest errors" on the part of state and local welfare agencies, whereas the remaining 50% of the blame was placed on recipients. Principal reasons listed were "failure by recipients to report changes in family size or income and agency errors such as inadequate determination of eligibility, failure to follow up and misinterpretation of policy."[3] Additionally, potentially eligible people were not enrolled. The question can be raised in every such instance as to what is the line between private and public information necessary to identify all the appropriate beneficiaries and only them. An extremely pertinent example of public data disclosure is that related to Missouri Senator Eagleton's psychiatric care history and the issues of who should know the information under what conditions.

Experience with data and compliance errors such as these should provide data that can be used to cut down the size of programs in the area of health program services. The problems of compliance will continue to occur. The question remains how best to administer the services to minimize the errors, whether they be created by fraud or honest mistakes. The other implication seems to be made that perhaps local and state agencies are less qualified to control the quality of social welfare programs than the federal agencies.

Cornuelle[4] expresses the feeling that the original American dream of both a free and humane society was only a reality because most public needs were met outside of government. He says that the "independent sector" (the individual) is better able to solve public problems because it both limits government and solves public problems directly. Compliance problems plague American society in regard to every piece of legislation that is passed. What the founding fathers did not account for are the reasons why people do or do not obey or comply. Schattschneider[5] proposes that people only "obey for the same reason that the crew of a ship at sea in a storm obey the captain." They obey because it is essential to survival in the face of danger.

Public support for law enforcement is one of the front-line issues in the United States today. Emotions, prejudices, preconceptions, illusions, and misconceptions of all kinds are involved. Each person perceives a desire to do what he or she wishes, to be relaxed and expect a friendly world around him or her. As the past in this country has often been glorified and idealized, one is prompted to ask whether the pilgrims at Plymouth or the authors of the Constitution believed that they were creating a utopia in the face of danger. Nathaniel Morton, who served as secretary and record keeper for Plymouth Colony, wrote in 1620 of the "hideous and desolate wilderness full of wilde beasts and wilde men" in which they had settled.[6]

Americans have had problems understanding government from the beginning. They seem to be a schizophrenic kind of people who live in a constant conflict between theory and practice and a state of ambivalence toward their own political attitudes. They seem to want and yet rebel against law enforcement; they want government and yet seem not to believe in it and think it should be minimized. In spite of how much Americans

may cherish the small government of George Washington's day and in spite of the resistance it has experienced, as a governmental structure and power the federal branches have mushroomed for reasons that are not accounted for in the Constitution or in the political theory and ideals behind it.

Reacting to the revolutionary and psychorevolutionary movement described by Reich,[7] Knopfelmacher[8] of the University of Melbourne, Australia, proposes the dilemma and an analysis that are of interest here. He says that at the present time the system of law enforcement in the United States permits more dissent and violence than that permitted in other highly industrialized, English-speaking areas of the world. On the other hand, Americans have a continuing nostalgia and feeling that government is really dispensable, or if not dispensable it should be kept at a minimum. This provides a link between both conservative and liberal elements in American society. In spite of the nostalgia and fear about government control, no gross challenge of the social order would ever be permitted because it would be quickly squelched by enforcement of law and order. Stating that the problem is how to safeguard liberty while maintaining the managerial state on which American culture depends, he says, "Whenever a Reichian Consciousness III switches on the light on his desk to write an essay against Consciousness I and II on his electric typewriter, he votes against his essay with his typewriter keys."[8]

Knopfelmacher[8] continues by saying that the fear of being swallowed by totalitarian despotism, of which USSR still remains the most threatening, maintains the open societies and its allies in a state of cohesiveness and in control of internal conflicts. It is the power of determination against terror and totalitarianism that continues to ward off the force that the enemy possesses in the form of a mass internalized sense of civic responsibility. He proposes that the only counter to tyranny requires Reichian (industrial) Consciousness II. Civic consensus and loyalty to one's land, virtues of various kinds, and utilization of the good and bad within individuals make a nation survive. If this were lost, as he perceives it would be in Consciousness III, society would experience internal disintegration and social parasitism to the point where people would be consumed by tyrannical societies that are based on order, hierarchy, myths, uncontrolled violence, and oppression.

Unless the entire spectrum of factors affecting who gains and loses what, is considered and a plan is custom built around them, any major public health program will be an irrational and financially disastrous one. All concerned parties will have to study means of communicating issues and concerns. American corporations continue to report their earnings in the form of the historical dollar figures. Although their reports continue to show shareholders an increase, the figures become meaningless in themselves, since the dollars reported continue to lose value. In reality, after paying taxes, dividends, and expenses, the earnings of American corporations may well have sharply diminished net earnings. When real earnings decline, their power to meet public demands and needs is decreased. They cannot expand so that new jobs cannot be created nor can inflation be stopped. Rising prices in and of themselves are only a distortion of the total picture. It might be pursued further to the illusion given by prosperity, which comes when money policies become easy for the borrowers. The prosperity that they perceive will be returned with interest, which will be in the form of less valuable dollars. To bring attention by the public to the sobering facts, there was first created the Accounting Principles Board. This body attempted to address the perceptual problems being referred to, but to no avail. A second body, the Financial Accounting Standards Board, was then created by the accounting profession in hopes of stimulating a realistic comprehension of the facts.

Several responses are observed at times of crisis. One is that just described—an unwillingness to acknowledge the facts. Another response is a turn to the use of humor. Perhaps not since the great depression of the 1930s has such a depression pervaded the emotional tone of conversations, exemplified in individuals' strategies for survival and in so much loss of sleep. During the 1930s, in the midst of tense times and bread lines, some good laughs were produced by such people as Will Rogers. He needled politicians, and as a partisan Democrat, some of his jabs or stabs at the Republican party, at presidential conventions and elsewhere, might be really in tune with headlines in recent years. Humor such as his seems to improve with age, since it reinforces the old adage that history repeats itself. Included might be his quip related to dubious activities of top government officials, ". . . You see, there is a lot of things these old boys have done that are within the law, but it's so near the edge that you couldn't slip a safety razor between their acts and a prosecution."[9] Or, reflected at Spiro Agnew's tax litigations: "The income tax has made more liars out of the American people than golf has."[9] In times when people are anxious, they look for facts, data, on which they can base actions. As Will Rogers also said, however, "All I know is just what I read in the papers,"[9] implying that they are an unreliable source of facts.

The basic issues with respect to the nation's health largely depend on who is being asked to question. Somers[10] has described the responses as follows. The physicians reply that they are overworked and troubled by political interference and malpractice insurance. The poor black mother points to the impersonal care, inconvenience of care, and drug addiction. Health insurance company executives outline the problem of their relations with hospitals, the overuse by physicians and patients, and the political criticism they receive. Farmers say that physicians are scarce, that worthwhile health insurance is hard to buy, and that their work is hazardous to their health. Administrators of hospitals complain that they are unable to control the medical staffs, that they are unable to satisfy the patients because they are overly demanding, that third party payments are inadequate, and that they cannot keep their beds full. Congressmen are faced with rising costs of government programs, with conflicting pressures for further government programs, and with occupational health hazards. Boiled down, what seems to concern the greatest number of Americans today are the physician shortage (no mention is made of nurse shortage, perhaps because nurses are seen as an impersonal extension of the physician) and costs of health care generally.

The complexity of the issues and the pressures of the powers behind the issues have inhibited the federal government from directly attacking anything more than the financing of care and some associated compliance measures. As an example, even a strong supporter of massive reorganization such as Senator Edward Kennedy seems impelled to revert to financing measures to gain some colleague support. The life-style of patients and the environment broadly affect how any one individual looks at the major health issues. Ghetto residents and persons living in a rural isolated area may each be concerned with the unavailability of care, quality of care, and costs, but some of them may resist comprehensive federal health programs because they are accustomed to getting along independently and want to be able personally to buy what they need. They resist paying for care of others with lung disease who choose to "live off others" (welfare) in the city, where pollutants aggravate if not initiate the health problem for which they require care and who choose to spend the money on cigarettes that they get by "living off others."

Comprehensive care has become a cliché, and most people expound on the need for such care. To obtain it, as an ordinary citizen, is another matter. An easy formula is not readily engineered. At best it can slowly evolve, providing it is possible to teach and learn to establish meaningful professional/client (patient) interpersonal relationships and to satisfactorily prepare the necessary health professionals who accept-

ably meet individuals' needs. In addition, health care teams must be developed. Their development, far beyond the development of the concept, depends on health professionals' (physicians and nurses being only two components of the team) accepting one another and working together in a manner satisfying to all.

Nurses tend to want to blame physicians for the problems of the health care team. Many of the troubles are self-induced. Many nurses claim that their significant contribution to the health care team is that they "care." They tend to forget that despite the noncaring nature of the health care *system,* there are many individual physicans who indeed care for their patients. In nurses' loud proclamations of concern they can alienate many physicians and the patients who appreciate them. The ultimate criterion of good health care is not always described by elaborate research studies but in terms of patient (client) satisfaction. Although not readily accepted by some health professionals and too easily capitalized on by others, people do not necessarily equate the most sophisticated treatment technique with satisfaction.

Health care has traditionally been sickness oriented. It has been designed to restore or cure whenever possible and to ameliorate or manage when conditions are chronic. When neither of these approaches works, it is directed toward dignifying the condition and easing the death process. Few would agree that they are satisfied with the system. Most believe that the present system is not working well, and some go to the extent of identifying it as a crisis in health care.

Finances

The crisis is so labeled by identifying the shortage of health professionals and personnel and resources with inaccessibility to health care, particularly in the densely populated inner city and sparsely populated rural areas. Costs of services and hospital care continue to spiral, with little evidence that things will change. Increasing utilization of existing health resources by certain segments of the population is enlarging the proportion that health consumes of the total gross national product. The entire health system is fragmented, and the points at which individuals enter are uncoordinated. In spite of much increased medical care, the life expectancy and various indexes of health have not been significantly improved.

Considerable federal and state support has been given to the training and preparation of health professionals. The overall ratio of physicians to population is not significantly out of line, for example, but rather, the ratio of family physicians (general practitioners) to population has an impact on entry into the system, costs, distribution, and overall meaning of statistics. If it is true that the United States spent more per capita and a greater amount of its gross national product on medical care than any other country in the world, one might naturally be concluding that

more physicians are needed. However, questions arise as to whether it would be better to recruit (or accept more applications to medical schools) and to subsidize more medical education or to prepare more nurse practitioners and/or other health personnel. It might also be suggested that the government play a more direct role, paying less attention to the American Medical Association and other professional organizations, and cut back on support for health manpower education.[11] In place of these types of activities it might be suggested that government funding be put to use in building low-cost housing or in food subsidy programs. This, in fact, may be the position currently being taken, since appropriated dollars are decreasing (Table 3).

Interpretations of data vary and are dependent on a multiplicity of factors, one of which is whether the picture is viewed from the

Table 3. 1974 funds for nursing—with and without allowable cuts*

	1974 Budget request	1974 House allowance	1974 Senate allowance	1974 Conference agreement	Effect of $400,000,000 reduction
Nursing support					
(a) Institutional assistance					
(1) Capitation grants		33,800,000	38,500,000	36,150,000	34,343,000
(2) Financial distress grants		5,000,000	10,000,000	5,000,000	4,750,000
(3) Special projects	15,000,000	20,000,000	22,600,000	20,000,000	19,000,000
Subtotal	15,000,000	58,800,000	71,100,000	61,150,000	58,093,000
(b) Student assistance					
(1) Direct loans	21,000,000	24,000,000	24,000,000	24,000,000	22,800,000
(2) Scholarships	11,000,000	19,500,000	21,500,000	20,500,000	19,476,000
(3) Traineeships		11,500,000	15,900,000	13,700,000	13,016,000
(4) Loan repayments	1,600,000	1,600,000	1,600,000	1,600,000	1,600,000
Subtotal	33,600,000	56,600,000	63,000,000	59,800,000	56,892,000
(c) Construction assistance					
(1) Grants		20,000,000	20,000,000	20,000,000	19,000,000
(2) Interest subsidies	1,000,000	1,000,000	1,000,000	1,000,000	1,000,000
Subtotal	1,000,000	21,000,000	21,000,000	21,000,000	20,000,000
(d) Educational assistance		7,569,000	9,720,000	7,569,000	7,191,000
(e) Direct operations	3,348,000	4,119,000	4,119,000	4,119,000	3,914,000
Total	52,948,000	148,088,000	168,939,000	153,638,000	146,090,000

*American Journal of Nursing **74:**192, Feb., 1974. Copyrighted February 1974, The American Journal of Nursing Co. Reproduced with permission.
The 1974 budget bill signed by the President permits the administration to cut the HEW budget by $400 million, but no more than 5% for any one program.

standpoint of a provider or recipient (yet one might be both).

With decline in the value of the dollar and inflation, sales of all kinds of goods and services have declined. This extends into many areas. For example, sales of used machine tools during February, 1974, rose 16% from the previous year and increased 2.2% from the previous month.[12] Examples of demand for used tools include lathes, milling machines, and various other tools used in metalworking shops. Because of labor and material cost increases, people become more interested in doing work themselves that they would earlier have hired others to do. Those who need the tools to make a livelihood are more likely to replace worn-out ones with used ones when the prices are greatly increased. Currently democracies in industrial countries throughout the world are having difficulties. Countries throughout Western Europe have governments that are struggling with uncertainty as to whether they have popular support. Before eliminating democracy from the board as a workable form of government, however, this state of affairs must be compared with other types of government. It continues to appear to most American citizens that not only do democracies provide more freedom than other governments but that they better meet their material needs as well.

Inflation can be blamed for much social instability, this ultimately resulting in political instability. The means of curbing inflation then must be addressed. As Greenspan has outlined,[13] the problem is more a political one than an economic one. It is realized in an unwillingness to forego short-term benefits for long-term benefits, maybe living by the old adage, "A bird in the hand is worth two in the bush." One might attribute a part of the problem to the unwillingness of people accustomed to comfort to rough it a bit temporarily (a part of the culture). Leaders able to rise to the occasion have been lacking (probably because they too are a product of the culture in which they grew up), and no earth-shattering threat has rallied everyone with differing views and stations of life together. Technology has played its part.

Although energy has received a great deal of attention in the headlines of the world, perhaps an equally or more critical issue is that of inflation. Inflation has accelerated at an ominous rate. Nations within the Organization for European Economic Development had an annual inflation rate of 5.5% during the last half of 1972, increased to 7.5% during the next six months, and then to 10.9% in the last three months of 1973.[14] In 1975 it may be significantly higher. During the last period, Germany had the lowest rate (5.5%), whereas Australia had the highest rate (16.3%).[15] This trend continues to the present.

The shrinking purchasing power of consumers is in the areas of goods and services, but it includes agricultural products (food) as well. Industrial wholesale prices have gone up so that the increased prices are not due to industrial profits. Reported profits of businesses do not entirely support the assertion that the rise in price is due to racketeering of business. It is not possible, nor is it the intent, to identify the villain and the victim.

The magnitude and complexity of the problem is great; the solutions cannot be arrived at easily. Any intervention will have direct and indirect impact on individuals, the community, and the society of nations as a whole. After-tax profits cut down purchasing power, which in turn results in unemployment, and the cycle is established that grows larger and larger. Inflation, however, can only be countered through fiscal and monetary restraints. To be implemented and effective they must be well thought out and have citizen support and confidence. Current practices reveal a lack of social commitment to any one solution and alternating concern over recession, or depression, and inflation.

Energy

The most difficult problem facing the nation either internationally or domestically has been the energy situation, described by Senator Henry Jackson, who is the person recognized by federal congressmen as perhaps most informed.[16] Americans have always enjoyed an abundance of everything—food, land, minerals, and energy. They are now being made to realize that their life-style in an atmosphere of plenty to which they accustomed themselves must be adjusted because the limit has been reached in certain areas. With only 6% of the world's population the United States consumes 30% of all fuel. It has been likened to an addict caught in an endless cycle: the more energy, it gets the more it demands.[16]

From available facts it does not seem that a worldwide shortage of energy supplies exists but, rather, that political and administrative factors have consummated in the present energy crisis. In reviewing the federal administration in the United States, it is apparent that until the situation reached a real crisis stage, there was reluctance to confront the inevitable. This behavior is evidenced in the attitudes of the general public as well, which previously considered with little sincerity operating costs (energy) of the multiple energy-consuming items they purchased. The question of responsibility for the state of affairs arises, with the public blaming oil companies and oil companies blaming the government, which regulates the oil industry through taxation, permits, licenses, and the like. Little responsibility is readily assumed by the citizenry, as people continue to keep the house flooded with light while they are absent, overheat every room, drive "gas-hogs" a block for a package of cigarettes, and wear sweaters at work in office buildings that are overcooled by huge air conditioners. In addition to these examples of waste, gadgets such as electric toothbrushes, hair combs, and blowers, and tie racks are commonly owned.

Change with regard to energy use and planning for the future is now unavoidable. Attitudes toward consumption must be changed; this includes all aspects of the society. Even if it is technically and economically feasible to substitute one material or method for another, it is useless without social acceptance. The latter is more difficult to predict, especially when changes are initially introduced. Once socially accepted in one country, it is more likely to meet acceptance in

others. Examples in other areas are liberalized marriage and divorce practices as well as "free" medical care, which, later introduced in the United States, became accepted. Privately and government-funded surveys and studies have increasingly been utilized to determine the impact of changes on various components of society and must necessarily precede innovations such as in the present area of energy.

Societal impact is of grave concern to government because it must guarantee its citizens the essentials of life, that is, those necessary for survival. Only then is growth and prosperity possible, ultimately leading to programs that improve quality, such as environmental esthetics. One difficulty is locating the point at which survival-environmental issues and esthetical issues separate. The Pilgrims were concerned with the survival aspects and considered available energy potentials as unlimited. The post World War II boom strained certain previously plentiful resources. Pollution of water and air began to draw attention. When the oil shortage became a serious reality in certain areas of the country, building the Alaska pipeline seemed a ridiculously expensive venture to many Americans. Only when oil was unavailable, could the government consider increasing the permissible levels of air pollution resulting from burning coal.

Various dilemmas must be concurrently addressed. A steep increase in fuel consumption is anticipated during the coming decade or two. Physical resources are adequate, yet there is a shortage of available energy in terms of acceptable price, effects on the environment, geographical and political factors, and technological capability. Areas of the world with the richest supply of fuel oil have been shunned as political enemies. A case in point is the United States' position in the Arab-Israeli conflicts. To admit dependence on the abundant supply of Arab oil necessarily weakens American political muscle in opposing Arab tactics as well as jeopardizing Israel's confidence in United States support. Short-term solutions must be considered also because they might well have an impact on other areas of the world that have a similar crisis. Increasing imports increases dependence on foreign sources, which are potentially unreliable as well.

A logistic problem is the time necessary to build necessary refineries, ports, and nuclear plants and to develop oil fields. Three to ten years are required to complete these necessary program components. Increased exploration for oil within the United States is expensive so that increases are passed on to the consumer. Alternate sources such as solar energy are not yet proved, are costly, and are not considered as a possibility in the near future. Efforts, however, must necessarily be directed toward increased domestic production, new sources as well as conservation of energy if the United States wishes to be independent and not at the mercy of foreign sources.

Energy conservation will undoubtedly be a major national goal. A magnitude of changes are necessary by every individual to conserve energy. Appalling wastes now exist in a nation where otherwise puritan values pervade, increasing as the supplies became easier to obtain and inexpensively acquired. It is now clear that the life-style that developed resulted from very short-sighted private and public policies. Less was wasted when people had to cut the wood they used to keep warm. Lest those in health care say, "But our area is not wasteful," they should be reminded of the source of the plastics so tidily disposed of day after day in hospitals across the country.

In the years ahead efforts will be directed toward insulating homes and buildings better, by minimizing leakage of outside air by way of excess ventilation and windows, and by eliminating inefficient and excessive equipment and lighting. It is possible to tighten and enforce tightened standards for new construction, but a major problem is that of older construction that still has years of functional and/or economic life before being replaced. Increased use of mobile homes may be curtailed; although they provide quick, inexpensive housing, they consume large quantities of

energy because of the way they are constructed. In the past emphasis was placed on substantially increasing lighting, minimum square window area, and ventilation in office buildings and places where people work. These now ironically become questionable standards. Possible new strategies might include tax incentives for energy conservation and eliminating discounts for high volume users.

As stated earlier, no physical shortage of energy currently exists. That, however, must be qualified because some resources are heavily used and are being greatly diminished. The resource that remains the most plentiful is fossil fuel, coal, which is dangerous to mine, leaves areas unattractive (especially when strip mined), is bulky to transport, and creates pollution of the air (sulfur, particulates, and nitrogen oxide), which rapidly exceeds tolerable public health standards. That coal with the least sulfur emission is the Rocky Mountain area and would create huge transportation costs for utilization in the East Coast. Too well known are the working conditions in the coal mines, health and safety problems, and disasters that occurred in the past. The Federal Coal Mine Health and Safety Act of 1969 was passed to improve health and safety conditions. Although the cost for meeting the standards may be little, assuring enforcement of the improvements at all times creates a much greater problem. Enforcement provisions were a major issue during bargaining in the 1974 coal strike. If new coal fields are opened, it will be necessary to consider the desecration of land created by large developments in the past, provision for an influx of workers and families (housing, schools, roads, shopping provisions, recreation), and opposition from the population in the area along with guarantees against ghost towns when the mines are exhausted and moved. Alternatives such as use of fuel oil, Arctic drilling, and nuclear underground methods to develop natural gas provide some possibilities but have their various limitations.

A comprehensive plan in the form of a national resource policy is probably a long time away, not because of physical or economic reasons (although they are real and significant factors) but because of political reasons. From the past one can be all too aware of how slowly political processes move toward decision making in any area. Finding a long-range, overall solution to the energy problem will surely be no exception. National policy making has traditionally been fragmented and has not taken into consideration the somewhat subtle interrelationships, the indirect (or even direct) effects of policy in one area on policy in another area. Examples might be extended but include those mentioned earlier—environmental effects such as pollution, land desecration, ghost towns, to mention only a few.

Major shifts have occurred from the use of wood to coal, coal to oil and natural gas, and now to atomic fuels. In many of the shifts the political process involved is referred to as pork barrel, logrolling, or cutting up of the pie. The improper or corrupt disbursement and dispensation of publicly owned land and resources by governmental administrations can be extended to the leasing of mineral rights, franchising of public utility companies, licensing of atomic power plants, and other such projects. During the gasoline shortage, it began to appear that the public was becoming more aware of the political dynamics and the actors on the stage. Increased sensitivity and growing awareness of supply limits and new demands are vital, along with knowledge of the political alliances of entrepreneurs, corporations, and complex coalitions into new governing, regulatory bodies. The Tennessee Valley Authority, first established as an independent government corporation, a regional resource-conservation agency, and producer of hydroelectric power to increase economic development was gradually developed by its board of directors into a major commercial producer of coal-generated electricity. Its ever-increasing demands for coal resulted in the environmental and general disruption of Appalachia.

Regulations

The states, which all vary in their policies and values, relinquished much or withdrew as larger public projects such as the Tennessee Valley Authority evolved. The interstate highway program of the 1950s and 1960s serves as another example of far-reaching consequences on such factors as use of domestic oil, land desecration, and the dying of big city centers. Yet the states' policies and values were not sufficiently consistent or were federal bodies such as the United States Bureau of Public Roads provided with authority and responsibility to decide on a comprehensive policy that could prevent the unintended consequences. The United States Bureau of Mines, likewise, has not yet sought or achieved multistate policies to regulate coal strip mining or to coordinate various efforts to extract subsurface fuel or research the potential of fossil fuel while preserving the environment.

United States politics, built on the pluralist model, assumes that policies are the result of conflict resolution in the form of a compromise or several small compromises. When it comes to dealing with natural resources that do have some real limits, compromises that satisfy industry, business organizations, and private interests have led to the state of affairs that the nation presently faces. Compromising on matters affecting delicately balanced areas of nature in which balance, once destroyed, can never be restored is no compromise at all. This cold fact must be realized by all concerned before the compromise concept will be abandoned. In the meantime, because a majority is needed to initiate or continue a program and many diverse interests are vested in relation to the nation's resources, many attempts to address what may be critical problems will meet with vetoes, thus blocking action, unless some link weakens in the veto pattern. An example is the overturn of the Supreme Court decision blocking the Alaska pipeline by shared jurisdiction with the legislature that overturned the decision, accomplished by exempting the pipeline decision from the Environmental Protection Act. Furthermore, in light of the public's increasing demand, any policies that throw energy and environment into frank confrontation will result in victory for those on the side of energy.

The development of more comprehensive energy policies brings to the fore a need for more centralized decision making and administration. Always controversial, it is especially certain to be threatening at this time when the centralization tactics made by the previous President have come under increased attack. In spite of bureaucratic resistance from government's civil servants, agencies, congressional committees, and state and local authorities, there have been slow but deliberate moves toward more centralization with regard to energy and environmental resources. Toughening of air and water pollution legislation was followed by creation of the United States Department of Natural Resources and by passage of the Environmental Protection Act of 1969, the federal land use bills of 1971-1972, and the Land Use Policy and Planning Resistance Act of 1973, in addition to presidential appointment of a national energy coordinator.

State officials and many congressmen resist centralization as interference with what should be the power of the states. Across the country, corporations shopped around among the states to find those that would make special allowances in their environmental standards to attract industry. On the other hand, state groups that directed efforts toward conservation of resources were able to make a significant impact to prevent resources' exploitation and federal intervention through maintenance of resource conservation and planning at the state level. The traditional belief in the sanctity of private land ownership is not readily overcome, even with much public education through modern communication media, until energy and environmental problems combined reach emergency levels. Even apparent emergencies can lead to strange decisions. The taconite ore iron mines in Minnesota were closed on court order because of litigation disclosing the dis-

charge of high quantities of asbestos into Lake Superior. This contaminated water is utilized as the drinking water source for the city of Duluth and its neighbors, and there is significant potential for an increase in the rate of development of carcinoma in the public as a result of the asbestos. Nonetheless, the mines were reopened in less than a week due to efforts in behalf of the suddenly unemployed workers. In publicity related to the battle there was little evidence of serious consideration by many health professionals of the relative benefits of current work and income as opposed to shortened life span and malignancy.

Social change

A little conflict is necessary for change. However, at the present time dangerous turbulence has mounted as the result of unresolved conflict among the races of American society, air pollution crisis in the cities, academic institutions in a "generation gap" crisis, economic crisis, the worldwide food supply problem, and bitter disagreement over foreign policy and military overseas activity. These all remain unresolved and are proliferating. The urgency for some control of the conflict has caused men to use brute force to remake American thinking. Such intense polarization has not been experienced by this nation since the period preceding the Civil War. The force has been directed largely at American institutions, perhaps because they are seen as making changes last. It may be, however, that breaking down whatever can be reached, without rationale or reason, is simply a phenomenon of unresolved conflict. The point seems to have been reached where society is unable to depend on the self-correcting strengths of American democracy. Government has intervened because society's natural strengths were too weak to moderate the conflict or make compromise. The nation has been preoccupied with a broad expansion instead of focusing on "integrating" or conciliating on the home front. It is probably now time to turn inward for self-evaluation and adjustment before the nation can progress toward a better life for all.

Civil rights has been a struggle in the United States since its beginnings. Meyer[17] contends that the Constitution was written twice to achieve civil rights. It was first written in Philadelphia in 1787 and included the first eight amendments, and it was rewritten in 1868 with the adoption of the Fourteenth Amendment. The first resulted from victory through the Revolution; the second resulted from the war between the North and South but was not enforced even by the United States Supreme Court. Another revolution was necessary, begun and carried on chiefly by blacks to return to the intent of the second Constitution. To date it has been possible to return to the point on paper but yet not totally in fact. The same phenomenon could be framed in the case of women, who were granted their rights in the first Constitution (1787) and again with the constitutional amendments in 1866. A third attempt is being made through the Equal Rights Amendment. One wonders if a hundred years later the civil rights of women guaranteed on paper then will be realized in fact.

One can hardly refute the principle of participatory democracy as the critical focus within modern constitutional government. One might raise the question with DeGrazia[18] concerning whether actual expectations of ipso facto participation are naive. "Involvement" too frequently is getting on bandwagons, which satisfies the ego and is done in terms not of representing the self as a person with political postures but substituting nonnegotiable theoretical principles and institutions. It then becomes somewhat similar to people doing incapacitating meddling into business about which they know little. Certainly the health care workers have accused others of doing this. In recent events this is what has been occurring too often. It hinders the work that must be done, dissipates and obscures responsibility, and limits and complicates government. It becomes almost a form of "sick" entertainment when other outlets would be more creative expression of

themselves, their emotions, amusement, and inspiration. There must be ways in a democracy for life not to be dull, which acknowledge rank, opinion, and interests that hold people together and eliminate what appears to be a destructive, brutal system.

A current example illustrates that society is still in the same proverbial "box." With school integration in both the North and the South, following recent court-ordered desegregation, the actual situation is perhaps little better than before. Several reasons are presented. Parents are enrolling their children in private schools either because of their feelings about integration or because they fear that their child may perhaps become one of a white minority within a large classroom of black children. They fear the quality of their child's education will of necessity be poorer because the black children need so much additional teacher energy to complete the required assignments. However, public school boards of those schools have a high percentage of white members whose children do not attend them. Taxes are paid by all, at least idealistically according to ability to pay. A teacher of one such school is quoted as saying: "The people paying taxes need to be represented on the board too. Wasn't that one of the things we fought the American Revolution over—taxation without representation?"[19] The "box" is created by an evaluation of *who pays taxes,* since the wealthy frequently find shelters to avoid them and the poor (a group composed of far more blacks than whites) are either unemployed and on public tax assistance or pay very little. The question is whether there is, in fact, taxation without representation.

There are changes within the educational system as well. Colleges and universities in the past assumed responsibility of supervising student conduct *in loco parentis.*[20] With changing moral and social standards there was a trend away from educational administrators' presumed obligation to parents that their children be guaranteed minimal disruption while pursuing academic study. There may, however, be a return to a modified parental role as students take issue with uncontrolled freedom. One coed has filed a $1 million damage suit against Vassar College. She claimed she flunked out because the college did nothing to prohibit her roommate from continuously having all-night pot parties.[20]

The antiwar protests did not die after the Vietnam pullout. The sociology of peace making, peace and conflict studies, and world order studies have grown rapidly.[21] Some universities are now offering minors in the area of peace or are developing peace studies degree programs. It has been referred to as a truly liberal education and relevant to all areas of life. Literature in the field is extensive. However, peace study still presents a tough struggle for academic acceptance for reasons such as the change-resistant nature of universities and its threat to previously existing departments so that jobs and status are at stake. Compromises have been made in some institutions so that courses in peace making are taught by regular departments. One advantage to that approach is that the ultimately earned degree is in an acceptable field such as history, which is helpful in obtaining a job. The content is being also developed for high schools and elementary schools. One author* of an elementary textbook in conflict-resolution points out that as early as first grade the content is useful to children to deal with family squabbles. He considers that more relevant than the traditional "mickey mouse" stuff which kids are taught.

Population control

The kind of health care needed in years ahead will be greatly affected by the age and attitude of the population. Whereas around 1960 the average family had three to four children, there has been a rapid decline in the birth rate to the point where the average family now has fewer than two children. In

other areas of the world it is absolutely critical for survival that control is gained over the rate at which the population increases. Yet what happens in other areas affects this nation as well. Thus the life of every individual is influenced. In the United States the declining birthrate has had both a negative and positive impact. Hospitals that were built to accommodate the needs of a large number of new mothers and their infants now have empty beds. Schools built with tax dollars to educate large numbers of children are being closed, and teachers are unemployed. Many more women are free to enter the labor market and are seeking constructive ways to occupy their time and use their talents because they are not needed to cook and sew for their large families. The natural resources and environment are taxed less when the numbers of people using them decreases, making it a better world in which to live. Because Americans have learned to be great consumers, the resources in their country are taxed more heavily by every individual than are those of other countries where people have always lived to expect less. A striking example might be to compare individual expectations of average Americans with those of people in India.

When the United States does achieve a zero population growth, the age of the population will shift. With the recent decline in birthrate the children who are born will benefit from the large number of people from the baby-boom era who have become taxpayers. Better education and standard of living should thus be available to them. Better social legislation, retirement benefits, pensions, and health care will undoubtedly be demanded. With fewer young people crime in the large cities may even decrease as well as automobile accident rates (provided the older driver is indeed a safer driver). Recall, however, that the same boom population will eventually reach old age, with a potential for excessive drain on social and health resources if current concerns of the aging remain the case.

Whether or not the allegations made by

*Lawrence Senesh, a University of Colorado professor, referred to by Martin.[21]

radical historians are altogether true, many Americans are listening and changing their notions about the nation's past. More are viewing America not as a land devoted to the ideals of equality of men, of small business and small farmers, of overseas activities promoting democratic principles for people of other lands and "making the world safe for democracy," but as a gigantic corporate venture. The reality lies probably somewhere in between. Knowledge of the political processes and specific issues can enable one to work toward bringing the actual state of affairs in line with one's desire.

References

1. Wall Street Journal, Aug. 11, 1971.
2. World sees U. S. as Mecca of health care, AMA head says, Los Angeles Times, Oct. 3, 1972.
2a. Stuart, B. C.: Who gains from public health programs, Annals of the American Academy of Political and Social Science, **399**:148, Jan., 1972.
3. Welfare study finds 5% weren't eligible for April payments, Wall Street Journal, Jan. 4, 1972.
4. Cornuelle, R. C.: Reclaiming the American dream, New York, 1968, Random House, Inc.
5. Schattschneider, E. E.: Two hundred million Americans in search of a government, New York, 1969, Holt, Rinehart & Winston, Inc., p. 22.
6. Op. cit., p. 28
7. Reich, C. A.: The greening of America, New York, 1971, Bantam Books, Inc.
8. Knopfelmacher, F.: The dropout as revolutionary, Wall Street Journal, Oct. 25, 1971.
9. Ketchum, R.: Will Rogers, the man and his times, Boston, 1973, American Heritage Publishing Co.
10. Somers, A. R.: The nation's health: issues for the future, Annals of the American Academy of Political and Social Science **399**:160-174, Jan., 1972.
11. News, American Journal of Nursing **74**:192, Feb., 1972.
12. Used machine tools had sales rise of 16% in February from 1973, Wall Street Journal, March 27, 1974.
13. Greenspan, A.: The politics of inflation, Wall Street Journal, March 19, 1974.
14. Smith, W. D.: Shortage amid plenty. In Connery, R. H., and Gilman R. S., editors: The national energy problem, New York, 1974, The Academy of Political Science, p. 44.
15. Sargent, F. W.: The need for a new perspective on energy. In Connery, R. H., and Gilman, R. S., editors: The national energy problem, New York, 1974, The Academy of Political Science, p. 25.
16. McCracken, P. W.: 1974's basic problem—inflation, Wall Street Journal, Feb. 21, 1974.
17. Meyer, H. N.: The amendment that refused to die, Radnor, Pa., 1973, Chilton Book Co.
18. DeGrazia, A.: Politics for better or worse, Glenview, Ill., 1973, Scott Foresman Co.
19. Maxwell, N.: Friend of foe? Schools in South said to be harmed by some boards, Wall Street Journal, Oct. 27, 1971.
20. In loco parentis: review and outlook, Wall Street Journal, Oct. 27, 1971.
21. Martin, R.: To the three R's, you now can append a P; it stands for peace, Wall Street Journal, March 5, 1974.

UNIT TWO

POWER

It is said that the best way to get along in the world is to do what is expected of you. But it's a lot more fun to do what is suspected of you!

DAL DEVENING[1]

5

TYPES AND SOURCES OF POWER

Power is defined as the ability of one person to influence another in any situation. It may be based on skill, circumstance, or brute force. The methods generally accepted by political scientists as appropriate for the attainment of power are through receiving votes and by having position and ability to affect policy making. Power, according to some, differentiates those who "have" from those who "have not." An individual's achievement of increased power results from the loss of power by other individuals who possess it. Inherent in this process is conflict. Theorists in various fields have indicated that a little conflict is a good thing and that conflict or dissonance is necessary for progress and for psychological and intellectual growth.

Power may be described as being of two types. One type of power is unique or original and puts the individual who possesses it in a class set apart; the second type of power places the individual within a group among those with distinguished ability. Persons in political leadership positions have been of either type, and any one leader is not necessarily both. The point might be argued; however, one might classify an individual such as Abraham Lincoln as an originator and Thomas Jefferson as having distinguished ability but not originating power. In making that distinction one reflects that experiences of past times and nations would qualify men to plan for the future. Jefferson envisioned that the children of his generation would be connected with agricultural occupations and that by useful facts from the past they would be able to determine their own future happiness. Facts from history could be used to provide ideas which were perceived as power greater than that of property itself and would make for equality in society. Some great minds of the past centuries have functioned from the historical perspective and have given birth to ideas that derived their power to address the present from a sense of the past.

The social struggle by underprivileged groups against special privileges and political dominance of an earlier aristocracy has been the basis for upheavals and revolutions throughout the centuries. Serious economic and social antagonisms were underlying factors in the American Revolution and have from time to time surfaced whenever power (in whatever form) has become concentrated into an intolerably few privileged hands. It is not intended here to pursue a lengthy explanation of the American Revolution. However, recent historians (Bailyn et al.[2]) have certainly emphasized the role which ideas played at the time of the Revolution, indicating that a profound instability was prevailing. The colonists placed great emphasis on corruption, disruption, and hostility. They viewed everything suspiciously, as possible conspiracy, since they seemed to envision the creation of an almost unrealistic great society. Several hypotheses have been set forth, but one need not for the purposes of this discussion discount either hypothesis referred to here. It is relatively insignificant whether one believes that colonial society experienced a severe erosion of its own internal cohesion from the landing at Plymouth Rock to the time of the Revolution or whether one agrees that the social structure of the colonies was becoming more rigid with resultant intense social strain leading to the time of the Revolution. Either or both sets of dynamics may have been occurring simultaneously. Rapid economic and demographic development place strain on any society. Supplemented with other developments, a state of perpetual instability and disorientation is increased to the point beyond which some release or restructuring must occur. Factors that contributed to the instability prior to the Revolution included the splintering of religious uniformity by the spiritual "Great Awakening,"[3] increased social differentiation with increasing divergence in terms of individual wealth,[3a] competition among the colonies resultant from men's quest for more land, wealth, status, and supremacy,[4] and development of new towns and cities with cultures and life styles that differed from those of the earlier rural communities of the colonies.

The American Revolution was not merely a war for independence from Great Britain but also was a social struggle by groups of underprivileged against the privileged, politically dominant aristocracy of the colonies. The masses had become severely resentful as wealth and power was ever more concentrated in the hands of fewer and fewer. The ties of community and political supremacy among the traditional elite were splintered as they attempted to hold authority and maintain their position. Settlement in new geographical areas and attempts to extend authority into new economic areas created additional strains. New men challenged relentlessly. Although historians differ in their emphasis, one result of the Revolution was an internal social and economic leveling.

Not unique to the era of the American Revolution were the destabilizing effects of rapid change and the frustrations brought about by a closing society. The readers are reminded that change, even rapid change, may not necessarily create social instability and that society must be homeostatic or in equilibrium to be healthy. If change is institutionalized and widely accepted, it may indeed be a stabilizing factor. A slowing down of change may in fact create serious social upheaval. Neither is it necessarily true that rapid economic and population growth along with increased social distinctions automatically result in decreased social cohesion. Furthermore, although rapid upward mobility and demand to participate in political decision making created conflict during the early days in American history, these factors cannot be disregarded as having relieved perhaps as much social strain as they created. No matter how critical problems are resolved, whether in reference to the Revolution or present-day unrest, it is always questionable if any or all factors can be assigned a weight and one can be labeled as the major cause. It is frequently said, however, that whenever major discontent arises in society, the intensity and extent can be seen in terms of an increase in the crime and insanity index (of both individuals and the total society).

Although it is difficult to understand complex social, political, economic, and religious changes, effort to do so cannot be abandoned. Evidence to date would certainly support the presence of social malintegration, both before and after various major revolutions or changes. To view the revolution or change, one must abandon the intense search for ways of linking the complex network neatly together and, rather, focus more broadly on the whole situation, since various things will surface during a period of social strain that during normal times would be hidden or obscured from view.

In this context, conflict is one type of power; it is not the length of the conflict but its intrinsic factors that make it so. It is likewise a mechanism for shifting power. Thus revolutions have been powerful in shaping societies, including not only this nation but others as well. Thus several revolutions have recently been proclaimed in the United States: the black revolution, the student revolution, the youth revolution, and the women's revolution. From a study of revolution as a theoretical concept it has been learned that revolutionary situations can be created. Knowledge of power dynamics and the necessary components makes it possible to create deliberately not only violent revolutions but also planned change, since revolution has come to contain an assortment of meanings. Revolution or change occurs as power shifts. With this is the idea of cycles of change, circularity, and turbulent ups and downs. The meaning of the word *revolution* has shifted from a description of internal change by means of violence to include the attainment of a specific range of goals not necessarily through violence. Violence as a component of revolution might be aimed at the leaders and personnel within a govern-

ment, a regime, or system in which power is distributed or aimed at society in which dominant values or power structure are significant. Thus one speaks of the scientific revolution, the sexual revolution, the population revolution, the educational revolution as well as the industrial revolution, the military revolution, the Protestant revolution, and others.

Study of causes of revolution (change) have received more emphasis than other aspects such as classification, the dynamic processes, and the long-range consequences of revolutions. However, few experts agree on even basic factors of causation. For example, de Tocqueville believed that revolution would most likely occur when oppression was lessened, whereas Marx contended that intensified oppression or exploitation brought on revolution. Brinton[5] stated that the psychological and economic factors which attract people to a revolutionary cause are actually better described as a quasi-religious faith. Perhaps the greatest flaw in the Marxist model is an oversimplification or oversystematization of economic factors as sole source of change in social structure, state, and ideology. Money is an important source of power, but there are sources of power that are less directly economic.

Major European revolutions such as the French, Russian, German, and British revolutions are widely renowned for their deep and widespread revolt. Although not uniform in nature, such movements have usually the features of complete rejection of the existing world order with an anticipation of a future world purged of all the present old evils and a somewhat prophetic world transformation derived from Judeo-Christian beliefs. Often for such revolution there is a charismatic leader, who may be viewed as a prophet. Secular revolution and religious movements frequently occur simultaneously, perhaps intertwined if not dependent on one another. Such revolutions may occur as oppressed masses strive for an outlet, a means of expression, yet they have not achieved political consciousness or political organization. A few fanatical members among the masses are able to arouse hysterical, irrational revolt against the socioeconomic status. It is less than realistic political struggle and a far cry from democratic planned change.

Although stressing money as a source of political power and lack of it as cause for revolution, social change must be considered in the context of existing values and politics. One example is that of the current United States situation in which the citizenry has tasted liberal programs that upgraded the welfare of the society and its members during the Kennedy administration and Johnson's Great Society era. These administrations were followed by an administration that gave little or no emphasis and support to those programs that were generally expected to continue. The result was a sharp discrepancy between public expectation and accessibility. Programs of the Ford administration show few signs of changing this condition. An acute discrepancy thus exists between mounting wants and expectations (values) and the possibility of their satisfaction, and the resulting anger, frustration, and discontent are all conditions favorable to violence and revolution. Whether this will occur has been described in a theory of relative deprivation[6] and defined in terms of the amount or extent of the discrepancy between what people perceive or hold as expectation and the likelihood of their obtaining what they expect. Many of the current problems may be a manifestation or syndrome resulting from or related to this discontent.

Of course, it is important to distinguish long-term preconditions and dynamics from immediate agents that by chance precipitate revolutionary situations. Eckstein[7] proposed eight preconditions, pointing out the factors that act to stave off or encourage revolution. Those factors discouraging the outburst of revolution are the coercive capacity of those in power, effective repression, concessions made as adjustments, and diversionary mechanisms. Favoring revolution are inefficiency of the elite, disorientation processes, subversion, and the ability of the insurgents to produce violence. By the careful evaluation

and weighing of these eight aspects, it is suggested that the likelihood of revolution can be predicted. It must always be kept in mind, however, that revolution and violence are not necessarily identical.

In the case of American society, where revolution is identified with various forms of violence, the reader must make a clear distinction between violence and revolution. In situations where political or collective strife in the form of banditry, labor struggles, lynchings, and food, race, and other riots are common, a distinction must be made between those acts that are precursors to revolution and those that are not necessarily so or that would require additional circumstances. Revolution and various forms of violence may have similar or identical features; understanding is necessarily dependent on further observation and study.

To "modernize" is revolutionary, depending on the context and description of what occurs. It may be instant, large-scale, or ongoing change. Ability to absorb the change as rapidly or slowly as it is introduced influences the social reaction. The social reaction depends on the capacity of a society to synthesize ingredients of stability and instability. In contrast, societies that are traditional in nature are likely to lack the political mechanisms and organization to carry the responsibility placed on them by overwhelming demands for major revamping and are thus unstable; they become disorderly and in some cases prime targets for major revolutions.

Modernization can be construed as a form of revolution. To modernize in eastern (Oriental) culture seemingly means first the shaping of new institutions (new power groups) and then the overthrowing of the existing order, whereas in western culture mobilization of citizenry and overthrow of the old order (old power groups) follow the downfall of what is the old order. The problem inherent is that it is difficult to categorize societies or cultures clearly because many are in the gray or unclear areas. Is modernization a cause for revolution? All one can actually say is that the rapid social and economic change inherent in modernization is most likely going to produce instability and that instability is a factor which is connected with revolution.

Although revolutions involve the large masses, *alienation* is a concept or descriptive term for large portions of the present society. If withdrawn and alienated, how do these large segments of people suddenly involve persons to support a cause and bring about a turn of events? There must have been some element of power existent or available to the alienated group.

A functioning social system is not necessarily void of change but is one in which change takes place as an equilibrium occurs among the various sectors supporting and opposing it. Values both inside and outside must change. The system discontinues its functioning when sectors or subsystems of the entire system are unable to adjust and adapt and achieve a point of equilibrium. If subsystems are unable to adapt, the results are disorientation and hostility. Those in power must respond either to resist the change, control its direction, or assimilate it. Thus the negative and positive aspects, or the ingredients, of revolution determine the outcome—revolution, change or no revolution. Something will happen in any case.

Much of the foregoing discussion may seem to be generalizations. This point of view is reflective of the general nature of theory currently available even from theoreticians such as Johnson,[8] who made ambitious attempts to apply social systems theory to revolution (change). Societal dysfunction and disequilibrium are not synonymous, and not only is the formula for each extremely vague but also indications are lacking that are sufficiently clear to enable one to distinguish between and among various indicators or variables. A number of seemingly promising ideas for developing neat formulas have been presented, but no clear adaptable plan that is measurable can be obtained to date. Thus we pursue an area that is not clearly tested and found true but must present a gamut of approaches from other areas that may or may not be applicable to the reader's own specific situation.

Men such as Locke, Adam Smith, and Jefferson deemed man to be inherently self-sufficing and equipped by nature with both the instinct and reason that could make him autonomous. In hindsight, however, it can be seen that these founders of liberalism were unconsciously abstracting certain moral and psychological attributes from a social organization and considering these as a timeless natural quality of the individual, regarded as independent of the influences of any historically developed social organization. Given the image of man as inherently self-sufficient, given the view that the importance of communities and groups was merely secondary and a shadow of man's actual reality, it was inevitable that the strategy of gaining freedom should be based on objectives of release and emancipation of man from fettering institutions. Fromm and Tillich referred to the need for meaningful objects of devotion. These need not be personal objects but symbols with which to identify the objects that are meaningful. Such is necessary in any system that effectively provides mental health services.

A growing concern is that of building a society in which all persons can attain their potential and individual power. Society yet remains plagued with individuals obsessed with the search of ever-increasing power, seemingly indifferent to the results of their actions. Historically the situation is perpetuated until, continually frought by conflict and dissonance, a few of the least internally devastated turn to revolution.

Naturalists of the last century were greatly intrigued by their observations of the interrelations and coordination within the realm of nature. They described a vast system of dependence, interdependence, and independence, which they called the "web of life." Interdependence is described in Darwin's classic illustration of the cats and the violas and red clover. He found that humble-bees (bumble-bees) were almost indispensable to the fertilization of the heartsease, since other bees do not visit this flower. The same thing is true with some kinds of clover. Humble-bees alone visit red clover because other bees cannot reach the nectar. The inference is that if the humble-bee were to become extinct or extremely rare in England, heartsease and red clover would become very rare or might actually disappear. However, the number of humble-bees in any area depends greatly on the number of field mice that destroy their combs and nests. It is estimated that more than two thirds of them are thus destroyed throughout the countryside. Near villages and small towns the nests of humble-bees are more numerous than elsewhere, and this is attributed to the number of cats that destroy the mice. Thus next year's crop of clover depends on the number of humble-bees in that district. The number of humble-bees depends on the number of field mice. The number of field mice depends on the number and enterprise of the cats. The number of cats, as someone has added, depends on the number of old maids and others in neighboring villages who keep cats. The exact nature and quantity of power held by any one of the insects or animals are difficult to identify or understand without consideration of the total picture.

Food has recently been labeled a potential political tool[9] and source of power. Because of the natural land potential and technology and application of scientific agricultural principles, the United States has been able to produce more food than its population consumes. Since the depression of the 1930s, farmers have maintained a position of being one of the nation's most powerful pressure groups and through various ways have gained insurance against serious economic fluctuations. Food programs were developed, one being The Food for Peace (PL 480), under which surpluses were distributed abroad. Using food as a means of obtaining commodities that are in short supply (such as oil) is one alternative. Agriculture Secretary Earl Butz is quoted as stating that the food program is no longer a mechanism for disposing of surpluses but for humanitarian purposes and national defense (strengthening the arm of countries that are political allies). Feeding the world's needy has long been a United States concern, and recently it is becoming recognized more as an international and not solely a United States responsibility. Feeding the impoverished in the United States has taken on increasing import with acknowledgment that its resources do not allow feeding all those with hunger in the world. In addition to all this the United States population has increased greatly, and people are migrating from farms to cities. Agriculture as a pressure bloc has lost considerable clout to labor and industry. The interrelationships of power are intricate. The potential for gradual change or revolution in food distribution is also a real one. Available theory does not make the situation readily understandable.

Rational and irrational aspects of power and conflict

The political process, although not usually viewed as a psychological one, is either a conscious or unconscious process. If considered a conscious process, it concerns itself with rationality, theoretical concepts that comprise political science. If considered as an unconscious process, it concerns itself with the irrational elements of interpersonal relationships and practice. Rational or irrational, the process of interpersonal relations is a political one, comprising a dynamic struggle for order and subordination of some elements in favor of other elements, but one in which at any given time some hierarchy of persons prevails. Those who rise in the political process must rise (1) by birth or (2) through the ranks, usually slowly. Some are endowed with ability to rise faster and higher than others. People have been institutionalized to think that certain ones among them possess the right to prescribe to others, to specify directions for achieving a state of existence, and to test or evaluate the extent to which they have accomplished that for which they set out. Thus power is granted as well as sought after and taken. Whether persons submit, are "to be helped," "directed," or "taught" depends on the degree of submission. There are social compensations for sacrificing autonomy within society as well as a political reward—power.

The devaluation of objects, human subjects, or situations by individuals in search of ascendency, that is, power, can be observed in the otherwise most sensitive people. It is regular and normal that human needs for recognition, fellowship, security, and membership must be met. However, this is inadequate. A historical tragedy is that States most successful in meeting the needs for recognition and security have also been most tyrannical and despotic. This can be seen in nations under dictatorships.

During the eighteenth century man focused on freeing himself of his historical bonds with state, religion, morals, and economics. Man's nature, originally good and common to all, then should develop unhampered in what was conceived of as democracy. In democratic society all persons have been philosophically viewed as having equal, ultimate worth. Documents indicate that in action even the great hallmarks of American democracy, the town meetings, imposed restrictions on all people with regard to qualifications for voting and participation in policy making. In some of the colonies only landholders and males could determine policy for all others. It meant that under no circumstances could women determine their own future.

Mental health professionals, both for themselves and in behalf of patients and potential patients, must answer the question of how the personality accommodates itself in the adjustments to external forces. Schools and colleges in recent years have greatly diminished the emphasis on history as a part of the curriculum. The impact that this may ultimately have on the distribution of power is the diminution of the number of persons who, through the use of past events, plan for the future.

The distribution of money-based power has changed little over the past generation. Five or six out of 100 families in 1974 are estimated to be in serious financial trouble, as opposed to three families in 1973. "Serious financial trouble" is defined as owing more money than they are able to pay. An example[10] is given of a 27-year-old salesman who had an income of $40,000 in 1973, more money than he and his wife had ever known. They developed a feeling of power and set forth to purchase a $60,000 home, new furniture, clothes, and a Lincoln Continental equipped with all the extras including telephone. They accumulated $40,000 of debts that they could not keep up during the turbulent economy and inflation. The wife went to work, their house went for sale, they traded the Lincoln for a small foreign car, and amidst frequent periods of depression they remain essentially broke. This unfortunate situation might be contributed to by the overwhelming attempt in the United States to get families to buy on the installment plan and by the vulnerability of Americans to suggestions to use this approach to obtain what appears to them as power.

In the light of the preceding material, those individuals who are originators are left with the potential of achieving power in American society. One fallacy, however, occurs in this logic. The fallacy lies in the fact that an assumption is made about the rationalism or reasonableness of those intellectual concepts which are developed. To be conceptually and theoretically sound, intellectualism cannot be equated with rationalism and may indeed be seen as reducing man to the form of a machine, therefore limiting his freedom and dignity. Members of some professions have gained power as a result of brilliant new discoveries, and others have achieved power through the outlining of principles that can be viewed from a historical perspective and applied to present and future problems. The two approaches have been antagonistic to one another; various professions have focused on one or the other as being of greater import.

People face a decrease in value of their purchasing power because of a complex network of political and economic dynamics. Their response is recognized in various ways.

One is in shopping patterns. One supermarket has found that 25% of its customers are shopping less frequently, whereas another supermarket chain states that its customers are buying less.[11] People depend more on shopping lists, planned menus, and pocket calculators as they make the grocery dollars stretch. Fewer convenience foods are bought, coupons that save a few pennies are used, and less expensive brands are in greater demand.[11] Studies such as this are common and are a part of regular bookkeeping procedures; when explored in the light of everyday events, the findings provide assistance in understanding the changing times and political underpinnings. They provide access to power for some.

Advertising may be initiated by one or a few individuals and may be a means of gaining increased support from sympathizers. On the other hand, it may be the end result rather than the means. One example is that of the gay liberation movement. Not long ago advertising for the movement was unheard of. In the past year or so small articles or news items appeared through various media on the subject. The National Gay Task Force placed a full-page advertisement in one edition of the *New York Times* and was financed by a loan from a supporter with hopes of raising funds and broadening its base of support through political and educational activities.[12] The use of an accepted approach, the advertising media, to gain a base for power has been harnessed by a group that has been kept powerless primarily because of multiple non-national responses.

Constructive or destructive power and conflict: range of normal

Nietzsche described the full development of the individual as a result of the most ruthless struggle of individuals. Socialism believes in the suppression of all competition (conflict) for the same reason. However, be that as it may, in any position the same motive is at work: the person resists being leveled down and worn out by a social-technological mechanism. The same factors that have united with exact and minute precision to form life itself are also united in the form of personality, a structure of the highest order. There is that which is the "general human being" in every individual, but as well there is the qualitative uniqueness and irreplaceability.

As the environment of individuals more and more takes on the form of an impersonal, causal, and mechanical structure, one might expect to find simultaneously a steady heightening level of individual self-discovery and self-consciousness. Detachment from his world then becomes the only way in which the individual can win a form of mobility and freedom. Only when the world is organized and defined in objective and impersonal terms, does it and the individual become separated. In other words the individual's community becomes ever more remote to him. The deepest problems of modern life derive from the claim of individuals to preserve autonomy and individuality of their existence in the face of overwhelming social forces, historical heritage, external culture, and technology impinging on their lives. There is perhaps no psychic phenomenon that has been so unconditionally reserved to recent times as the blasé attitude. This is not only a current ill of American metropolitan society but can be seen in history as man continuously strived to liberate himself from his historical bonds and to distinguish himself from others.

Frequently mental health professionals treat persons who perceive their power or position in life as being so insignificant and what they have and what they want as being in such conflict that doing away with themselves seems to be the only solution. In part because of their involvement with such powerless people, health organizations can become powerless or be seen as powerless.

Not only has the private health sector been criticized in recent years, but the power and support maintained by the public health system is likewise unfavorable. This can be recognized in various ways. Although public health nurses twenty to thirty years ago earned greater salaries than nurses in private settings, this is now reversed. What public health officers today earn as much as their colleagues in private practice? Local, county, and state public health systems have lost considerable muscle, as has the public health clinic system. The distinguished public health service medical officers corps was dissolved; public health service hospitals are closing. Most recently federal support to schools of public health was cut sharply. Public health as a specialty area began fifty years ago when its charge was clear—check the spread of communicable disease, educate the public, provide health services to persons not receiving private care (especially mothers and children), and eliminate environmental hazards to health. When the distinction between public health and private health was made and public health became a specialty area, its practitioners worked together, even in professional education programs, quite separate from their private counterparts. They made little effort to build alliances with health professionals in the private sector. The fear of those in the private sector that they might lose patients contributed heavily to this. When the struggle for support became critical, those in public health had few dependable allies in the health system, and the general citizenry had few positive data that stood on their own merit in support.

This situation is not unique to this one field, but public health serves as an example. Whenever one component of a total system breaks away from the mainstream of the overall system, it can anticipate the ultimate loss of power. It has then a hard road to travel, with expenditure of much extra effort, before its skills and performance will again be acknowledged as being in its golden era. Public health has before it the many challenges of environmental and population growth, which include monitoring and participating in the planning and delivery of comprehensive health services, particularly in the mental health, drugs, alcoholism, and control of accidental deaths. Public health personnel, including educators in schools of public health, will need to provide services in

these areas so that they can readily be seen and to focus less on their statistics' gathering and theorizing activities.

Power is never in a permanent state of equilibrium. There are changes in physical environment, such as seen in clinical settings and in people's movement from place to place and position to position. There are social changes, cultural changes, changes in size of groups, and changes in the extent of group power.

Money per se will become a less powerful factor in obtaining political office as various pieces of public disclosure legislation are enacted. Records of expenses and donors are recorded, and contributions to election campaigns and trust funds of political officers become subject to public review. Whereas cold hard cash no longer is a direct means of electing the person who best represents one's interest, other powerful methods will undoubtedly be discovered. One must watch to learn what methods will be developed.

"Credit," not cash, is a valuable source of power in American society today. Many Americans carry little cash but a sizeable collection of credit cards with which they purchase everything from meals to wheels.

It can be expected that subsequent elections will reflect the increased public awareness brought about by factors such as the Watergate scandal, and by tax evasion by high-level governmental administration, as well as reflect improved educational levels of the citizenry. The candidates for national election in 1976 will receive careful scrutiny, and undoubtedly there will be less credence given to the glowing promises made by political candidates. To support this, the pollster Lou Harris[13] provides the data in Table 4.

In his discussion of civil disobedience (one form of power struggle) Cohen[14] rejects such arguments as civil disobedience implying contempt for law, and he accepts selfish interests as prime. He contends that as long as lawful channels are open, civil disobedience cannot be justified in a democratic system. He does not rule out civil disobedience as a tool when no other avenues remain.

Table 4. Changes in the electorate (1968-1976)*

	1968 (%)	1976 (%)	Change
Shrinking in power			
Under $5,000 income	25	19	−6
Small town voters	22	11	−11
Union members	23	15	−8
Education not beyond 8th grade	19	11	−8
Democrats	51	41	−10
$5,000-$9,999 income	43	23	−20
Increasing in power			
College-educated	29	40	+11
$15,000 and over income	12	25	+13
Independents	18	28	+10
Suburban residents	26	34	+8
Under 30 voters	18	27	+9
Professionals in occupation	9	20	+11

*Harris, L.: Coming soon: educated, elitist electorate, Parade Magazine, Spokesman Review, p. 23, June 9, 1974.

In using money as power, Americans are finding themselves less and less powerful as they bargain for what they want both abroad and in their own country. In less than ten years the dollar has lost nearly one third of its value to the purchaser.[15] In the case of the purchaser being the government it would appear that taxes will need to be increased if government must continue to pay the inflated prices. Actually therefore taxpayers would appear to be hit doubly as they are required to pay higher prices and higher taxes.

Cohen's[16] final paragraph perhaps states it best: "If law is the skeleton of justice, however, it is not its heart. After the context is known, the laws distinguished, and the levels of authority and conflicts of jurisdiction made clear, the moral task remains—that of determining whether, in that context, given those facts, a given law ought deliberately to be broken. That is what civil disobedience is all about."

Control exerted by a group leads to countercontrol. The resultant conflict is an issue of surviving and perishing as groups become stronger or weaker. A new value emerges when survival is perceived to be threatened.

Two or more groups may then share the practice of passing the value of survival on to others within their respective groups, and an evolutionary process goes on. The more who carry out this practice, the greater will be the chances of survival by a group. Pressure groups join together when their joining is perceived as being of mutual benefit. To the extent that members get what they need and avoid what is dangerous, the more they are helped to survive and transmit their power. Two kinds of evolution are thus going on simultaneously and are closely interwoven. However, the better educated and aware members of the current generation are unwilling to be satisfied with less than full equality and participation in their society. Questions that arise include: Is it possible for human beings to live without power and its inherent interpersonal struggles? Perhaps humans can if this happens in the coming century. Power will not be based on domination of one person over another but rather on a cohesion based on integration. Perhaps a new social order will evolve from the many hundreds of rebellions that consist of an interlocking of classes and nations.

The dynamics of interaction between the world community and its natural environment may, in fact, be the phenomena of concern rather than those discussed in this text and countless political writings of today and years past—power, class, conflict, political behavior. Prescriptions for building the world community vary in their degree of complexity. One such prescription by Brucan[17] calls for a combination of Marxism (the world viewed as full of conflict, instability, and action) and cybernetics (interactions and variables in a systematic complex that is controllable and described) to accomplish the ultimate goal. Such a philosophical presentation can be neither excluded nor ignored in the context of the discussion in this book.

References

1. Wall Street Journal, Nov. 9, 1971.
2. Bailyn, B., et al.: Pamphlets of the American revolution, Cambridge, Mass., 1965, Harvard University Press.
3. Heimart, A.: Religion and the American mind: from the Great Awakening to the Revolution, Cambridge, Mass., 1966, Harvard University Press.
3a. Main, J. T.: The social structure of revolutionary America, Princeton, N. J., 1965, Princeton University Press.
4. Bailyn, B.: The origins of American politics, New York, 1968, Alfred A. Knopf, Inc.
5. Brinton, C. C.: The anatomy of revolution, New York, 1938, W. W. Norton & Co., Inc., Publishers.
6. Gurr, T. R.: Why men rebel, Princeton, N. J., 1970, Princeton University Press.
7. Eckstein, H.: Internal wars: problems and approaches, New York. 1964, The Free Press.
8. Johnson, C.: Revolution and the social system, Stanford, Calif., 1964, Stanford University Press.
9. Rosenfeld, S.S.: U.S. food: a political tool or to feed the hungry? The Kansas City Star, June 2, 1974.
10. Austin, D. W.: More consumers find their debts outpacing their ability to pay, Wall Street Journal, June 4, 1974.
11. Business bulletin: Fighting inflation, Wall Street Journal, June 6, 1974.
12. Gay rights group stating its case in newspaper ad, Wall Street Journal, June 6, 1974.
13. Harris, L.: Coming soon: educated, elitist electorate, Parade Magazine Spokesman Review, June 9, 1974.
14. Cohen, C.: Civil disobedience: conscience, tactics and law, New York, 1971, Columbia University Press.
15. Inflation jolts taxpayers, Spokane Daily Chronicle, May 30, 1974.
16. Cohen, op. cit., p. 214.
17. Brucan, S.: The dissolution of power, The Center Magazine, Santa Barbara, Calif., Center for Study of Democratic Institutions, vol. 5, Jan./Feb., 1972.

It's possible that some diplomats see
both sides of a situation just so
that they can get around it.

MURRAY COHEN[1]

6

FORMAL POWER STRUCTURES

The entire field of health care, and especially public or community health, even in a democratic society, is heavily involved with bureaucracies and the formal power structure. The nature of those structures is such that just as circumstances which sponsor creativity in artists are not necessarily creative, it might be also said that although improvements may be made in health standards and practices by public health teams, the circumstances producing them may not be democratic. If the public health worker is not a mature, morally responsible individual, the tendency will be to plan and act compulsively and impulsively, which will not encourage the self-fulfillment of others, even though such actions may lower disease incidence and improve the health of the mass of humankind.

Public health should not be a concept separate from people; public health *is* people. Involving citizens, lay committees, parents' groups, and volunteers in community health programs may be democratic. In itself this is not necessarily democratic, as no one approach automatically is. If these groups are used in a manner that manipulates people or if they comprise rule by minority groups, one can no longer say that this approach is democratic. The goal of such groups is to help people develop a sense of awareness of health problems and to help them work together toward a satisfactory solution.

The solutions arrived at by such groups, it may be argued, may not be scientifically sound. This is the chance society must be willing to take. This chance is minimized through education. Classes and discussions conducted by health personnel to inform and educate the public on various aspects of health, although not automatically helpful, can be "freeing" if they allay unfounded fears and anxieties, give information to people so that they can make better judgments on issues that intimately touch their lives, and prevent misguidance by "pseudoscience." In a democracy freedom must be allowed to exist as long as it does not obviously harm people, as can happen in the practice of quackery and "cures" on an uninformed public.

The public should also be better informed about the working of that part of the government which operates to guard and improve their health. They should know how major health-related regulations, for instance, communicable disease regulations, work and why. They should know how they can change these laws if they can be improved for the common good. In a democracy these formal channels of communication are necessary.

Public health is one area of government that maintains many controls which may be argued to be for the common good. Reporting and isolation of persons with communicable diseases such as tuberculosis is an example. With the advent of drugs for the treatment of tuberculosis, communicability of patients was reduced and isolation measures could be altered. Controls therefore were no longer needed to the extent that they had been previously. However, even today if tuberculosis patients do not cooperate and take the prescribed drugs, and therefore remain contagious, they may no longer have a choice because they are endangering the health and welfare of others. In a disease such as cancer, on the other hand, where the patients harm only themselves by not following the treatment program, they should be allowed to do this. Even in this situation, if they are morally responsible individuals, they will ensure provision for their closest of kin, who may depend on their earning capacity, companionship, and guidance.

In so-called underdeveloped countries, particularly where people have lived for centuries in superstitious, unhealthy environments, the public health team is faced, first, with gaining the confidence of the people and, second, with changing habits and customs. To gain the confidence of the people, huge "crash" programs such as leprosy treatment have been used. If democracy means choice, the question can be raised as to whether it is democratic to establish such a program without the involvement of the people's choice. The

rationale often used here is that the people cannot make a choice until they have first experienced some improved health conditions. The public health team, therefore, by studying the circumstances in the country or area, must be sensitive to what the people's major concern is and start their program planning from "where the people are." As the people gradually experience better health and become educated, they should be encouraged to participate. It might be added that unless the leader or group of leaders in the area, who are usually aware of the needs of their people, see the value of the proposed program, the public health team may not even begin such a crash program. In this sense there is some local participation from the beginning. If freedom is earned and men are "ends" and not "means," one goal of public health workers is participation. The participation is a learning process and is as important as the end result, whether it be reduced infant death rate or better nutrition. As people learn to think rationally, their health habits and customs tend to change, but only when the emphasis is on the *process* of learning, can it be determined whether only health was taught or whether something was also taught regarding democratic principles.

The goal or purpose for which public health may be said to exist is, "To live and then to live well—first to guarantee life and then to promote the good life. These have ever been the tasks of man, and this their order. Neither task has been possible apart from cooperation."[1a] Neither is possible apart from the power structures of society.

People often use the terms *bureaucracy* and *formal power structures* to refer to governmental units with their implicit red tape. It is this built-in rigidity and insensitivity to human beings against which various youth groups have been directing their revolt. In the 1930s and 1940s social and economic conditions were unquestionably poor, but somewhere beneath it all was a hope and belief that things would be better. Now things have become considerably better for many, but there is apparently a concern, especially among young people, that those earlier adverse times may return and they will not be prepared. Looking up the mountain in the 1930s and 1940s was certainly different from fearing a fall from the top, as seems to be occurring in the minds of many today. Facing a possible fall, the young look at the system that must save them but fail to be reassured by its ability to do so. Some would advocate the rejection of private organizations and turning to government for a means of meeting social needs. Others would reject government and reaffirm their faith that a free society depends on free, private institutions. Both approaches can be unreliable and insensitive, but they work as well as those individuals inside and outside their systems make them work.

There has been a strong urge from one generation to the next in the United States to reject in toto the patterns and norms of one's elders and to destroy them with the hope of finding comfort. It is no doubt true that each generation must believe in itself and see bright visions of the future. However, to feel a sense of reward, it is not always necessary to destroy that which their elders established and to build something new. Frequently a well-used older home with its refinement and its functional problems already worked out, is more able to provide a good life than an exotic new home that hasn't yet demonstrated its structural and functional weaknesses.

Bureaucracies and formal power structures must occasionally go through a period of "having their nests stirred up." As blacks in the 1960s stirred the whole American nest, so was the American federal level of government stirred, in particular that of former President Nixon and a few others. On occasion, nests have been stirred up in health care, when misuse of funds, frank mistreatment, and gross errors come to the fore. When the individuals doing the stirring are inside the nest, they are in a somewhat precarious position, since they themselves may fall out along with some others. Inside the bureaucratic system persons too readily learn to conform, placing responsibility on the "system" head or

elsewhere. Thus complaints often appear like fingers pointing from windows at various levels within towers standing opposite one another. Pointing fingers (complaints) at other towers is less dangerous than pointing at one's boss if one wishes to maintain one's position.

Frequently new bureaucracies and power structures are established to improve on previously existing systems. As various certification programs for nurses are developed by the American Nurses' Association, appropriate examinations must be developed and administered, records must be kept, and compliance measures must be outlined and enforced. The concept of improved nursing care in specialty areas is undoubtedly a good one. It is difficult at this time to know whether the new certification plan can be underwritten financially or justified in terms of significantly improved nursing care. The question remains to be answered when a larger number of certificated nurses enter practice settings. Hopefully it will show that this method of testing for competency far excels any other. Then, however, what must happen to structures such as state boards and the National League for Nursing? Can they still be justified? If so, how? If all the systems remain operational, what was created was merely more complex red tape for the nurse to cut through in order to become eligible to serve society. The additional red tape, however, may be merely an indicator that the nurse can tolerate red tape rather than that she excels in an area of specialization.

The impact of events and decisions at one level or in one bureaucratic system on others may be profound. During the summer of 1973, a band of about 2,000 roving hippies, calling themselves the Rainbow Family, set up camp along the Popo Agie River at Lander, Wyoming.[2] The city engineer reported their behavior as "savage" and described their running around naked, shooting dope, and polluting the water. The city of Lander uses the river to obtain its drinking water. With some alarm on the part of townfolk, the city engineer tripled the dosage of chlorine to assure adequate protection against pollution. He soon required a renewed supply of chlorine but could not get any more for about a week. The people became aware of the growing shortage of chlorine in the United States. Fortunately the hippie organization migrated onward at about the time the city ran out, only to affect other areas. The chlorine suppliers blamed the shortage of chlorine on the fuel shortage, yet only about 5% of the total amount of chlorine is consumed annually by municipalities, the major portion being used in private industries for the making of paper and plastics. With electric power plants running at or above their capacity for lighting and power, chlorine production received another setback, since it requires large quantities of electricity. Complete analysis of the interrelated bureaucracies in an incident such as this is impossible. One point of importance is that economics is deeply involved.

An early analysis of bureaucracy is that done by Weber.[3] Among the characteristics he lists are rule-ordered, fixed jurisdictional areas, a consistent distribution of authority, hierarchical ordering of components, and the use of document-based management. From his point of view bureaucratic structures are examples of the complex relationship between social and economic factors, in which seemingly behavioral phenomena are deeply influenced by economic motives and realities, and vice versa.

Various secretaries of defense have maintained that the United States must arm while in the process of disarming through agreement with other countries. The rationale given for large expenditure of taxpayer dollars for military hardware and manpower is to maintain a sufficient might so as to offer no temptation to any other strong nation that might wish to overtake the United States. The response to such behavior can readily be anticipated: relentless effort on the part of other nations to build up their military strength. The question is then periodically asked by Americans as to whether their nation is falling behind other nations militarily,

and the cycle continues. American leaders have declared that the United States must never become less than the strongest nation in the world and that cutting military spending is self-defeating.

The recent unwillingness of the United States Department of Defense to adopt a less expensive model of military attack aircraft at a time of serious budget cutbacks provides one example. Having built a plane with good performance, the designer of the new prototype is thoroughly frustrated. Ironically, the department's refusal to accept the less expensive, less complicated model occurred at the same time that many people called for simpler, cheaper war planes. From available data it is impossible to describe the details, but the conflicting behavior is symptomatic of some hidden motives, such as keeping away threats from certain pet projects. Recently, public disclosures have increasingly revealed the vast network of ties between the governmental defense bureaucracy and the defense industry—economics and sociology mixed.

Until recently, India took a negative stance with regard to nuclear testing by nations that currently had no nuclear capability. Suddenly India pursued nuclear testing and received a great deal of criticism from other nations for doing so. Their own action will detract from subsequent opposition as other nations express a desire to blast off nuclear weapons. The question arises as to how to stop this never-ending mutual paranoia among nations and their citizenry. Taking the risk of losing to a potential enemy by laying down all arms is too frightening for most to consider.

The similarity or relationship of status symbols with power provides interesting speculation. Buying a $10,000 Mercedes-Benz on monthly payments when one's colleagues are driving United States Cadillacs is only one example. Ownership is not synonymous with what is purchased on a time-payment plan; yet how few people clearly make the distinction and label the apparent wealth as phony. The same type of person or family may sport a new motor home, the current ultimate in status symbols among the "average" Americans. The reverse of this is exemplified by those who seem unable to avoid making money, or as the expression goes, "Everything he (she) does turns to gold." Many of these persons are unpretentious and live simply, oblivious to the status symbols currently in vogue. It is organizational and organized pressure on the individual that can distort his economic status, and it is economic success that can sometimes free one from the pressures of bureaucracy.

Bureaucracies and formal power structures are frequently accused of inactivity. In 1971 a group known as Health Employees for Change accused the Nixon Administration of inactivity regarding helping to fight lead poisoning in children and sending health students into geographic areas where they were sorely needed. The group contended that their position represented the concerns of not less than 60 to 100 employees within the Health Services and Mental Health Administration as well.[4] The administration's response was that, indeed, what the Health Employees for Change wanted were important concerns but that other issues must take priority. The typical demands made on a formal power structure are specific, and specific responses are expected. The Health Employees for Change based their charges of inactivity on observations that former President Nixon had not mentioned lead poisoning in his health message of February 18, 1971, and that he did not request funds in 1972. The typical response to such charges is that other matters were considered more urgent; to the group making the demands this is an ambiguous and difficult response to counter except by stepping up their campaign to such a peak that they can be no longer ignored.

The Health Professions Student Assistance Program was begun in 1963. A government study conducted by the General Accounting Office recently showed that funds to assist low-income medical and dental students with their education have not significantly increased their numbers or encouraged graduates to move into practice in rural and needy urban areas.[5] The study revealed that there were cases in which students were receiving funds even though their parents earned $49,000 a year and had net assets as great as $820,000. Problems such as these are likely to occur when monitoring of the funds is largely left with the schools or when sufficient allowance is not made in the budget for outside monitoring.

Bureaucratic merger

The review of one attempted reorganization in a large bureaucracy, the health-related departments of Los Angeles County, provides ample illustration of the complex power relationships of formal organizations. On February 24, 1970, the Los Angeles County Board of Supervisors approved "in principle" the development of a single Department of Health Services, which would fulfill the functions of the existing health, hospitals, and mental health departments. This merger represents one attempted solution to the problem of providing adequate health care to the population of a large metropolitan county. The study, planning, and decision making that preceded this decision by the Board of Supervisors illustrates some of the issues and interests that might affect any such major decisions.

The trend of coordination and integration of services is highly evident in this decision to merge health services in Los Angeles County. (See chart, next page.) Consumer participation, another important current trend, is much less evident, a point that may lead to the conclusion that the planners did not see a need to consult the consumers regarding their perceived health care needs because they believed that the needs of existing bureaucracies and power groups were of greater importance.

The Los Angeles County Department of Health is the second oldest full-time county department in the United States and is the sole provider of preventive public health services to all inhabitants of unincorporated areas of Los Angeles County in addition to the citizens of all but one of the seventy-seven incorporated cities through twenty-three

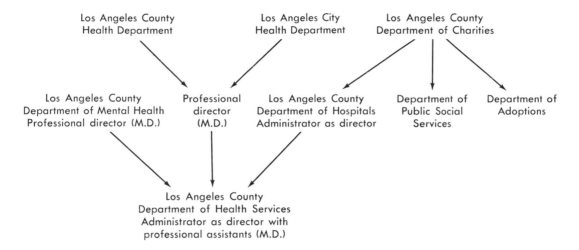

health districts and forty-eight centers and subcenters. The Los Angeles County Department of Hospitals was created in 1966 after the reorganization of the Department of Charities into Department of Hospitals, Department of Public Social Services, and Department of Adoptions. The Los Angeles County Department of Mental Health was created in 1960 under California's Short-Doyle Act, and it had 550 positions and a budget of $29.6 million in the 1969-1970 fiscal year. The policies reflect three goals: primary prevention of mental illness, increasing the resources of other community care givers, and treatment of persons suffering from acute or chronic mental illness.

There may be three sources from which the idea of the merger grew (although it may be questioned whether they are, indeed, separate sources or different manifestations of the same or similar sources):

1. When one member of the Chief Administrative Officer's staff was asked, he said "It was all my idea," citing his involvement in the study of health services through the organization and management studies of the Los Angeles County Department of Health.

2. Another study[6] of this merger indicates that the force was the economic combination of rising medical costs and the precarious position of local governments described by the Citizens Economy and Efficiency Committee in the early 1960s on the basis of the advice of a committee of prominent physicians, including the Director of the State of California Department of Public Health, Dean of the University of Southern California School of Medicine, Dean of the UCLA School of Public Health, and Dean of the UCLA School of Medicine.

3. The third force providing impetus to the merger came from the Department of Hospitals and its predecessor, the Department of Charities. Under their prodding, a motion was unanimously carried by the Board of Supervisors that stated "It is ordered that the Chief Administrative Officer and County Counsel be, and they are hereby, instructed to prepare the necessary legislation to implement and otherwise carry out the needed merger of County Health Department with the County Hospitals, under the supervision of Hospitals and Health Department Director."*

A Health Services Planning Committee (HSPC) selected by the Chief Administrative Officer was appointed by the passage of the supervisor's motion. It included the directors of the three departments, the deans of the medical schools and school of public health, the presidents of the medical societies, the

*Minutes, Los Angeles County Board of Supervisors 816:251, item 158), Dec. 27, 1966.

medical examiner, the chairmen of several citizens' advisory boards, and the head of the local interagency planning groups. The additional appointees of the supervisors were all health professionals, including one administrator and one psychologist. Note that all of the bureaucracies threatened were well represented.

A designated steering committee carried on with two tasks: (1) decision on the course to be taken and internal organization and (2) its relationship to the steering committee of the Southern California Regional Health Planning Organization, which was working toward a planning grant under PL89-749.

When the steering committee next met, the assigned staff suggested a two-phase study approach. Phase 1 would include task force study of specific problems such as (1) district boundaries, (2) number and types of departments providing health services, (3) relationships between private and public sectors, (4) consumer concerns, and (5) need for indirect services. Phase 2 would include actually planning comprehensive services based on the data collected. Later the steering committee had determined that only the first three areas listed for study needed attention and that three task forces were to study these issues. ("Consumer concerns" was one of the areas dropped!)

The chairman for Task Force I was a person who had been involved in the matter of establishing boundaries as they related to her work on the Mental Retardation Services Board. The President of the Los Angeles County Medical Association, whose position put him in intimate contact with a major portion of the private sector of Los Angeles County, was the Chairman of Task Force III.

A lay member (who later married one of the county supervisors) was chosen as chairman of Task Force II. It was the consensus that the work of this group (dealing with organization of health services) was at the heart of the planning committee, since it dealt with questions such as which departments should be consolidated, would restructuring the organization meet needs, and what were

the relationships between interdepartmental coordination and organizational consolidation. This threat to organizational boundaries could be expected to make people concerned and even prepared to oppose the final report, whatever its recommendations. It would also seem natural that this group would become the focus of any leftover reactions created by the earlier moves to unite the Department of Health with the Department of Hospitals. Those who selected the "consumers" to speak to Task Force II seemed to have exercised care in the selection, since those who were present represented limited geographical areas and were all associated with established organizations.

In September, 1969, Task Force II met once more and reached two significant conclusions.* The first was that *"it would be better not to turn over administration of Personal Health Services to any of the three existing departments, with their present responsibilities and institutionalized concepts."* The second was that *"a single health service department should be recommended as the ultimate organization of County health services."* Each of the departments then presented position papers regarding the entire issue of the merger. The Department of Health suggested that they assume responsibility for personal health care (except for physicians, who would be under the Department of Hospitals). They stated that "unilateral Hospitals Department direction and control of the neighborhood health centers or any portion thereof is not acceptable to the Health Department."† The Department of Hospitals suggested that the Southeast Health Center should be used as the basis for promoting "the integration of the present dual departments of health and hospitals into a single comprehensive health system . . . this can be accomplished by ordinance . . . or preferably by legislation

---

*Minutes, Task Force II, Sept. 19, 1969.
†Health Department position paper on interdepartmental planning for a model southeast coordinated comprehensive health center, p. 4, Sept. 22, 1969.

creating a single Department of Health and Hospitals under the strong leadership of a generalist administrator . . . for the present to maintain . . . mental health as a separate entity."* The Department of Mental Health, with clearly spelled-out individual missions and bases of community interest and support, should *not* be agglomerated as a large "super" department.† The Department of Public Social Services presented a position paper‡ dealing with issues of coordinating their programs with those of any department or agencies providing health services. The final version of the Health Services Planning Committee's report indicates that all the draft recommendations except one received unanimous approval. The one that aroused controversy was recommendation number 2§: "The County should go on record immediately as being committed to a phased reorganization of the functions of the Health, Hospitals and Mental Health Departments into a new Department of Health Services as soon as it can be accomplished." This was approved by the Board of Supervisors in February, 1970.

The first progress report on implementation was due in June, 1970. However, it was not until December 1, 1970, that the board considered a *Progress Report on Implementation of Recommendations of the Health Services Planning Committee,* dated November 24, 1970.‖ The specific recommendations were that the Board of Supervisors reaffirm its intention to create a Department of Health Services, that the Chief Administrative Officer and the three department heads

consider the Public Health Commission recommendations within their ninety-day report, and that the County Counsel and the Chief Administrative Officer include one item of legislation in their package to the 1971 California state legislature.* These recommendations were approved.

The next progress report outlined a three-phase implementation program: (1) the county should establish the Department of Health Services to include a director (an administrator) and each of the existing department directors who would be his deputies; (2) a pilot health service delivery program would be operated in one region of the county as a one-year test of the new department's plans; and (3) the implementation of the consolidated Department of Health Services would begin in January, 1973.

"Bureaucracies seldom fade away and almost never die."[7]

Communicating with bureaucracies

The Ralph Nader organization has been an instrument that has gained great popularity in people's search for a way to penetrate bureaucratic systems. As was mentioned earlier in this book, attorneys have more than their proportion of members in governmental positions all the way to the top. An unusual number of persons with law backgrounds have been incriminated in recent government scandals. Public distrust has gradually built

---

*Position paper on reorganization of health services, County of Los Angeles Department of Hospitals, Sept. 23, 1969.

†Mental health policy regarding proposed interdepartmental comprehensive care center, Sept. 23, 1969.

‡Statement of position for the Department of Public Social Services, Sept. 12, 1969.

§Los Angeles County Health Services Planning Commission report on study of health services in the county, p. 6, Feb. 24, 1970.

‖Minutes, Los Angeles County Board of Supervisors, Nov. 17, 1970.

---

*Legislation requested in the progress report was designed to alter the requirements for the positions of County Veterinarian, County Health Officer, and Director of the local mental health services. The wording of the bill limited its applicability to Los Angeles County and specified that if the county consolidated any offices, the occupant of the consolidated post need not have any qualifications required of the occupants of the separate offices if there is no one qualification which applies to all of them and if there are division heads within the consolidated offices who have the qualifications required to handle the functions of the previously separate office. This bill eliminated the necessity of having to locate a qualified physician-psychiatrist-veterinarian to head the new Los Angeles County Health Department. In the opinion of many it would open the way for a public administrator to be its head.

up pressure to toughen discipline of lawyers. It seems to have taken the Watergate scandal to give increased impetus to this movement. Mounting dissatisfaction with attorneys' fees was a beginning of antitrust action and a break into the tight state bar association, a mighty power structure of the past. As with health services, the wealthy are able to obtain good legal services, and poor people currently obtain better legal service through government-sponsored, legal-aid projects.

Among lawyers there are some older members who are sometimes referred to as "fat cats," who like members of other professions, are more interested in their own well-being than in providing service. Often members of the Association of Trial Lawyers of America, these practitioners act together in a formal power system to fight federal no-fault insurance legislation because it would significantly decrease legal fees that they would receive as a result of personal injury litigation. The reason given, however, for their opposition to the insurance plan is that more experience with that type of approach is needed before legislation can be supported.

Surging inflation and elimination of the price control programs are adding renewed vigor to labor's previous weapon, that of strikes, a means used by laborers to fight an unyielding power structure. Unemployment is continuing to increase, yet workers are turning down wage increases. It would appear that any or no wage increase would be accepted in view of a complete wage cutoff through unemployment. For the last few years labor strikes seem to be in essence a strike against the government. If offers are unacceptable they are turned down, even with the risk of losing a job. The reasoning seems to be that one loses a job that pays inadequately to cover living costs, then lets "government" provide support, since the adequacy of public assistance can probably be little worse than "unjust" compensation for long hours on a hard job.

The Social Security Administration has been the target for bitter miners who have long sought some improvement in disability benefits for those who contract "black lung," an occupational hazard among coal miners. After several days of tests at a hospital in Appalachia,[8] one man with thirty-one years in dusty coal mines was told he had no black lung disease. He was, however, forced to retire early because of fatigue and shortness of breath. He and others like him have lost faith in what they thought was a great legislative victory, the passage of the Federal Coal Mine Health and Safety Act in 1969. The legislation was to establish improved mining standards and black lung compensation programs for workers and their families. More than half of the applicants for black lung benefits in 1971 were turned away by the Social Security Administration. In dealing with such a gigantic bureaucracy, the miners' lobby group, the Black Lung Association, says that the miners' only recourse is to strike. The objections raised include the disparity in rejection rates among applicants for benefits in various states (from 54% rejected in West Virginia compared to 70% approved in Pennsylvania). Miners also claim that physicians in the coal mine areas are influenced by the coal mining industry (allegedly because of concern about money when the programs became state administered and mining industry financed on January 1, 1973). The Social Security Administration was accused of basing decisions to reject applicants for benefits on insufficient or slipshod diagnosis. The miners based the crux of their contention on the fact that one single x-ray film and one breathing test served as the only tools for making the medical decision. Some said they saw a nurse and had an x-ray film taken but never even saw a physician. The United Mine Workers played no active role in the controversy, claiming that they set up a mechanism for miners to file claims and beyond that they are not concerned.

The Social Security Administration and the Public Health Service, after receiving complaints from 100 miners whose applications had been denied agreed "to determine what other tests might be used in the future" (almost conceding inaccurate diagnosis but not really helping the thousands of rejected miners). Meanwhile, as might be expected, the head of the Social Security bureaucracy asserts that the Social Security Administration "is administering the law as passed by Congress. . . . It is difficult for a man to understand that he can be totally disabled but not by pneumoconiosis and thus not receive benefits."

Regulation of prices, wages, hours, and other factors has become common to everyone's life. Federal regulatory agencies have substantial power, and their twisting, bending, and turnings would perhaps be amusing were it not for the impact that each move has on various aspects of people's lives. Their erratic pattern of behavior seems to continue straying further from any form of consistency, and even from the economic rationale that gave them birth in the first place. It may appear that some agencies fail to have any economic rationale at all by which they operate. Railroads were recently permitted to raise freight rates by 10% but were then restricted by the Interstate Commerce Commission from spending that increase on improving roadbeds and equipment. Furthermore, the 10% increase could not apply to recyclable materials, that is, scrap metal, which was the Interstate Commerce Commission's way of being congenial toward environmental control efforts. So it seemed that the Interstate Commerce Commission was saying that railroads could be saved from further bankruptcies but only if they allowed the Interstate Commerce Commission to manage their money by regulation. By encouraging spending money on roadbeds and equipment rather than long-term planning through paying more competent managers, the commission can keep its own political problems down.

The dairy industry in 1971 funneled donations into about fifty various "front groups,"

such as Americans for Greater Public Awareness, Organization of Citizen Politicians, League of Involved Citizens, Supporters of Rational Federal Reorganization, or Committee for Political Integrity. The names in no case convey the entire purpose of the associations. The power structure involving dairy farming and agriculture then became silent while suspicions rose and investigations were underway. The contribution of funds by the milk lobby followed a reversal in former President Nixon's decision regarding price supports, and the price of milk and dairy products rose. The contributions were apparently a symbol of gratitude on the part of the dairy industry for the backing of the administration.

This has obviously not been a complete course in the power potential of bureaucracies and the pervasive nature of large organizations in the American culture. It has highlighted some of the issues, however, and may serve to make the reader more alert to possible uses and abuses of organizational power.

References

1. Wall Street Journal, Jan. 10, 1972.
1a. Smith, T. V.: The American philosophy of equality, Chicago, 1927, University of Chicago Press, p. 277.
2. Gapay, L.: The latest shortage could contaminate your drinking water, Wall Street Journal, May 6, 1974.
3. Weber, M. (translated and edited by H. H. Gerth and C. W. Mills): Essays in sociology, New York, 1946, Oxford University Press, Inc.
4. Health group accuses Nixon of inactivity, Los Angeles Times, May 14, 1971.
5. Gold, H. C.: Lag, abuses in health plan, Kansas City Star, June 2, 1974.
6. Marshall, D.: Merger for health, an attempted innovation in the organization of Los Angeles County health services, HSMA Health Reports **86:**867-878, Oct., 1971.
7. Clark, L. H.: There's no easy way to live with excessive power, Wall Street Journal, Feb. 2, 1971.
8. Harwood, B.: Bitter miners assert the "black lung" law is filled with loopholes, Wall Street Journal, Sept. 24, 1971.

WALL STREET JOURNAL[1]

7

PRESSURE GROUPS

Today's world finds individual units of the American population involved in a process of competitive cooperation formulating the interrelations and the character of the economy. Ecologists, sociologists, planners, political scientists, and various other professionals have each applied the term *community,* a unit with a given habitat and inhabitants competing for interest and acceptance of their own approach. In a broad sense a community as a unit is composed of plant, animal, and human components interacting in a struggle for survival and dominance. The dynamics regarding the desire for dominance operate in the human community as in the plant and animal community. The struggle of industries and commercial institutions for strategic locations results ultimately in the major outlines of urban communities. The slum, the rooming house area, the shopping center, and the central bank each owes its existence to the factor of dominance, that is, overt conflict. The area of dominance in a community is usually the area of highest values, which determine the location of social institutions and business enterprises. Both are bound up in a kind of territorial struggle, within which they are simultaneously competing but interdependent. It should be said again that competition which functions to control and regulate the interrelations of human beings tends to assume on the social level the form of conflict. That there exists an intimate relation between competition and conflict is indicated by the fact that wars frequently, if not always, have or seem to have their source and origin in economic competition, which in that case assumes the more sublimated form of a struggle for power and prestige.

Among the health professions dominance is established in terms of money and social value of the array of complex assets that men attribute to them. Dominance, moreover, is indirectly responsible for the phenomenon of succession. That pattern continues unless forces intervene, perhaps competitive with it but having to cooperate with it. Certain discoveries, inventions, and catastrophies play a part in bringing about serial changes in the dominance pattern. More directly, in health care systems, physicians have collectively dominated and thus have tended to succeed themselves. The outline of human health services, however, may ultimately be determined from the struggle of the various professions for a strategic location in the system. The additional question may be cautiously posed as to whether the struggle among the health professions is not only a struggle for power and prestige but also a conflict to control and regulate society's actual "need."

The American Association for Social Psychiatry has suggested outlining criteria that make men equal professionally. Even with these criteria it must be pointed out that there are still few women among the professionals. In these changing times women also offer their contribution and desire to share the responsibility in the political process involved in policymaking. From the viewpoint of political science and nursing we anticipate this to be a stressful period because it becomes necessary that those who originally held power relinquish some. Interdisciplinary experiences, when begun early in the student's professional preparation, have demonstrated that professional boundary watching and achieving and maintaining power in pressure and special interest groups do not become the focal point. Rather, significantly greater energy expenditure is directed toward addressing the situation they face, and the improvement of the individual's worth and power becomes more equally the responsibility of all health professionals. One definition of politics is that described by Machiavelli,[1a] who believed that those in power strive to maintain power and that this

is their sole consideration. He further believed that the desire for conquest or power is a natural human desire. Moral considerations are excluded as being irrelevant and extraneous; if a king is powerful enough to conquer, he has the right to do so. Machiavelli provided examples of strategies used throughout history to achieve power and observed that when a person rises to power, he stays on the wings of popularity. The best strategy is for the person to make himself a voice of the people and therefore prevent would-be rivals from seeking to undermine him. If allies are necessary, there are ways of manipulating them and subsequently getting rid of them; in current political terminology this is the process of co-optation, similar to the group process labeled manipulation. To have a reputation of virtue and kindness is good, but the actual virtue itself may be a dangerous thing. Cruelty when it accomplishes peace and order may in fact be kindness.

Although we concur with Machiavelli that order and survival are basic needs within a society, this is so not only for those in power but for all. Humanity should not be forced to obey through fear of punishment, deceitfulness, or other means. Individuals with power have been allowed to test how far they may go in breaking rules, being deceitful, and utilizing devious means to achieve and maintain power. Some have gone so far as to establish a political morality apart from ethical morality. It can be carried to a point where justice is reduced to a mechanical process and society is simply a system of forces in which the loser is always wrong and fact (synonymous with force) is right.

Data regarding the materials from which people learn about their world support this. The subject of evolution and the teachings regarding the biblical account of creation to schoolchildren serve to point out the dynamics involved with pressure groups. The business of producing science books became a lucrative business in California because of the shifts of power between and among pressure groups. Finally it was suggested that there should be a special California science text-book, which balanced the theory of evolution with the Bible's presentation. A framework for texts suitable to various grade levels was established by the State Advisory Committee on Science Education, and a copy was sent to every major publisher in the country. Notorious for doctoring up history to sell their books, publishers were caught in a conflict between a restriction to the letter of the advisory committee in the case of California's science texts and a chance to earn millions of dollars if their proposal was selected. Among other possibilities, pressure groups maintained that an illustration of the first page of the Book of Genesis should be incorporated in the work in addition to a Michelangelo painting acceptable to the evolutionist faction. One can wonder if it is ever possible to be sure of anything.

In overview, worldwide at this moment the power of the United States is returning to a range of normal rather than being focused on a grandiose, unreal image of self among the peoples of the world. It demands a look at rationality and being of equal status with citizens of nations throughout the world. It brings to bear national ego deflation, if one can be so honest, and bringing oneself as a person down from a plane comparable with Superman or the angels to the ranks of all other people on earth.

From modern social psychiatry we have learned that people are not self-sufficing in social isolation, that their nature cannot be deduced simply from elements innate in the germ plasm, and that there is an indispensable connection between humankind and such social groups as the family, local groups, and interest associations. No conception of individuality is adequate that does not take into consideration the many ties which bind the individual to others throughout life. Individuality cannot be understood except as a product of normatively oriented interaction with other persons. Whatever may lie neurologically in the human being, a knowledge of actual human behavior in society must take into consideration the whole of norms and cultural incentives that are the product of social history. The normative order in society is fundamental to all understanding of human nature.

The intensity of personal incentive, whether in the context of therapy or day-to-day life of the normal human being, fluctuates with the intensity of meaningful social relationships. This has been shown in various studies of motivation and learning, from character formation, from observation of personal morale in all kinds of stress situations, and from the dropout rate of nurses from professional practice. John Dewey, a century ago, recognized that the mental and moral structure of individuals, the pattern of their desires and purposes, are drastically altered with every great change in social constitution. Individuals who are not bound together in association, whether domestic, economic, religious, political, educational, or, one might say, professional are outside the natural "web of life." It is absurd to suppose that the ties holding individuals together are merely external and do not combine the mentality and character, producing the framework of personal disposition. Along with creativity it must also be added that the freedom of persons is crucial. Power is associated with freedom to move not only in the vertical dimension by mastering the inherent conflict in doing so but also in the horizontal dimension. For example, nurses should not need to move (apparently vertically) into the physician role to attain power, but rewards may come from moving horizontally within the profession. Such achievement is not the sole consequence of innate individual forces, nor is such movement simply the result of processes of separation. All health professionals must acknowledge their interdependence before reaching out to the patient, family, or community.

Most accomplishments in the social system could not have been done apart from such communities as guilds, colleges, philosophical societies, institutes, or associations. Small groups can be as deadly as large ones, but unlike more formal types of associations, small and informal groups are unlikely to last for long when their purpose is dead and their fellowship dwindling. They cannot be saved by rules and regulations, legislation, by-laws, or dues invested when their true inner resources run out. One goal in the development of groups must be to build systems in which the majority of its constituents believe it is indeed *their* system—conflict consists of differences in small degrees sufficient to stimulate progress. There must be a place for the "human role," which provides self-esteem, personal identity, and power not only to clients but to professionals as well. In this situation each member does not depend on others for self-esteem; each expects others to perceive his/her value, that is, inherent power, and not have to create it through conflict.

The interdependence that has existed through the years is becoming more evident. Politics, within the range of normal, describes interdependent relationships in which power and conflict are interchanged to enhancement, not destruction, of others. Recent events in American history alone serve as evidence of the hostility, alienation, and waste of human energy that can emerge outside the range of normal.

Grass roots decisions are not necessarily democratic. In experience with the Tennessee Valley Authority (TVA) it meant bowing to the United States Farm Bureau, which did not care about poorer farmers, and bowing to southern sentiment in that black agricultural colleges were excluded from the fertilizer programs and so on. Grass roots may mean rule, from the local level, of a few people with purely selfish interests. Often the ones whom the program is especially set up to help are helped the least. It tends also to strengthen organizations that are devoted to the larger, more prosperous members of society. When leadership and goals are not clearly defined, an organization may develop but often not in the direction it was intended. Power to decide what is to be done therefore often comes from not too well-meaning outsiders by co-optation, disguised under the grass roots approach.

Co-optation may be informal, sold on the grounds that it will utilize local institutions and create democratic partnership with them. In TVA it meant sharing power of the TVA board with land grant colleges and through them with the United States Farm Bureau. Formal co-optation, a means by which local citizens are encouraged to participate in applying general program policies to varying local conditions, results from the agency's lacking a sense of belonging or from its inability to mobilize community action. "Substantive participation" by local people is desired, but in formally co-opted organizations there is a tendency either for the unorganized public to be used as a reliable instrument for the achievement of administrative goals labeled "democracy" or for local participation to degenerate into mere involvement, in which the administration makes the decisions and the local people provide a "front" for the organization. The grass roots approach may be a cover-up for an administration's need to gain power in what appears to be a democratic manner. There is also necessity to guard against democratic participation breaking down into administrative involvement.

Tugwell and Banfield[2] state that if most farm communities are to have democratic administration, it will need to come from Washington. Public policy cannot be made by special interest groups. Grass roots planning cannot rightly be done without hearing the voice of the urban as well as rural citizens, so that the perspective, in the end, involves the entire organism rather than only one or a few of its members. What is needed is that the interests of all people are protected against local interest, even at the expense of coercing local interests if necessary.

The romantic, verbal expressions, and clichés about the small town conceal its political dynamics. The same few people hold many positions, and newcomers have difficulty getting into an area of interest in the political realm because the same few achieve "honorary" positions. A distinction may be made between formal leaders and real leaders at the local level. Small businessmen hold some formal political positions, and their perspective is dominant in village politics. The real leaders are those who act as political brokers, who are regarded as reliable in telling the small businessmen what is in their best interest. The real decision makers occupy no important formal positions that are relevant to the decision. These are the informal leaders.

Other dynamics of the town include the low-tax, cut-cost orientation, which means that tax funds collected from the large urban centers are needed to subsidize local programs. The do-nothing, status quo attitude causes the more progressive community leaders to form extra-legal organizations to solve local problems. There is a lack of interest in local elections, with stimulation directed toward state and federal elections. Local businessmen want the supply and service orders but cannot compete with outside establishments in terms of prices.

The self-image of local townsfolk is of interest. They view "success" in terms of the things that spell immediate reality, since opportunities for them are limited to that environment. They accept and understand that deviants in the community as quaint, colorful, or humorous and do not label them as abnormal persons as long as they are not threatened by them.

Through their work, work projects, home, car, and social events the small town residents solve their personal conflicts regarding aspiration and achievement. Regarding life in their community, they tend to use unconscious mechanisms of compromise, self-deception, and self-avoidance to handle their everyday problems in such a way that they receive some satisfaction, recognition, and achievement. It is imperative, however, to remember those people who would gladly move from the hustle of the big city to become the "big frog in a little pond" rather than being the "small frog in a big pond." The small town represents domination by a few, with more people and interests being represented by state and federal levels of government. One

raises the question about the fairness of tax dollars paid by urban residents being shifted into tightly held rural pocketbooks, where it becomes of greatest benefit to the few wealthy individuals who are in control.

The existence of pressure groups and special interest groups reflects both diversity in opinion and dispersion of power among the public. The amount of power varies with regard to factors such as personality, expertise, and specialization. In the area of public policy the interest groups form around the subject matter of legislation being considered, and the power held by the various groups will be unequal, based on their involvement in the matter at hand and the nature of that involvement. Among the specific factors that affect the relative position of a special interest group are the following:

1. The offices held by its members. This covers the associational network through which one moves in the formal social structure and those on whom one may have some influence.

2. The position held by its members. The position held defines one's vantage point with regard to the flow of information, and the more data that can be accumulated the more strength a group holds.

3. The status ascribed to its members. Status is defined by one's position in voluntary interactions as well as the formal relationships of the social structure and will reflect the ability of the group to mobilize additional support. It is based on formal factors, prestige, and achievement of the individual members.

4. The resources, including money, commanded by the group. The greater the availability of resources, the greater freedom there will be to pursue the desired goals.

With specific reference to the development of legislation the first three factors play a role in the development of ideas, in the amassing of support, and in the passage of laws and their subsequent implementation. Money is of particular importance in the second and fourth steps, the amassing of support and the translation of the mandate into action. This is not necessarily saying that dollars buy votes but that it is considerably easier for those with abundant resources to make their views and desires known to others in positive ways. Given the preceding analysis, it is rather clear why neither nurses nor their average patients have had major impact on many health-related issues.

Establishing priorities at conferences and funding the projects from various interest groups provides a perfect example of the competitive aspects not only within government or other areas within society but also specifically in health. At the 1972 American Public Health Association convention in Atlantic City, New Jersey, nearly 200 scientific sessions (from the nineteen sections of the association) were conducted with nearly 10,000 health professionals and consumers in attendance. Subjects included sickle cell disease, abortion, sterilization, and environmental aspects, after which recommendations were made to the federal government administration regarding national policy. The decisions as to which topics would be discussed, and from what angle, were based on the relative power positions of those involved in program planning.

Diseases that previously killed or crippled many persons in their childhood have been conquered. This does not mean, however, that millions of children in the United States receive the advantage of immunizations, checkups, and medical attention except when a crisis arises. This is especially so among those in the poor, near poor, and lower middle class where infant mortality is far greater than among children from the middle class. In 1965 federal matching dollars were made available as an amendment to the Social Security Act to local health departments, medical centers, and community hospitals for the establishment of improved health care to mothers and children. As late as July, 1973, however, only fifty-six demonstration centers had been established throughout only thirty-four states, caring for only 10% of all the mothers and children who were eligible.[3] Why? Families are called and reminded,

transportation is provided, and the American Academy of Pediatrics vigorously supported the program's extension. Manpower is one problem; there were not enough physicians to staff the undertaking. Nurses, physician-assistants, and others were prepared to screen and provide many services that were earlier given by physicians. This in turn required reeducating physicians so that they would let go of certain activities which they had always done themselves and concentrate their effort on the problems which require their level of diagnostic skills and treatment. Children still are not receiving the care they need. A more effective strategy is essential to reach the millions who presently are doing without. Children are not a likely pressure group to bring about change because their voice and vote are absent. Unless adults take on the challenge, the situation will continue.

Business and labor have been strong pressure groups in the United States, holding large concentrations of economic power. Economists such as John Galbraith contended that permanent price and wage controls were the only way to control these excessively powerful factions. This has been a dilemma of nations everywhere: private enterprise taking over government in a fascist state and government taking over private enterprise in Communist states. American tradition has held to the tactic of compromise. However, few Americans seem to be concerned that the increased federal intervention, no matter how structured or unplanned, may well be directing the nation toward a state of totalitarianism which the American tradition of compromise would supposedly avoid. To control massive concentrations of power the government amasses ever greater power of its own. The danger is that there is a built-in impulse for power to grow and if in government hands, it also is likely to reach out more.

Industrial lobbies have been able to maintain extraordinary power at state levels. An example is the insurance lobby in the state of Illinois.[4] One of the nation's largest insurance companies has been represented by one who is also a member of the Republican State Central Committee, the party's official organization in that state. His telephone calls were among the first returned by state legislators. In 1973, when a Senate-House investigation was to be formed to look into alleged irregularities in the insurance business in Illinois,[4] little or nothing happened. It was explained that the insurance power bloc has veto power second only to that of the Governor. This kind of power exists in other areas of industry as well. Industries can have a tremendous influence at the state level because legislators largely depend on lobbyists for data on which to make decisions. At least in the case of insurance the situation is not unique to the state of Illinois. However, insurance is one industry that despite increased federal regulation, has primarily been left to state jurisdiction, derived from an 1868 United States Supreme Court decision that upheld the right of states to grant licenses to all companies writing insurance policies within the state.

The Ninety-third Congress will perhaps go down in history for various reasons but particularly for one extremely basic reason—the quiet change in its makeup that has taken place. For the first time more members of the House come from suburbs than from central cities or rural areas. This represents a change in the interest groups represented, as a result of population shifts, and the representation of very different constituencies, although all are lumped as "suburbia." One can, however, anticipate that members of Congress may take a solid united position on some issues. Those dealing with regional planning, aid to education, environmental protection, and others in which they have acute personal and constituency interest will receive their support. This need not always be at the expense of central cities, but it would be if it involved redistribution of monies from their suburban areas to central cities. Because suburbanites tend to be of a younger age, their legislators are usually united in efforts that reflect modernizing trends.

At times the work of a pressure group can backfire. Like many suburban towns the state of Oregon has systematically campaigned to keep out people from other areas because the residents did not want the state's popular and much envied environmental programs to be undone. The Governor of the state, Tom McCall, was telling tourists to "come see us, but for heaven's sake, don't stay."[5] All the "unselling" resulted in a population influx that already is causing problems. Urban sprawl is taking away 8,000 acres of prime farmland a year near cities, and there have been moratoriums on sewer hookups in the suburban areas of Portland, creating squabbles over "toilet rights." Resentments are building, especially toward California immigrants who make up 77% of Oregon's population increase. The negative invitation to visit but not stay did certainly have a powerful impact in the opposite manner. Recognizing how to capitalize on this boomerang, the Oregon Ungreeting Card Company in Eugene has expanded its production of over a half million cards to also making T-shirts, bumper stickers, and posters that together are grossing $25,000 to $30,000. Currently the company is also selling "ungreeting" cards for California, Washington, Colorado, Texas, Arizona, Nevada, and Idaho, with Hawaii being next. One might anticipate that the ungreeting card program will be a powerful tool for attracting new residents rather than discouraging them.

Pressure groups change with the times. As the population curve skews in the direction of the aged, senior citizen groups increase, as do demands for housing designed to accommodate the special needs of senior citizens. Colleges and other organizations are sought that will provide creative learning and recreational experiences for the older citizens, and pressures mount for health and welfare programs that persons can afford who must live on savings and stationary pensions.

Taxpayer suits increase as concerned citizens seek out ways to contest the actions or inactivity of government at federal, state, and/or local levels. These suits are called public-action suits because the plaintiffs sue not in behalf of themselves as individuals but as a representative of the general public. A Manhattan lawyer filed such a suit to prevent the state of New York from carrying out its plan to buy Yankee Stadium because he believes it to be a bad business deal. He contends that "many decisions that affect all of us are made by bureaucrats whom we never vote for, have not any other direct influence over."[6] Not a large number of such public-action suits are won by the plaintiffs for several reasons. Only a small number ever come to trial, and few of those that do are won because they are poorly prepared or because they do not show direct violation of law or dereliction of duty on the part of public officials. Furthermore, judges usually rule in favor of the public officials if they are able to show that they had good reasons for actions taken and that opposing views were considered.[6] Sometimes public-action suits drag on for years, but sometimes they reap greater returns than were ever anticipated. Ecology-oriented suits exemplify this, and a contaminated body of water may ultimately prompt a much broader water clean-up program.

Women are becoming an increasingly powerful pressure group. In years past the League of Women Voters was considered influential in obtaining legislation. This has been expanded in various ways. Women may gain more political muscle as a result of the fact that most men have not done as well when it comes to the honesty issue. In Connecticut a woman Governor was elected in 1974. More women are being employed in universities, in research projects, and in minority programs such as a Chicano Center. In 1972 the University of Southern California appointed a woman as head of their Department of Pathology. More women are entering the field of dentistry as dentists and dentist-specialists, whereas earlier most women interested in dentistry found that they were essentially limited to the area of dental technician. The University of California at San Diego conducted a recruitment program urging girls to enter the medical field as physicians and recruiting them especially through candystriper or volunteer groups.[7] Along with gaining access to new jobs, women are making an impact to liberalize abortion laws, family planning programs, and similar areas. The spin-off is the development of pressure groups dealing with broader issues. A new organization called the National Alliance for Family Life was formed to combat what the members see as an overemphasis on sex and a downgrading of marriage and the family. It focused also on changing the outdated attitudes held by professionals working in these areas.

Professionals and professional organizations are gaining greater inroads as pressure groups. It was the United States Public Health Service that exposed the forty-year experiment during which about 500 syphilitic victims in an institution in Tuskegee, Alabama, were given no treatment (as part of the experiment), and perhaps 100 or more of them died. The end result of this entire public exposure was a program of financial compensation to those subjects who survived or to families of the deceased. An official of the Maryland Department of Juvenile Services used statistics in making a case against continuation of that state's reform school programs by pointing out that it costs more to keep one youth in a training (or reform) school than to support him through three years of Harvard.[8]

A clinical psychologist in New York countered the popular notion that families are going downhill because of failure on the part of institutions in American society.[9] Coming to the support of parents who are frequently accused of poor child rearing, he made such points as mothers who have to work *must* leave their children in the care of others during their early years, which are the most important. To offset this it was advocated that companies give female employees maternal leaves up to two years and guarantee that the women can return to their previous positions. Psychiatrists and other groups have changed attitudes and treatment of homosexuals by emphasizing that it is nonsense to say homosexuals are "sick."

The introduction and proliferation of multiple group therapy and learning approaches by psychologists such as Carl Rogers has had a powerful impact in many settings. Used initially in treatment settings, they became popular as an approach toward improving employee relations, student relations, and social relations. It is not the intent here to make an evaluation of their effectiveness in accomplishing a treatment goal but rather to point out the power gained by psychologists through this demonstration of expertise. Grantsmanship and the ability to get federal and foundation support has likewise become so important that those with such skills have had sufficient call for providing assistance to individuals and agencies in developing grant applications that they have started up grantsmanship centers and charged tuition.

Between 1957 and 1969 the number of black farm workers declined by more than half a million.[10] During the same period, domestic labor declined significantly, with skilled blue collar labor declining the least. Unemployment has also declined throughout the 1960s. In 1957 only 10% of black families earned $8,000 or more (1968 dollars), but by 1968 the percentage earning more than $8,000 increased to 32% (43% for families in the North and West). When asked whether conditions were improving, eight out of ten black respondents spoke favorably about economic improvement and attitudes. Group pressures in favor of black and other ethnic minorities have focused sufficiently on the "raw deals" that these minorities receive in many areas. They have, for themselves, been almost totally successful in eliminating the administration of (or at least the reliance on) intelligence tests in public schools, grades earned in school as a prerequisite for college admission, and degree requirements for employment in many positions. In 1972 five faculty members quit their jobs at a state college in California in protest of the college's alleged lack of minority programs.

After the University of California at Los Angeles fired black professor Angela Davis because of her radical partisan statements in public and in the classroom, they expressed a desire to rehire her. Meanwhile she was found to be on the fringe of a plot to help prisoners escape from a county courthouse, charged but acquitted of murder, kidnaping, and conspiracy, toured the Soviet Union collecting medals and awards, and chose to return to her own country, the United States. Since she continued in her totalitarian spirit, maintaining her allegiances and contempt for democratic freedom and processes, the question remained as to whether she should be welcomed back into the university. Although philosophers have made statements that question the democratic system, to what extent can and should one's freedom and liberty be permitted to go under the Constitution?

At essentially the same time the Dean of the School of Dentistry at the University of Southern California was charged with giving preference to minorities over better qualified white students in addition to appointing a Jew as department head. Concern was expressed that the school's reputation was being threatened because the scores on state board examinations were no longer as high as they had been earlier. The Dean's response was that the charges were coming from alumni who wanted to dictate the academic and research programs at the university and were occurring at cocktail parties or other meeting places.[11] In his defense 450 of the 600 students in the School of Dentistry signed petitions to have the Dean retained. The University Senate confronted the attack from conservative elements in alumni and fund-raising groups—that the school's academic standards were declining—with a resolution "to affirm the academic integrity of the school of dentistry and to support the dean."[12] The university administration responded to the charges by publicly announcing that they would "probe" into the entire situation.[13]

Corporations such as General Electric, RCA, Westinghouse, and others have developed or are developing programs to recruit minority engineers. One pours $100,000 into minority education in an attempt to increase significantly the number of minority engineers among their ranks.[14] New York municipal workers are no longer required to pass an oral examination to demonstrate their ability to speak "American English," a change that came about as a result of pressure from the workers' union after a Taiwan-born engineer failed the examination.[15]

Private elementary and secondary schools along with institutions of higher learning have served as a strong pressure group aimed at getting tax support to supplement their educational efforts. They are reinforced by religious leaders not directly connected with schools. To date, their efforts have reaped benefits beyond indirect aid such as busing of parochial school children in public vehicles, loaning of textbooks to Federal Title I compensatory education programs (under PL89-10) operating within private schools, and the receiving of special grants and scholarships of various kinds. The question of constitutionality still remains, and the separation of church and state is debated in the light of the original intent.

Education programs are increasing their efforts to get student and parent involvement in decision making. It is not only so that they get the best decisions but for purposes of public relations and attaining a higher level of community support. Community support is essential to eliminate the criticism of schools that is currently so pervasive and serves to deter passage of wage increases and benefits. School staffs are criticized for being outdated and stuffy. The California State Department of Education adopted a *Handbook on Morality for Teachers* so that school personnel might be assisted in understanding "the legal rights and responsibilities of school personnel and students in the area of moral education, civic education, and teaching about religion."[16] If schools become inert to avoid attack from the community for wrongdoings, this may be one way to overcome the inertia. Being clear when their behavior is legal and right *may* make school personnel more confident and promote creativity.

Schools are pressured by many groups.

One spokesman for the United States Commission on Civil Rights reported that a civil rights study showed that Mexican-American students in schools receive less positive teacher attention in class than do Anglo students.[17] The "permissive" education view is questioned, the value of "grants" to subsidize college programs is questioned, and an overhauling of the funding system is called for to eliminate disparities caused by unequal local tax bases from area to area. Militant students have forced universities to yield some of their power and authority and to look at what is their true function. Lawmakers react to student, parent, and community disenchantment with educators by putting a crimp on the life-style of college executives and cutting their housing allowances. Some define the problems more broadly to include in the blame a complex mixture of campus history, state fiscal problems, faculty attitudes, and the personalities of college and university presidents. Arguments ensue between university administrations and boards of regents regarding quality as opposed to economy. Laws are formulated that require teachers, principals, and even the superintendent of public school districts to receive a regular evaluation of performance. Violence on campus has served as another pressure, with targets of shoot-outs being such persons as the dean of students. Students' demand for nontraditional education resulted in programs in which on-the-job experience counts toward a degree. Data from various studies have indicated that education does not have a significant impact on earning power and that the development of better jobs will keep numbers of students from wanting to pursue a college education.

Can the school system, colleges, and universities recover their standing as academic institutions of superior quality? Only if they can get out of their state of bewilderment and are clearly able to define their societal mission. Although the Los Angeles City Board of Education receives numerous pressures and community support is sought, the members announced that principals, not advisory councils, will run their schools. School administrations, not parents, are to be recognized for their expertise and then expected to adapt their school programs to the interests and characteristics of local communities. The decision was based on a legal question of whether schools have the authority to delegate authority to advisory groups and the tendency for *advisory* councils to be *decision* making having no legal precedent. Teacher associations are unleashing grass roots power of community and school boards, implementing programs to help teachers learn how to flex their political muscles. Teachers are taught how to take polls, raise money, write advertisements, enlist volunteers, and even how to influence the press. Educators are beginning to make a rebuttal to people, saying that schools have become the scapegoat for the rest of society's sins of omission and commission and that they have been expected to produce social, moral, and psychological miracles in a few hectic, overcrowded hours. Leaders in the field blame the deterioration of public confidence in the schools on the inadequate, unfair, and regressive property tax on which schools must depend. Perhaps nurses have something to learn from this strategy.

Among current pressure groups are convict and prisoners unions, pseudopatients who feign insanity to get a look inside the system and possibly expose mental health care programs, and a Committee Opposed to Psychiatric Abuse of Prisoners. Once considered a source of free labor and "slaves of the state" by an 1871 court ruling in Virginia, felons in that state and elsewhere now sue for steak and wine. The Black Muslim movement's spread throughout penitentiaries across the United States is credited (or blamed) for this drastic change. Other pressure groups have linked poor health to crime, but the American Medical Association has made the claim that one reason for poor health care in the ghetto is that physicians "take their life in their hands" by setting up practice in the ghetto and that crime is keeping them out of such areas.[18] A former

employee testified before a special legislative committee investigating "suspicious deaths."[19] He described the conditions in two state-licensed homes and the treatment and violence used with mentally retarded persons there. Parents and families of mentally retarded patients in state hospitals reacted so violently to the governor's plan to close these facilities that the phase-out program was made provisional, to take effect only if given approval from the legislature. Two legislators asked by the governor to introduce legislation refused to do so because of their constituency reaction; they obviously understood the potential impact that sponsoring such a closure bill would have on their chances for reelection.

Opportunities for young people who want to learn a trade or specialized skill have never been greater. Unfortunately many lose out because they drop before finishing twelfth grade for their stated reason of wanting to "get a job." They join the labor force with no job skills or high school diploma, and their futures are dimmed. Simple high school is often not the answer either because students go through a general program with no vocational training. They receive a sufficient academic base to continue their education within a college, but there a large number of them stop. This means that about 2 million people a year enter the labor force without any special job training. The result is extremely high unemployment rates among the young. Fortunately educators and government are determined to change things. There is an increasing focus on a balance between academic and vocational education in various grades at school, along with the generous amounts of federal support dollars being poured into the effort.

The Consumer Protection Agency pressure group has developed almost like a Frankenstein monster to haunt Congress, with women's clubs and Ralph Nader putting it together in an almost evangelical fashion. The problem is beyond politics short and simple. Furthermore, consumers in this evangelistic group do not all hold to the same beliefs or have the same concerns. In earlier days if the shoe did not fit, the consumer could take it back to the shoemaker until it did. Responsibility was direct, and the purchaser's recourse was immediate. It is not so today. Trapped in a complexity of worldwide trade, the consumer feels as helpless as a fly in a spider web.

To eliminate some of the public's feelings of alienation from the decision-making arena, efforts have been directed at finding consumers to participate on so-called consumer group committees. Public forums have been conducted to identify such persons, but the difficulty continues in terms of assembling groups to represent the average person, minorities, low income groups, senior citizens, and foreign-speaking citizens. Blue Cross has begun issuing for general public use a *Shoppers Guide to Hospitals* with helpful hints such as selecting hospitals because they are teaching hospitals and more likely to provide quality at less expense, not necessarily selecting the hospital that is the biggest (bigness is not synonymous with best), checking if a state regulatory agency exists that can provide direction to a lower cost hospital, avoiding hospitalization on Friday because the hospital bill will be greater (laboratory work, x-ray examinations, and tests are usually not read and reported on weekends), getting routine laboratory tests done before admission, and not insisting on a private room. In response to such consumer education programs and demands, a considerable number of surgical procedures are on the list of "twilight surgery," a scheduling pattern which allows persons to receive elective or minor surgery with a minimum loss of time from their jobs and families by doing surgery during evening hours or after the usual work day.

Although Blue Cross was beginning this progressive program, it was also being charged with not paying California Medi-Cal claims submitted to their company by nursing homes and more than $500,000 to a university hospital.[20] These charges were made after the state had just agreed on a 5% hike in fees that could be charged for services rendered to Medi-Cal patients.

In the style of a father, various health professionals and legislators speak in favor of comprehensive health plans that will provide adequate health care for every citizen. The degree of genuineness of this expressed concern for people comes into question in case after case of shoddy practice, overbilling, and impersonal service. A former President's special health advisor said that Congress was deferring a workable national health insurance for purely political reasons. Advisor Roger O. Egeberg charged that the California Medical Association has become hysterical and hung up on health maintenance organizations, and as a result the federal government questions this approach as an answer. Such local and state experimentation programs should, however, be encouraged, he said, because the solution to health problems will never be solved in Washington.

Counterpressure

Pressure attracts counterpressure. The Roman Catholic Church and other groups have created the "Voice of the Unborn" in protest of liberalized abortion practices. In California the Reagan administration proposed the reduction of welfare grants to pregnant women. It was countered by some twenty-one groups, including pediatricians, welfare, church, children's, labor, nutritional, and other organizations.[21] Some males argue that the federal government in its support of women's rights and equal opportunity employment is creating a discriminatory backlash against males and reverse discrimination. A New York University professor organized 500 scholars into a Committee on Academic Nondiscrimination and Integrity aimed at proving that the United States Department of Health, Education and Welfare guidelines will lead to illegal quotas in hopes that Congress would lift them.

A county medical society denounced California's prepaid, low-cost health plan for welfare patients and, in an unsigned letter to its physicians, urged them not to participate in the state's new plan. Physicians were urged to stick together and fight a compulsory governmental medical system. American Medical Association President C. A. Hoffman, in a 1972 speech[22] exclaimed, "We must preserve the best features of our present system, including traditional physician-patient freedoms, and we must also redouble our efforts to eliminate any gaps in our health care system." Although it may not be viewed in like manner by consumers, the physician group proposes what would comprise an optimal health care system for catastrophic illness as well as improve care to the poor and disfranchised.

Medical care review has stirred a fiery debate among American physicians. Professional Standards Review Organization (PSRO) probably represents the last chance that physicians will have to put their house in order, and if they fail, government will come in. There is a powerful group within the American Medical Association that is pushing for an immediate repeal of a 1972 law that requires PSROs to review health care provided under federally funded medical care programs, and this group is also urging physicians to refuse to cooperate with PSROs.

Statistics are useful, and a good many are presented to serve various purposes. Some complex statistical indexes are available. One must be reminded, however, that statistics are always history, and that the newspapers are not in themselves history books but a place for live information. Newspapers serve as a basis of judgment as to what will happen tomorrow. Researchers support the efforts of school systems through the presentation of complicated data which indicate that school reform will not close the student gap and that school output is dependent on the abilities of entering children. Genetics, the environment, family background, and television programs are claimed to be causative factors. The question remains whether equalizing schools will end poverty. Lengthy investigations have been carried out with some indications that

equalizing schools will end poverty. There is relatively little relationship between a child's education, equal or not, and his economic achievement as an adult. Some would maintain that it is necessary to look at the whole concept of "equality" and what it entails, that if it is truly acceptable, the more intelligent, ambitious, and lucky must subsidize those with the least of these qualities through paying a sweeping price and socialism. The same or similar data might be used to question the development of national health programs for all members of our American society because health cannot be divorced from poverty and other factors.

In Minneapolis-St. Paul a kind of Professional Standards Review Organization called the Foundation for Health Care Evaluation has been in operation since 1970. The foundation is credited with bringing about a decrease in the average number of hospital days since it started. One problem, however, is that it may be given false credit, since the trend across the country has been that of decreasing the length of hospital stays. Establishing cause-and-effect relationships between and among pressure groups and their resultant effectiveness can lead to erroneous conclusions.

From whence one views it

Residents in an area in upper east side New York are protesting the opening of a McDonald's hamburger establishment, a nationally popular eating place for most Americans of the lower and middle classes.[23] The "upper crust" elite accustomed to prime steaks is up in arms, saying "We don't go to hamburger joints."

Tear gas and troops were brought in to calm campus and ghetto violence. Protestors claimed that the American government was engaging in a brutal suppression of human rights. The slightest action against the most violent demonstrators and students who were burning buildings was called horrible. Entire universities were shut down, and all students denied education for days and weeks. The fact that militants threatened the safety of all who did not agree was accepted and even considered morally desirable by antiwar, ultraleftist revolutionaries and their sympathizers among the citizenry. Now, after ten yeas, there is a lesson to be learned about the minds of progressive people. James Meredith, a militant who received nationwide publicity for his participation and leadership of protest groups, registered as a Republican.[24]

Violence is not a sign of power but a symptom of loss of power or fear that it is in the process of being lost. With pressure to increase numbers of minorities on campus in occupational areas including health and nursing, entrance examination scores were eliminated as were doctoral dissertations as a requirement for graduation. The faculty solved their problem by simply giving As and Bs and saying "heck with them." Citizens and students with various viewpoints ask the question, "What price a college degree?" and one might add, "What price increasing professionals?"

Trades and compromises were made between the Department of Defense and the House Armed Services Committee, which held opposing views. The House Armed Services Committee contended that the civilian scholarship plan would not produce more physicians than were produced otherwise. This committee wanted the Uniformed University for the Health Service but stated that legislation for the university and the scholarships must be passed separately. The scholarship program was scaled down, and limitations were passed on the highest rank that military medical officers could hold.

The medical profession has been a powerful group in terms of achieving what it sees appropriate, not only in behalf of consumers but also for the practitioners. In the view of some, the public's tendency to sue and threaten to file malpractice suits is not always in its own interest because the lawsuits and threats deter the training of physicians' assistants to relieve physician manpower shortage.[25] Responsibility for malpractice coverage for physician assistants has made physicians hesitate in utilizing them. Meanwhile newly

trained physician assistants have been unemployed, the health manpower shortage was not alleviated, and the number of lawsuits filed against physicians continued to climb.

The American Medical Association opposed the Democratic Party's compulsory medical insurance plan, which would allegedly come under the state's iron thumb and be a direct infringement on the "inalienable rights of the men and women of the medical profession, . . . the bleeding hearts of both parties are giving away a lot of gifts nowadays that are not theirs to give. In the end we all get robbed."[26] The response was that undoubtedly the American Medical Association would not disappoint people; it would surely fight. While it was putting up a good fight, however, the people would be paying medical costs that continuously rise at a rate which is twice that of the cost of living. Furthermore, went the response,[26] if the medical profession does not wish its " 'inalienable rights' (whatever they may be) encroached upon by legislators and outsiders, they had better come up with a decent medical care plan of their own."

Hospitals and their administrators have been labeled as a powerful monolithic system. They have put considerable pressure on the entire society, and although only one factor, they have done their part in the creation of ever-rising costs of health care. Only one example is a community hospital accused of Medicare fraud charges to the tune of $100,000 in false claims.[27] Free care is said to be a myth in view of long lines and red tape at university and other public hospitals. Following the pattern of crisis clinics, more hospitals are giving medical care in the evenings and nights. The Cost of Living Council was told by a former government economist that federal price controls on hospitals are fostering multimillion dollar cost overruns on patient bills through statistical rationalization of ever-increasing prices for hospital care similar to price maneuvers at the Pentagon. This council joined the Ralph Nader Health Research Group and a health consultant from the Wallace-Elijaber Fund, Inc., in proposing a formula to better control charges for hospital services and restriction on daily rates.[27]

Medical rights for teenagers are gaining. Their health is affected by increased freedom that they now have, with drugs and sex probably causing the major problems. Many young people under the age of 18 years are not living with their parents. Lawmakers have and continue to support ways of protecting minors through such provisions as health care and abortions without parental consent.

A state Senate committee in California was told that serious deficiencies exist in hospitals but that the state and medical profession fail to act.[28] State agencies seldom or never revoke a hospital's license to operate, even if care is extremely poor. The state medical association and Joint Commission on Accreditation of Hospitals refuse to make findings public and to make available a mechanism whereby patients can evaluate the quality of hospital care. Some deficiencies with which the system was charged include physicians without a state license being permitted to practice, physicians practicing with false credentials, physicians bilking insurance and Medi-Cal programs by ordering laboratory tests that the diagnosis does not call for, and physicians paying "bounties" for patients funneled to them by salesmen (to fill their empty hospital beds).

The pharmaceutical industry has been condemned for putting $1 out of every $4 back into advertising and promotion, thus contributing to the vast overuse of drugs in the United States.

In the struggle to cut costs the Office of Management and Budget has questioned the value of the federal health professional training grant program on the grounds that it is geared more toward helping in the education of highly skilled specialists who either go into research or command exceptionally high incomes if they go into private practice. Physicians and nurses were said to be trained incorrectly and that changes must be made in educational programs to emphasize the giving of basic medical care under supervision and

to concentrate on producing practitioners to deliver primary care.

The current movement of citizen involvement is aimed at protecting the consumer, at the meaningful participation of the citizenry, and at peace and social justice. Inherent in this overall movement is an almost unconscious assumption about the persuasive power of "information." An overall strategy used by pressure groups in this movement is that of manipulating information and changing the general views of what is logical or rational. To accomplish this, validated information is assembled, restructured, spread widely, and amplified. It is then woven in various ways into the complex of political power to affect social and economic decisions. Leaders of citizen groups have an awareness of the fact that the formal power structure of institutions is designed to screen out any information perceived as irrelevant or threatening to the purposes for which the institutions were organized. They therefore select, conceal, distort, and impound information related to their processes of planning and establishing goals. A restructuring is required in terms of symbols of advertising and communication. Values of society shift about in what seems to be a large ocean of free ideas. It is these values that must be altered by "information"—hopefully the most accurate information possible—and must serve as a basis for action, that is, change. Accurate forecast of the social future is impossible because the interaction of interest (pressure) groups is so complex and the processes emerging are so difficult to detect that no current methodology is capable of accomplishing the task.

Interest groups form strange combinations. An example is that of the white woodcutters in Mississippi who turned to the National Association for the Advancement of Colored People (NAACP) for emergency support when they and their union went broke. Yet it is known that some of those seeking NAACP help were former members of the Ku Klux Klan. The county welfare department had turned down the woodcutters' applications for food stamps but subsequently denied doing so. The NAACP representative was Charles Evers, Mayor of Laurel, Mississippi, and black candidate for Governor. He joined some of the white strikers in making a protest trip to Washington, D. C., and he is credited by them with getting the food stamps. In spite of all that transpired, the racial harmony that appeared (on the surface at least) in Laurel was not held in great esteem by other residents of Mississippi. One large Mississippi paper, the *Jackson Daily News,* ran a cartoon with a caption "At the Bottom of It," showing a pile of logs labeled "Laurel Pulpwood Agitation" stacked on top of a Communist banner. An accompanying editorial also pointed to the close watch kept on the Laurel events by the Kremlin, and a question was raised about Moscow's level of pleasure or displeasure with the turn of events at Laurel. This type of response might be seen as an attempt to force the groups apart again and to prevent a disruption in the usual dispersion of power.

Nurse students are taught early in their professional preparation that a legitimate respect is due the physician and that only on extremely good grounds are his orders questioned. They are also taught, openly or subtly, that any other person, such as an osteopath, chiropractor, or dentist, does not deserve recognition as being "medical." The enculturation process is so pervasive that many nurses on graduation hold a severe negative attitude toward these practitioners. Recently, however, osteopaths and chiropractors (and perhaps dentists in some areas) have become organized into pressure groups designed deliberately at breaking into the inner circle of the medical and/or health care field. They are, in fact, sharing with nurses the position of the second-class citizen reaching for an "equal" role in the provision of health care. The very disciplines that nurses have learned to shun may provide great support, as in the case of the Washington State Nurse Practice Act. Few if any nurse leaders in that state would deny the important role which Senator William Day

played in gaining passage of a revised, expanded role for the nurse in the licensure law; Senator Day is a chiropractor by profession. More chiropractors, osteopaths, and dentists participate actively on comprehensive planning committees and view their participation as a means of achieving recognition in the total health care system.

Pressure groups lose power through splits in their ranks. On many issues the American Hospital Association (AHA) and the American Medical Association (AMA) have taken a united position. At a critical point in time, however, the new president of the 7,000-member AHA accused the AMA of tunnel vision during a worsening health care crisis.[29] This came after a period of feuding between the two associations over roles and particularly over the shape that a national health insurance program should take. The AHA chief asked where the AMA was while the cries for better health care continued to grow and people clamored for outpatient services, lower costs, health education, and mental health care. He answered the question: "I'll tell you where they are—where they've been all along—under the umbrella—representing the physician and physician interests."[30] At such a time nurses might make political partners (or as some political scientists have said, "bedfellows") with a usually unlikely group, the American Hospital Association.

Power is often equated with self-interest, and self-interest in a religious sense as wickedness. Writers as early as Helvetius pointed out that self-interest is a universal characterisitic of man. One often hears of persons who are referred to as "power hungry" or highly obsessed with interest in self. This image is a negative one and might be similar to the image of those labeled "wicked" in the religious sense. However, to be considered virtuous, persons do not necessarily need to sacrifice personal pleasure. The difference is that the behavior or activity from which they receive pleasure (and at the same time are granted power) is in the interest of public welfare. Nurses obtained pleasure (power) by becoming head nurses who were shuffling papers, but they were not considered virtuous by the public because the pleasure gained from shuffling paper (power) was not conceived to be consistent with the public's welfare.

Change does not take place merely through the passage of laws but through the development of new values. An example of changing values is seen as nurses and physicians currently ponder their duty when dying patients plead to have treatment ended. The burden of guilt commanded by prolonging the life of hopeless cases through costly complex treatments will continue until euthanasia (the act of inducing death for merciful reasons) engenders sufficient public support for acceptable alternatives. The use of a "living will," which is legally binding, has been one suggested approach so that health professionals will not continue to incur civil or criminal liability but will allow patients to determine their own destiny when, according to sound professional judgment, there is no reason to continue life unless the patient chooses.

In nursing, changes will take place through an enculturation process of neophytes. Resistance comes not only from among the elders within the ranks but also through such factors as the effects of commercial advertising, that is, the nurse in white on television. Decreasing enrollment in colleges and universities will have its effect on change in the health care system and on nursing. Many of the bright and ambitious will decide not to go to college but to become tradesmen. Power then might no longer belong to the "educated" lawyers, social engineers, but to the many alert working people who dominate by numbers alone, if no other way. These are the young people who are questioning the earlier established ways of dealing with social ills. Will they be able to make their voice heard? Likewise, nurses have not been the ones who were given the responsibility for shaping public affairs. Can they now join the socially conscious and make this a better world?

References

1. Pepper and Salt Cartoon, Wall Street Journal, Oct. 31, 1972.
1a. Machiavelli, V.: The prince (translated and edited by Datnold, C. E., and Crocker, L. G.), New York, 1963, Washington Square Press.
2. Tugwell, R. G., and Banfield, E. C.: Review of *TVA and the Grass Roots* by Phillip Selznick, Public Administration Review **10**:47, Winter, 1950.
3. Velie, L.: Needed: quality health care for *all* our children, Reader's Digest, June, 1974.
4. Loing, J. R., and Klein, F. C.: Industry lobbies are active and powerful at the state level, Wall Street Journal, June 6, 1974.
5. Immel, A. R.: Try as they might, folks in Oregon can't deter new residents, Wall Street Journal, May 22, 1974.
6. Prestbo, J. A.: More citizens sue to force governments to stop or start acts, Wall Street Journal, April 16, 1971.
7. Osment, N.: Woman doctor at UCSD urges girls to enter medical field, The San Diego Union, Oct. 29, 1972.
8. Reform School: higher than Harvard, Los Angeles Times, Sept. 13, 1972.
9. Olson, L.: Institutions are not helping families, Long Beach Independent, Feb. 28, 1973.
10. 5 Quit posts at college in black protest, Los Angeles Times, Sept. 28, 1972.
11. Trombley, W.: Dental leader denies charges against dean, Los Angeles Times, Oct. 17, 1972.
12. Trombley, W.: Won't yield to pressure groups, USC head says, Los Angeles Times, Oct. 12, 1972.
13. USC orders probe of dentistry school, The San Diego Union, Oct. 15, 1972.
14. Minority engineers, Wall Street Journal, June 18, 1974.
15. American English, Wall Street Journal, June 18, 1974.
16. Morality handbook adopted for schools, Long Beach Independent, Jan. 13, 1973.
17. Olmo, F. D.: Anglo pupils favored over Latins, unit says, Los Angeles Times, March 20, 1973.
18. Brown, P.: AMA chief links poor health care to crime, The San Diego Union, Oct. 17, 1972.
19. "Violence" in home of retarded, San Francisco Chronicle, Nov. 17, 1972.
20. Claimants rap new Medi-Cal payment system, Los Angeles Times, Oct. 24, 1972.
21. Doyle, J.: Blast at cut in aid to pregnant, San Francisco Chronicle, Nov. 17, 1972.
22. Government inroad fought by doctors, The Register, Oct. 6, 1972.
23. Newman, B.: To some New Yorkers Ronald McDonald is an arch villain, Wall Street Journal, June 21, 1974.
24. Editorial: Military might on campus, The Arizona Republic, Sept. 25, 1972.

25. Nelson, H.: Malpractice lawsuits called deterrent to full health care, Los Angeles Times, Oct. 10, 1972.
26. Editorial: Expensive medicine, Playboy Magazine, Oct., 1972.
27. Hertel, H., and Blake, G.: Hospital and chief accused of fraud, Los Angeles Times, Oct. 20, 1972.
28. Sweet, R. E.: Many hospitals in state said to have major flaws, Long Beach Independent, Oct. 12, 1972.
29. New chief of Hospital Association assails AMA, Los Angeles Times, Nov. 9, 1972.

8

POLITICAL PARTIES

In this chapter, after a brief history of the development of political parties in the United States and before pointing out some of the shortcomings of the system, some reflections on the current status of the political parties at the national and state levels will be given.

Although recent events have focused on developments to the contrary, party financing is national and mass based. Competition in areas of the two party system is expanding and should be considered as a positive factor. Party policy committees in Congress have moved toward a stronger position. The congressional seniority system has been altered significantly. This latter has occurred without accurate data concerning the support that senior congressmen now receive in their home districts in contrast to the time prior to the change. Significant evidence of a possible alternative has been the replacement of the senior senator concerned with international relations, not because of any wrongdoings but because of the bigger and apparent potential of his successful opponent.

Since leadership evolves from every social relationship, it is not for us to discern if it is good or bad, says Michels,[1] but to realize that a democracy always tends to develop into an oligarchy by nature of the leadership phenomenon. He contends that technically leadership is indispensable. Since government implies leadership in one form or another, we would have to disagree with Thoreau who maintained that the government which governs best is the one which governs least and best of all is that government which governs not at all.

After then reading theories from other authors such as Goodman[2] and Rossiter,[3] one is stimulated into thinking that political parties and politics are in fact desirable, since they give people some choice, by their act of voting, about which leaders they prefer to follow. In this way the leaders do not have complete power over the people they are leading without the risk of being put out of office. This does not, however, completely eliminate ulterior motives and unscrupulous behavior on their part. The present situation is undoubtedly far better than that under which the common everyday man existed during earlier centuries. Even with the pessimistic picture which Michels presents it would appear that the United States democracy can be justified by the fact that it does ultimately seem to determine a betterment of things, even though it is fruitless to think in terms of a particular goal or end result. It is the process of participating and searching and working toward the goal, and not the goal itself, that society must look to.

Michels's statements regarding leadership development and behavior provide the base for conceptualizing the dynamics in the health care system and what nurses need to know as they interact within that system, the society it serves, and their profession as a component of both.

Buddhist philosophy has long maintained that as individuals work on something and think they are reaching the goal, there is a point at which, when they momentarily believe they have reached it, it is gone. It is the working that is real, and the actual moment of achievement is an unrealistic expectation.

In a democracy there is always an opposing force. Although one can never completely be rid of anarchistic tendencies in society, as a result of various sociological counterforces there are ways to minimize their dangers. It is essential that institutions which educate health professionals and professional educators help to develop within individuals planning to work in the health care system an ability for intelligent criticism and control, thereby meeting societal needs. In so doing, all individuals gain increased power to improve their overall professional and economic status, since inferiority in political areas limits their ability to be critical and leaves them powerless.

Partisan politics and the dynamics of political parties are products of the process among individuals and groups that determines those leaders who emerge and the decisions that are made. We wish to place emphasis on the *process* and not the specifics of individual leaders or decisions. It is difficult to accept wholeheartedly the position taken by Michels that the end of democracy is inevitable. On the other hand, it is easier to accept Burns'[4] premise that as long as there is change in consensus and order in cleavage, the American democratic system will continue.

A political party has been defined in various ways. Key[5] says it is an authoritarian institution in which the power elite perform roles, that is, election and convention. These roles distinguish the party that is "in" from the rest of the electorate. Brogan,[6] a British author, described a confederate system in the American party system. The whole aim of political parties, as Hynneman[7] defines it, is one of legal government and power. No matter how one defines it, party politics is all a matter of gaining power and keeping it by getting and keeping their candidate in the office. Because various others also are seeking the same power, the political game is on. As long as the game is played by the rules and done with the consent of the people, the constitutional system will continue to function in the best interest of the whole.

One would have to disagree with Marxists and others who say that government is the strong controlling the weak. In a democratic system the weak control the strong (the persons holding sovereign power with the consent of the people). With the built-in checks and balances and the development of other means of expressing the wishes of the people (such as labor unions), it seems highly unlikely that any great change will be seen in the American system during the foreseeable future. This is said with concern that some readers may interpret this position as foolhardy in view of some recent events not exemplary of behavior that is desirable of leaders in a moral democratic society. The reader is reminded of an earlier statement that personal interests and unscrupulous behavior may sometimes come to the fore. These, however, will call to attention a need for responsible decisions in selecting candidates and solving issues.

The two parties are split with regard to the role of the "man on the street." The Democratic party makes the assumption that the man on the street can make rational choices and that his decision will be based on which of the alternatives will in fact get him the most. The Republican party makes the assumption that the man on the street can make economic choices (pocketbook decisions).

There is also a difference in how the two parties define the relationship between individual and government. The Democratic party concerns itself more with what is good for the masses, whereas the Republican party concerns itself with what is best for the individual and society. There is a somewhat subtle distinction to be deliberated here, in which one pits equality against excellence. Put differently, a distinction can be made between the description given from the viewpoint of the Democratic party regarding the role of government as arbitor and a description given from the viewpoint of the Republican party. There are differences in positions on economic issues and fiscal policy that change within the two parties from time to time, as well as shifts in the official stand taken regarding public and private rights and responsibilities.

The majority of people are left rather cold by such terms as *foreign trade, liberalism,* and *conservatism;* however, they are able to define the issues pretty clearly in terms of "party" when it comes to bread-and-butter issues. Although this also seems to be what the founding fathers saw as the real issues and what the parties stand for, there is more behind an individual's reasons for being either a Republican or Democrat. A Pennsylvania coal miner, whose grandfather was also a Democrat, believes in the Democratic party because he says, "they're for the working man." In addition he may be of Polish descent and adhere to the Roman Catholic faith.

Characteristics of voters of either party are of interest. Republicans vote more often than Democrats. Persons with money and those who own big houses vote more regularly. This may reflect economic differences; people in ownership and management positions can more easily vote without losing a day's pay. Idiosyncrasies of candidates are readily picked up by voters and influence their perception, loyalty, and vote. Examples include the grandfather image of Eisenhower, the heavy-haired look of youth by which Kennedy was portrayed, and the long hooked nose with which Nixon was portrayed.

History

Political parties are voluntary associations that have a distinct role in politics in democratic societies. They take over the helm of government through winning elections. Modern political parties win elections through the process of obtaining votes, which reflects obtaining dependable support. To obtain that support, it is necessary to mobilize citizens around interests and concerns. To understand American political parties one must review the contents of the Constitution and what the statesmen of that era knew about political parties from their experience with political parties in England.

Party is a synonym for faction and implies division. In the years prior to colonization, party politics (inherently partisan) were condemned as conspiracy and aggressively squelched. Political parties had to escape from this situation before they could act legitimately. This was accomplished by giving assurance that any strategies used to oppose certain individuals and policies were not in opposition to the constitutional order. From thence comes the term *loyal opposition.* It was in England that the term became useful and not self-contradictory. Through its growth, Parliament gained strength, and the House of Commons became the center of governmental authority. Ruling therefore was done through the Parliament, and tactics were required to win votes in the legislative assembly. It became necessary to develop a functional system of political parties.

British political parties of the seventeenth and eighteenth centuries, the Whigs and Tories, functioned mainly within the organization of Parliament rather than as organizations of the electorate. There was an electorate; however, its suffrage was limited. To obtain a seat in the House of Commons, it was necessary to win electoral support through a campaign.

It became obvious that what party organization accomplished in the House of Commons applied also to winning among the electorate. Party campaigning began some time before general suffrage gave every individual a right to vote. Incumbent members of Parliament found it advantageous to publicize their votes on critical issues. Gradually large-scale organizations developed from parliamentary party groups for the purpose of nominating and carrying out election procedures. By the time when the United States political system was outlined in the form of the Constitution, British party politics had become well organized and were considered an integral part of the governmental machinery.

In addition to their British heritage, the framers of the American Constitution had gained experience through their organization of factions and partisan groups during the Revolution and afterward in the states. American parties were as well organized as those of the British, with the additional advantage provided by broader suffrage, a broader overall concept of democracy, and a system of popular representative government. Initially the rival parties in America were labeled as Whig and Tory, referred to in the colonies as the "court" party (with loyalty to the royal governor) and "country" party (with ambition to strengthen authority of the colonial assembly). In contrast to England these parties were more than parties in each colony's House of Burgesses. Because of broader suffrage and political power being achieved more exclusively through consent of the people, American parties were more like the modern system and developed as parties of the electorate. The use of the party labels *court party* and *country party* was the forerunner of the labels *federalist* and *antifederalist*.

Throughout American history there has been disagreement in American political science as to whether the Constitution was, in fact, democratic. It has further been questioned whether the framers were "pro-party" or "antiparty." Being antidemocratic has been viewed as going hand in hand with antiparty. There is even lack of agreement as to the actual time when political parties arose, varying from the early colonial settlement period to the period of ten years or more after the Constitution was written. The former position is taken by those who believe that political parties changed the Constitution into a more democratic instrument. To pursue this argument seems inappropriate and unnecessary here. The point to be made is that the framers of the Constitution lived while political parties as institutions were in the process of development. Although they were familiar with parties, they could not expressly provide for them in the Constitution and also could not possibly have conceived of a national party system as it exists today. Although often misinterpreted or misguided, Washington in his Farewell Address seems to take political parties as inevitable and necessary; his concern seemed to be that national leaders would be able to distance themselves from consuming partisan animosities.

Although the Constitution does not delineate a system of political parties, there are philosophical and structural aspects within it that allowed for the shaping of the partisan system that developed. These include the protection of individual "liberty" and the permission to form voluntary political groups. The Constitution also outlines the delegated powers of representatives elected by the people. Inherent therein is the need for the mechanisms such as elections, which political parties and party organizations afford.

All national offices created by the Constitution are elective except for judicial offices, which are filled by appointment by elected officials. Members of the House of Representatives are elected by direct popular vote in state elections. This certainly served as a stimulus to the development and growth of the party system, much as it did in the case of the British Parliament. Members of the United States Senate were previously selected through a party process within state legislatures, but since the adoption of the Seventeenth Amendment, they are also chosen by direct popular vote. There is still no equivalent to the Seventeenth Amendment for the election of the President, but the party process rapidly took control of the electoral college and presidential politics. Many state legislatures, using the permission to do so that is given in the Constitution, turned the election of both senators and presidential electors over to direct popular election. Political party organization was further stimulated by this, since it increased the numbers from which a plurality must be derived. National party alignment evolved with the establishment of an office to be filled by a strong elected national executive. Federalists and Anti-Federalists, Democrats, Whigs, and Republicans all sought to organize nationally so that they might gain the majorities required to control the Electoral College and name the President.

The state political parties that existed before the Constitution continued as a form of political organization on the state level even with the new Constitutionally established federalism. Powerful state governments served as a continuous influence on the direction of the political parties. The same motivations provided by liberty and direct election of officials at the national level have been constitutionally multiplied fifty times under federalism. Local interests and democratic processes have been enhanced through this decentralization and unification, which operate simultaneously.

Because of the many offices to be filled and because of the frequent elections required for the staggered terms of office for President, senators, and representatives, the need for party organization was intensified. With constitutionally established separation of powers the executive and legislative branches of government and even the houses of Congress have at times been controlled by different parties. Moreover, the President has received opposition from those of his own party in Congress.

Although it may be difficult for foreigners to perceive differences between the American political parties, Americans quickly pick out characteristics that to them make the parties significantly different. Americans also can predict with nearly perfect reliability that the next president will be a Republican or a Democrat. The two party system, although an insignificant phenomenon in the minds of most Americans, is remarkable to many foreigners. Numerous minor parties have attempted to fill various elective offices, including the presidency, and have most often been temporary split-offs from one of the two major parties. They tend to occur because of some upheaval internal to the party and take the form of temporary withdrawal as more or less a punishment measure rather than an attempt to establish a new permanent major political party. Minor parties have on occasion controlled government on the local level. Such is the case with the Socialist Party, which successfully supported candidates for mayor of cities including Reading, Pennsylvania, Bridgeport, Connecticut, and Milwaukee, Wisconsin. Socialist voters in Milwaukee were successful to the point of electing a Socialist congressman. The Progressive party of Wisconsin presented considerable opposition to the Republicans during the 1930s, with Democrats running in third place. In somewhat the same manner and the same time Minnesota's Farm-Labor party functioned on the state level.

Although perhaps some have sustained the fantasy of revolutionary change in voters' behavior, the basic aims of minor party members are to draw attention to their issues and candidates, create factional power within the parent political party, and achieve ultimate electoral success (as opposed to immediate success at the polls). The American political system is unusual in that most modern democracies have multiple parties, with usually no one party obtaining a majority of seats in the legislature. What is considered a minor party or interest group and not taken seriously as a contender for political office in the United States would provide a serious threat in those democratic nations with constitutions under which major parties proliferate easily. It appears that although issues serve as an impetus to the development of new political parties elsewhere, they serve as an impetus to the development of pressure groups in the United States.

There seems to be a close relationship between the two strong major political parties and the influence of the presidency. Political leaders work intensely to plan and carry out the politics of the presidential elections, which are held every four years. This event engenders the greatest voter interest in the land and tends to unify the branches of government. In spite of technicalities of the electoral system, each elected official in the three branches of government assumes as a practical reality that a nationally distributed majority is required to win the presidential election. Only a major party with adequate internal unity has the ability to get enough voters in the necessary combination to produce a national consensus in the choice of President. Regardless of their sympathies, most third-party voters are aware that one of the candidates from the two major parties will win, and rather than throw away their vote to a party that cannot win, they decide to vote in favor of the lesser of the two evils (the Republican or Democratic candidate).

As mentioned only briefly before, the states under the federal Constitution each supply separate governmental bases for developing party organizations. Each party in all fifty states can become powerful regardless of national party defeats and without control from the national party. The two major political parties in the United States might be described as loose associations of state parties that are essentially functioning autonomously. State parties do not respond to national leadership as a matter of patronage and economic resource or threats of political

retaliation and reprisal. The President has access to state leaders and, being persuasive, can be heard. Presidential success is partially dependent on the popularity and competency with which the position of chief of the party is filled.

However, each of the two major parties is more than a loose association of state parties. Within each are also many subparties, which reflect a large variety of interests. Party unity and discipline among the subparties are, unlike the British system, generally not emphasized except as elections approach. Conflicts and differences within the parties may appear almost as important as conflicts and differences between them. Although American politics has always involved the conflicts that are internal to political parties, the basic rivalry has centered between the Democratic and Republican parties. It has been their responsibility to define issues, provide leadership, and determine public policy.

It is sometimes said that there is little difference between the two parties anymore and it really does not matter which holds power. From this comes the expression "like voting for Tweedledum or Tweedledee." However, if this were the case, the Republican and Democratic parties would have disappeared, as did the Whigs and Federalists before them. On the other hand, had the differences among them been too great, either or both of the present political parties would most likely have been destroyed by political fission. If one were to outline briefly the differences between the two major parties, it might be most accurate to say that as a rule the Democratic party takes an affirmative view of government and the Republican party takes a negative view. That is, Democrats emphasize what government *ought* to do and Republicans emphasize what government *ought not* to do. This essential difference can be traced historically to the beginning.

Among the men who provided theoretical knowledge and leadership to the framing of the American Constitution and form of government were those who feared strong government and those who considered it necessary if it were to survive over time. The issue of centralization and decentralization was uppermost in debates during the constitutional conventions, with Jefferson and Hamilton providing most of the leadership to the lengthy debates. Jefferson supported a decentralized form of government, with a high degree of power retained by the states. Hamilton stood fast on the need for strong central government and argued that numerous states in loose association could never become a federal system but rather, a republic. Several of their debates are contained in a collection of documents called the *Federalist Papers,* which each used to win support among the people for their positions. From Jefferson's view was first derived the label *Republican,* later called *Democratic-Republican,* and finally *Democrat.* Although the summarization is a considerably simplified one, the two opposite positions were called the *Federalist* and the *Anti-Federalist.* As time passed, it was found that almost total state autonomy was in opposition to the best interest of all in areas such as commerce, trade, and their strength and defense against external threats. As was mentioned before, the Federalist party gradually disappeared. The Whig party, derived from the British system, also fell by the wayside as the electorate demanded more direct involvement in political decision making rather than allowing it to take place within the congressional halls.

During the colonial period, there were those along the coast who were engaged in commerce, trade, shipping, banking, and professional occupations together with those formally involved in the government of the colonies. In the back country there were farmers, hunters, trappers, and stock raisers, and many of these were indebted to persons of the coastal area who had granted them credit. Thus began a bitter conflict between debtors and creditors. It did not develop into a totally distinct alignment of commercial interests against agrarian interests. It did, however, develop into alignment of the affluent against

the less affluent. Resentments of small shopkeepers, small farmers, sailors, ship workers, and artisans built up against rich fur traders, patroons, lawyers, and royal officials. At the same time trouble mounted between the colonies and England, as alliances between merchants, mechanics, and patriots clashed with those of the clergy, lawyers, officials, and others who were laughingly referred to as Tories.

Throughout the Revolution and afterward, alliances between country folk and city workers and mechanics grew stronger, and more opposition gathered by these alliances against wealthy merchants, slaveholders, and the total social elite. This alignment appeared during the struggle to draw up the new Constitution under the partisan groups called the Federalists and Anti-Federalists. It was at this point that two distinct parties appeared. In the Federalist group were men like John Adams (the first and only Federalist president) and Alexander Hamilton. Thomas Jefferson was perhaps the most noted leader of the Anti-Federalist group or, as they were often referred to, Republicans.

Hamilton was a driving man with strongly conservative views who was instrumental in laying the first tariff on imports to protect American manufacturers and, at the same time, provide financial support to the government. Although the idea was popular and passed, bitter controversy prevailed over the items that should be taxed. On another major issue Hamilton's group of Federalists ran into serious controversy—this time more directly with the Anti-Federalist (or Republican) group. The issue was Hamilton's proposal to fund the national debt, assume the debts of the states, and establish a central bank. Prior to this time there had been no power to tax, and bonds purchased (e.g., for $1,000) were sold for about one fifth of their original amount. The result was a boom of speculation, but argument continued about whether to pay the original owners of the bonds, as opposed to speculators, the face value or the current market value. Hamilton's argument was that to pay everyone the face value was the only way to attain the support of the wealthy. At this point the Anti-Federalist leaders, Jefferson and Madison, argued that only the original owners of the bonds should receive the purchase price because it would give substantial profits to wealthy speculators at the expense of the workers and farmers who paid the greatest amount of excise taxes. Hamilton's proposal passed, but Jefferson was outraged even to the point of calling it fraudulent. He pointed out that a few were accumulating great fortunes while the poor and ignorant were being bilked. It was this issue that has been given credit as being the critical factor in the establishment of the distinct and visible political parties, henceforth shaping the very core of the United States of America.

The controversy over Hamilton's proposal to establish a central bank under private management, a proposal to dispose of public lands in large quantities to large companies (rather than small farmers), and favoritism to the British in foreign policy clearly brought commercial interests into the Federalist party fold. Hamilton continued to hold extremely great personal political power. Meanwhile, however, Jefferson and his forces were organizing and mobilizing the citizenry at the grass roots. The Hamilton-Federalist camp was concentrated in urban centers, merchants' clubs, boards of trade, and professional groups, with a publication *The Gazette* serving as effective publicity and propaganda. To counter these important resources, Jefferson was determined to get the southern planters, farmers, small merchants, and laborers of various kinds into a solid organization and to make up in strength what they (the Anti-Federalists) lacked in prestige, money, and leaders. This was done by about a dozen men, utilizing a botanical expedition to arouse and mobilize the masses and lead them. A journal *The National Gazette* was started for communication in the same way the Federalists had *The Gazette.*

While the Jefferson-Madison team were organizing the grass roots group of Anti-Federalists (the Democratic-Republicans),

bitter internal conflicts were developing among the Federalists. Their bitterness toward the solid discipline of the opposing Anti-Federalists was also verbalized. By the end of Washington's second term as President the bipartisan coalition that he had started came to an end. The people then voted only for President, with the man receiving the second largest number of votes becoming Vice-President. Adams (a Federalist) won the presidency, and Jefferson (a Democratic-Republican), running a close second, became the Vice-President. A new era of American party politics began. Adams was in office only one term, partially because of difficulties presented him by Jefferson and partially because of dissension within his own party led by Hamilton. In the next election the Federalist vote came mostly from New England, and the Hamilton group representing wealthy commercial interests was dissolving. It continued on in a more humanitarian form, with support for Hamilton's policies being carried out by the Democratic-Republican party led by Jefferson.

The new political party, the Democratic-Republican, was made up of varied and sometimes disparate interest groups. Including small farmers, debtors, nonconformists, religious minorities, small merchants and traders, and workers, it was the party of the rank-and-file citizens in the lower socioeconomic levels of society. Because of Jefferson's commitment to an agrarian society, an uncomfortable alliance took place with southern slaveholders and plantation owners, who were absorbed into the party.

A prototype was thus established for the two major political parties that has carried on through the years. The one major group was formed from Hamilton's group of manufacturing and commercial interests. The other was formed from Jefferson's dream of a beautiful agrarian world. It is of interest that one reason why Hamilton viewed his party as being more beneficial was because it would provide jobs for women and children (almost all the unskilled textile laborers in England were women and children). The Federalists emphasized military strength, order, and a hierarchical system, whereas the Democratic-Republicans stressed freedom, equality, welfare, and opportunity for the individual. The Federalists emphasized strong government; the Democratic-Republicans emphasized the ultimate rationality and goodness of man, with government serving only at best as a necessary evil.

So it has been throughout the years to the present. The Federalists, Whigs, and Republicans have been leaders of business and industry, strongly Protestant, and including the professions that are high on the socioeconomic scale. From time to time they have received support from wealthy farmers and, from the Civil War to about 1930, the black vote. They continued in the tradition of Hamilton to support private enterprise and to oppose social welfare programs aimed at alleviating the problems of the poor. The Anti-Federalists, Jeffersonian Republicans, Democratic-Republicans, and Democrats have been small farmers, laborers, socially conscious intellectuals, nonconformist religious groups, Roman Catholics, and various minority groups. Hamilton's spirit continues in the present-day Republican party, and that of Jefferson in the Democratic party.

Both major political parties, now as since their beginning, have various internal conflicts. There have been periods during which one party was able to dominate the orientation of government. Examples are the so-called Democratic era, which broke up about 1860 over the slavery issue, starting the antislavery northern faction and the proslavery southern faction of Democrats. A Republican era began about 1860 and lasted until about 1912, when Theodore Roosevelt led some from the ranks into a Progressive faction, which became only a minor party but lasted for a sufficient period of time to allow the Democratic party to again take the reins. To the present time there is a coalition of southern Democrats and Republicans in Congress and among the electorate, pitting

liberals against conservatives on various issues. Another Democratic era began with the Great Depression and lasted until the Eisenhower administration of the 1950s, when again the Republicans gained strength. Except for four years out of thirty since the beginning of the Democratic era in 1932, the Democrats held control of both houses of Congress. From 1932 until the election of former President Nixon, the Democrats controlled the Presidency three fourths of the time. During the various eras, however, the President and the majority in Congress have not always had the same party identification. Such was the case, for example, as Democratic President Cleveland faced a Republican Senate.

The Electoral College system along with popular vote by the people determines the person who wins the office. States have a designated number of electoral votes that are cast in a block for one candidate. The electoral system exaggerates the geographical section as a factor in an election, as was the case with Lincoln. He received the overwhelming electoral vote of the northern states that could not be surpassed by the electoral vote of the southern states, from which were taken those border slave states supporting neither Lincoln nor his opponent. Lincoln, however, did not pull together a majority of the popular vote. Although his opponents together received more popular votes, the electoral system is such that Lincoln would still have been elected even if the opposition had been united on a single candidate against him.

National politics

Washington in his Farewell Address foresaw a nation of factions. Federalist Paper No. 10 discusses the danger of factions and how factions can be controlled. Jefferson first stated he could not agree but later understood the need for two parties.

Various reasons are given for the development of the two party system in the United States. Theories include the ins and outs, the haves and have-nots, the sun-moon theory, the political maturity of the founding fathers, and the homogeneity of the population (unlike the situation in France with its multiparty system). One other reason that might be added as a possibility is that Americans are practical people, in this aspect of life at least. They view partisan politics as spectators in a political arena, observing the players with interest as they would a horse race (or a cockfight?).

The Madisonian model of personal factions around office-holders and office-seekers buttressing the legal and political aspects of government has been instrumental in helping the constitutional system to remain and to do so in spite of major changes in most areas of American life since the Constitution was written.

In the American political party system one can observe a complex network of energies moving in every direction and in every level of government. In actuality the two party system is a four party system in which there are congressional Democrats, congressional Republicans, presidential Democrats, and presidential Republicans. These four work in a somewhat coalition fashion, checking and balancing each other. Without the two major parties, however, the number of choices that any individual might make would indeed be limited, since the making of choices indicates the way he wishes to be governed.

Many of the recent issues that have involved Americans and their political parties deal with the relationship between the individual and government. Various health and welfare issues are a case in point. Health proposals from the Republican party have tended to be prevention oriented, whereas those from the Democratic party have tended to be remedial or treatment oriented. The Republican party has asked what the plan would do for the whole society, whereas the Democratic party has asked what the plan would do for the downtrodden. Responses to problems and issues depend largely on whether the party is in or out of office. Both parties do achieve progress in areas of policy, and one often has to look closely to find the

differences. The differences are more distinct at times of election, when their party platforms officially and publicly present them. Regardless of the level of distinction or the exact nature of the issue and the solutions or alternative policies proposed (and/or passed), the basic question remains to be answered. That question is *whether, in fact, freedom* (to be healthy and to have three square meals a day, a satisfying employment, a useful education, or whatever) *can be legislated.* From what was said previously, it is more complex than passing legislation but depends first of all on societal awareness, then on the bulldogging of citizens to demand that to which they are entitled, and finally a compliance system that is effective and can enforce compliance and command negative consequences for noncompliance.

All political groups, including political parties, are a kind of interest group. Not all interest groups are continuously active in partisan politics. If everyone, however, agreed on what public policy should be, there would be no politics, no interest groups or political parties, and no politicians. Discussion of partisan politics entails a focus on differences of opinion. Sources of disagreement in political decisions have various roots, among which are economic factors, geographical-regional factors, ethnic and racial factors, religious factors, attachment to certain individuals, and purely rational differences in viewpoint regarding issues. It seems worthwhile to look at each of these factors briefly.

Economic factors make up perhaps the most common and fundamental lasting causes of difference. Individuals involved in various agricultural efforts have specific counterinterests; for example, those who have an interest in butter production oppose those who have an interest in oleomargarine production. There have been long bitter struggles at state and national levels on the behalf of each. Rich and poor are likely to view events and behavior differently. Industrial workers in the city tend to think differently from farmers about political issues. Small town merchants hold different views from those involved in international trade. It has long been known that there is a pattern of voting derived from these differences; some people can be predicted to vote Republican most of the time and some Democratic most of the time.

Economic factors overlap somewhat with geographical factors, especially in the area of agriculture. The convergent views of midwestern wheat farmers, Florida and California fruit growers, southern cotton and tobacco farmers, and western cattle ranchers serve as classic examples. Although some regions hold a common interest and vote in a geographical bloc, the homogeneity is usually created by an economic factor, as in the Tennessee Valley Authority region. On the other hand, northern and southern voters consider themselves distinctly different from each other, as do eastern voters and western voters. These feelings create a schism in the parties and make the hair of party candidates for office stand on end at election time. Geographical areas may acquire a uniform political affiliation as a result of common ethnic or racial factors. Long dominated by a certain culture, these groups tend to maintain certain common interests that influence their political behavior. This later may have been changed by the arrival of other new immigrant groups. Examples include the English Yankee-Puritan culture of Boston, which was changed by the incoming Irish, giving Boston a new political tenor. One political antagonism, and perhaps the deepest in the United States, arose from racial differences. Black and white needs and views served as a stimulus to the development of strong pressure groups, among them the well-known Ku Klux Klan and the National Association for the Advancement of Colored People (NAACP). Many Americans hold strong old-country ties. The isolation and sentiments developed throughout two world wars strongly affected the Irish-American and German-American antagonisms toward Great Britain. United States relations with Israel continue to influence the political behavior of Jews, especially in the large urban areas such as New York where this ethnic group is heavily concentrated.

Ethnic and racial factors are as difficult to isolate completely from religious factors as economic and geographical factors are from each other and other factors as well. Classic examples might include the Morman influence in Utah politics and that of the Catholic, Jewish, and certain black groups such as the Black Muslims in large urban centers. Religious factors played an extremely important role in the national elections of 1928 and 1960, when Catholic candidates were running for presidential office. Seventh Day Adventists and Jews oppose closing of businesses on Sunday in favor of a Sabbath closing congruent with their beliefs. Roman Catholics continue to fight for public tax support to parochial schools. Protestants do not generally unite in favor of their overall religious interest; however, with the establishment and increasing strength of the National Council of Churches they have the capacity to be highly influential. Prohibition, pornography, civil rights, and many other issues have been greatly influenced by Protestantism. Religious factors create an influence beyond that of the sect or religious body alone. Their distinctive moral and social codes and people's commitment to them is reflected in a fundamental way of thinking that pervades all of their political thinking.

Although leaders in one sense are merely spokesmen and articulate controversial interests, they are in themselves also an independent variable. Attachment to leaders has created controversy where otherwise no controversy existed. Likewise certain achievements are the product of the leadership of a place in a particular period of time. Among these are the post-World War I German resurgence resulting from the dominance of Hitler's twisted personality, which, regardless, aroused the masses of people to action, and England's courage and resistance in World War II, which was a reflection in the people of the forceful personal strength of Winston Churchill.

If an issue can clearly be differentiated into

component aspects, it is easy to predict the public's political decision regarding it. However, few issues can be so discretely taken apart. Examples in the health field include Medicare and national health insurance. The way in which one views these issues depends not only on what one has at stake but also on broader underlying attitudes such as the way in which one views big government, welfare for the poor, and the question of whether frugality and thrift are great virtues. Political predispositions toward liberalism or conservatism play their role, as do psychological frustrations and hang-ups, regardless of whether they are normal or abnormal. The amount of credence placed in social-psychological factors differs among political behaviorists and traditional political scientists.

Thus far the discussion on political opinion and decisions has focused on factors that are most nearly unconscious or irrational behaviors on the part of people. Some readers may be surprised at being reminded that we acknowledge any other factors in human behavior on the political scene (partisan or by its broader definition), aside from those which are conceived out of conscious drives for power or ulterior motives. We are well aware, however, that some political controversy and organization are the product of human intelligence applied toward the delineation of issues and a search for a solution to problems so that the outcome in terms of public policy will be for the overall good of human beings. Empathy and compassion are human qualities that transcend narrow self-interests and spur people on toward intelligent action. One can feel what other people feel without being in their shoes and have genuine concern for others who have material and other needs correctable through application of common justice. Certainly many of those who actively seek involvement in politics fall into the latter category. However, the failure to identify the former type is much more hazardous to the beginning observer so that it is necessary to devote considerably more attention to it.

If we say therefore that democracy cannot work without a party system, one needs to look at nonpartisanship and the nonpartisan trend in local government. Perhaps at that level, it might be more appropriate to use an approach such as Progressive and Conservative rather than to hold onto the Democratic and Republican labels. Local governments have different problems, and what is good for the whole community must be of concern. A Democratic approach or a Republican approach to financing a local sewage system seems absurd. Candidates in a nonpartisan type of local government are either self-selected or chosen by a particular interest group, which may be a union or whatever. The nonpartisan label is deceptive, however, and there is always an indirect connection with partisan politics.

Partisan politics also has a nonpartisan facet. President Truman said that a candidate must be partisan during the election campaign but is permitted to be somewhat nonpartisan while in office—that he must be such as President or he will alienate a lot of independent voters at the next election. Since it is known what type of person or group generally is sympathetic to either party, the real concern in the partisan game is the winning by either party of those votes that are independent, undecided, or easily categorized.

The states

State partisan politics differs among the fifty states for various reasons. One might take California as an example. Here the state politics differs from that in other states in part because of its third party movement, the Progressives, which led to a nonpartisan tradition. Because its population has been an expanding one and so varied as to background and geographical roots, the people tend to rely on newspapers for information while they are new to an area. The geography of the state itself is a factor, with its vast deserts, which are rich for agriculture only when irrigated, and the extensively long coastline and rugged moutains, which are sources of fun and recreation or barriers. A distinct north-south split exists with regard to orientation, cultural habits, and political affiliation. On the precinct level the turnover from election to election is frequently 70% or greater. Not only is this turnover created by immigration to the state but by internal mobility as well. Social characteristics are distinctive, with great personal wealth at one level and extreme poverty at another, congestion in the bustling large metropolitan areas, and absence of density in the deserts and mountains; these factors play a role in terms of another characteristic—a wide diversity of interests. It has often been said that California has a lot of crackpots among its population and government officials. It is probably a false idea; the eccentric character of some portion of the people is probably common to all states. Some states determine local policy from the state capital, whereas in other instances localities determine state policy. The differences occur with the variation in the degree of directiveness or permissiveness on the part of local or state governments. California falls somewhere in the middle between these two fundamental government approaches.

The nonpartisan heritage may be actually more in name than in fact. Nonpartisanship theoretically is based on government at the municipal level being similar to a corporation rather than a governmental entity. More accurately it may be a political entity in fact and a corporation in law. The corporation-like character may be desirable, since municipal powers are limited by government at the state level. As a corporation, problems are basically administrative, with boundaries set by the state. This makes "home rule"* more a state of mind than what the term actually says. The nonpartisan form of government does not readily lend itself to smaller towns

and cities. Part of this is because of the matter of recruitment. Recruitment of candidates for nonpartisan and partisan posts can be decided on either personality or issues.

Early in the century some took the position that local parties were necessary because no municipal questions could be solved without state and national parties into which local government must be capable of fitting. Another position was that it is the local party rather than the "boss" which is to be blamed for problems. Also to be blamed are those voters who vote a straight party ticket. Conservatives by nature look for and promote continuity and the status quo.

Partisan elections provide an opportunity for voters to vent their spleen and "throw the rascals out." When an issue is divisive enough, greater voter interest will likely be seen on election day, and a greater proportion of voters will show up at the polls. The anticipated result of this dynamic process will be that change will more likely occur and a liberal orientation prevail in the municipality. On the other hand, some political scientists have contended that nonpartisanship leads to conservatism. Going somewhat beyond that dichotomy, Michels[1] believes that all institutions tend toward conservatism.

The tendency in the American electorate has been that of active passivity. The electorate is influenced by various factors and is impressionable. Because of the relatively low percentage of people who turn out at the polls, particularly in nonpresidential elections and local elections, one might conclude that they stay home because they are relatively satisfied with the way things are going. They are giving consent by their relative passivity and their staying away.

Vigorous and courageous leadership potential tends to be neglected for several reasons. Individuals from certain areas of the country are not readily perceived as material for presidential office. Certain psychological factors influence voters against otherwise competent individuals (listen for expressions such as "I don't like his looks"). Men with various nationalistic, cultural, and religious orien-

---

*Home rule is established by municipalities giving assurance to the state and receiving permission from the state to run their own affairs in accord with state-mandated standards, established by constitution and law, rather than having the state operate within the municipality to provide services.

tations as well as financial resources have found them to be stumbling blocks to leadership positions. The situation with regard to gender is so blatant that one needs hardly to mention it as a stumbling block. The man with a rather local, rural, parliamentary orientation is most readily considered congressional material. If he is more urban in orientation and bureaucratic in his thinking, he may be presidential material. Few men who enter the congressional type of political life cross over into the race for the office of President.

The American electorate is somehow frightened by vigorous and courageous leadership. Change in thinking is slow. Although most people have a crisscrossing of interests and belong to several groups whose leaders and members influence them in somewhat a bombarding fashion, they remain politically immobile until they think through the issues and come up with an opinion that more or less fits into their previous pattern of thinking in terms of party lines. It has been observed, although not tested, that nonvoters (the nonparticipants) tend to be the less secure, less stable members of American society. If they do turn out at the polls, their votes may easily swing the decision regarding candidates and issues in the direction of the extreme, either left or right. The political parties try to recruit candidates who will support the interests of the greater proportion of the populace, the group in the middle on the standard curve. This group, moreover, wants men who satisfy their desires as they relate to change or who take a position not deviating greatly from the status quo. One might consider this phenomenon fortunate, since if this were not the case, there would be an overwhelming number of unhappy voters whose candidates lost, with revolution being a possible result.

"The governed" also seem to realize that regardless of which party wins an election, life goes on pretty much as before. It is not so much that there is a difference in what each party wants with regard to policy but rather in the approach used to achieve it. What

seems to be important to the governed is an assurance that they, the people, have the power to say "no" when they desire. The ability to give or deny their consent has been totally eliminated for some through such roadblocks as poll taxes (designed specifically to keep certain population groups from voting but forbidden in national elections by the twenty-fourth Amendment and in all other elections by a 1966 decision of the United States Supreme Court), gerrymandering (establishing voting districts in ways to assure the outcome of elections), unreasonable residence requirements, and complex absentee ballot procedures.

Problems

There are weaknesses in the American party system. Among these are such factors as (1) the party that appeals to the middle socioeconomic group wins (in reality this may be more frequently questioned in recent years); (2) the party that appeals to the predominant age group in the population at the time of election will be more likely to win; and (3) there is no party that exclusively protects the Yankee, Protestant white American male, although there are interest groups to protect blacks, the poor, and more recently women.

One rather obvious problem might be stated in terms of the working relations between the President and Congress. It has appeared that the President has been opposed in action by both Houses of Congress. He is no longer restricted so vigorously in terms of making recommendations and then, after the process of conflict resolution in congressional debates, giving his stamp of approval or disapproval. The President is expected to get legislation passed that is congruent with the philosophy of his political party or be defeated in the next election, yet he may be hamstrung in attaining it.

Being an effective political leader, it would appear, demands a quality not required of leaders in other walks of life. A paradox seems to be found in that political leaders must gain supporters, friends, and funds through a kind of socializing which is objective, never becoming involved emotionally with the problems of those whose support they desire. At the same time, they sip tea, shake hands, and give people the impression they are genuinely interested. It requires an unusual kind of person to shun involvement, to be impenetrable to those very feelings that give rise to the interest of others as one to whom they would be followers, and yet at the same time to seek the general good in spite of a genuine quest for political power. White[8] proposes that in the 1972 election one of the main reasons why Senator George McGovern lost was because he got involved with everyone's needs at a personal level, made rash promises, but was unable to follow through by gaining distance and proposing a plan for sound action.

It was earlier mentioned that vigorous and courageous leadership seems to frighten the American electorate. However, another paradox exists in the fact that although this may be true, those men who have been considered "the greatest" American presidents are those who have demonstrated great vigor and courage. These are few in number, whereas the large majority of presidents have been less vigorous but are held in high popular esteem by the fact that to attain election to the office of President is the highest honor in the land and requires the successful crossing of multiple hurdles. In any evaluation of a President, however, it should be kept in mind that a man's bumblings while in office should not serve as the basis on which his impact on history is judged. Men may be extremely capable and yet not reveal their level of capability in the office of President. Herbert Hoover and Thomas Jefferson (according to some) may serve as examples of such persons.

Rossiter[9] has labeled eight presidents as "major" ones and six others as having given strength to the office, even if only in a period of congressional ascendancy. Since his evaluation was done in 1960, it might well require revision, although we will not undertake that project for purposes of this book. The eight men whom he named as major

presidents are Washington, Jefferson (although Rossiter acknowledges disagreement with some political scientists), Jackson, Lincoln, Theodore Roosevelt, Wilson, Franklin Roosevelt, and Truman. The six men named for their contributions to the office of the Presidency are John Adams, Polk, Andrew Johnson, Hayes, Cleveland, and Eisenhower. The major presidents were each selected because they demonstrated unique leadership. Washington lent dignity, authority, and constitutionality to the office. Although he was an energetic and independent executive, he was able to see his role in the light of the Constitution. He acknowledged the confusion it created in his mind as he deliberated over decisions he must make; nevertheless he sought advice from those with opposing views. His serious deliberations offset the fears of those who worried about tyranny in the office of President. He proved that power can ennoble men as well as corrupt them. Jefferson, a great man even though not necessarily a "major" president, converted the Presidency into a political office and established that the President would provide leadership to Congress. After twenty years of congressional supremacy by committee Jackson remade the office of the President. Lincoln saved the government and the Union by means of an eighteen-day dictatorship during which he called out militia and did so with no concern that justification for this decision was needed. Theodore Roosevelt delineated the "bad guys" from the "good guys," made government more personal to people, made newspapers available to everyone, was a leader in diplomacy and great leader of Congress, and was sensitive to the pulse of public opinion. Wilson was perhaps intellectually and morally the best prepared for the office; during his Presidency the government reached a peak of morality. Franklin Roosevelt and Truman revolutionized the Presidency and provided presidential leadership in the legislative process.

The list of six presidents whom Rossiter named is congruent with and supports our acknowledgment of qualities that make men appear to demonstrate greatness in the face of grave odds. John Adams, difficult as it was for him to follow the strong Washington, did so in great style, in addition to moving for peace with France in 1799. Polk was somewhat a dull void between Jackson and Lincoln but developed harmony and efficiency among the secretaries of the Executive. Andrew Johnson is said to have had few talents but much courage, demonstrated in his protest against Radical Republicans in Congress. Hayes accomplished significant civil service reform and stopped the crippling railroad strike with militia. Cleveland demonstrated integrity and independence, which are exemplified by over 400 vetoes in his first term of office. Eisenhower, although a Republican following two "major" Democratic presidents, moved forward dramatically in the same tenor.

Another notable change has taken place in the Presidency, not in power so much as structure. There is an increased manpower within the Executive Office of the President, and the President is unable to function without the auxiliary help to extend his functioning. This is a problem to the extent that the staff may act in behalf of the President, with the President himself having little or no knowledge of what actually happened. Nevertheless, he is to be held accountable and may be accused unfairly. Party favoritism in appointment of staff also creates a loyalty not necessarily in the general interest.

The role of the President has changed considerably over time. In some respects the President's office is expected to be devoid of partisan politics and to be concerned only with the well-being of the entire citizenry. The President plays a major role in protecting the peace and carries the highest responsibility for establishing and maintaining peace. At the same time, when conflicts such as labor disputes are serious and crippling the nation, it is a function of the President to settle them. The President's role now even allows him to seek injunctions in federal courts. Since the Eisenhower administration and the Little Rock incident, the President commands leadership in the area of civil liberties and civil rights.

Party politics and the entire governmental structure in a democratic nation should allow for the expression of all interests among the electorate. Changes should occur within and among the levels of government that address existing needs. A question or problem might be raised—what of those interests and concerns that fail to be expressed, since lack of expression does not eliminate them? An additional question follows with regard to how "spontaneous" or how "controlled" is the democratic process of political parties.

In the United States the major function of the political party is that of nominating and electing its candidates to office, formulating platforms (statement of positions), and conducting campaigns. The system on the whole has served the country well, if one accepts its purpose to be the mobilization of the electorate with various interests and the working out of inherent conflicts among interest groups without revolutionary action.

References

1. Michels, R.: Political parties, New York, 1959, Dover Publications, Inc.
2. Goodman, W.: The two party system in the United States, Princeton, N. J., 1956, D. Van Nostrand Co., Inc.
3. Rossiter, C.: Parties and politics in America, Ithaca, N. Y., 1963, Cornell University Press.
4. Burns, J. M.: Congress on trial, New York, 1949, Harper & Row, Publishers.
5. Key, V. O.: Politics, parties and pressure groups, New York, 1947, Thomas Y. Crowell Co.
6. Brogan, D.: Politics in America, New York, 1954, Harper & Row, Publishers.
7. Hynneman, C. S.: Bureaucracy in a democracy, New York, 1950, Harper & Row, Publishers.
8. White, T.: The making of the President 1972, New York, 1973, Atheneum Publications.
9. Rossiter, C.: The American Presidency, New York, 1960, Harcourt, Brace & World, Inc.

THE NURSE'S DILEMMA

A halo is a fine thing to wear, but it's been known to slip and become a noose.

SILAS SHAY[1]

9

PROFESSIONALISM

Thus far we have discussed the political system and life within the American political system with an emphasis on health issues and nursing. This has been based on the assumption that the nurse has a contribution to make to the political system, based on her knowledge of and concern for the individual person's health needs. Such a stage of contribution and interdependence can only be reached after proceeding through the stages of socialization (dependence), professionalization (independence), and integration (identity). The process of socialization, which for nurses begins probably before entry into a school of nursing, makes the neophyte dependent on older, more advanced members of the social group for guidelines on many forms of behavior and thought. Particularly in the old hospital training school this was a well-defined process that accented the almost totally dependent state of the newcomer. It has been difficult for nurses to give up some of the security that can be derived from this

process. The beginning nurse today has often begun to leave this dependent stage before entering the school of nursing. Some conflict between student and teacher today may be a reflection of the contrast between the teachers' continued expectations that beginning students should be dependent and the students' attempted demonstration that they are prepared to begin independence much earlier.

The overt independence of a recognized professional identity is apparently a necessary swing to the opposite extreme from dependency, but it is probably appropriate to put some curbs on the ultimate extension. Although we know that many practitioners never reach this state, it is probably wise to have as a goal the achievement of professionalization within a limited time after completion of professional education. This should not be the false professionalism of impersonal, machinelike behavior and self-effacement. This is the identification of the self with the societally approved goals of the profession, coupled with realization that "I," an individual, can and should engage in a wide range of activities at my own initiative and discretion to achieve the goals.

At the point of integration and identity the skills and values of the individual have been integrated with one another so that the individual has enough self-awareness to readily make use of abilities in a positive way. The individual should also have acknowledged that identity and goal direction involve interdependence, which can now be handled without plunging back to dependence or overly demanding independence. It is our assumption that, at whatever point the reader is now, a desirable goal is the point of identity and ability to make contributions to the political process. It is the purpose of Unit III to articulate some of the issues that may arise as the skills (which include theoretical materials and intellectual capabilities as well as manual dexterity) and values of individual nurses and of the nursing profession begin to converge.

The words *profession, professional,* and *professionalize* are fairly common in modern English usage. Their connotations are so diverse, however, as to make it almost impossible to discuss the professional nurse or nursing as a profession in a coherent manner. Five possible connotations readily come to mind. The first of these is for *profession* to mean any occupation that requires some degree of effort or study in the process of becoming a member. This is seen in the phrase "Johnny is 'taking up' the profession of . . . (barber, beautician, doctor, mortician, teacher, druggist, nurse, secretary, engineer)." This use of the word appears to become more common as educators and employers speak of creating *new professions* to fill specific places in the employment market. Such groups are often associated with advanced education, especially in the growing junior college system, and cover extremely diverse areas including computer technology, health fields, penology, social service, and others. Increasing numbers of social critics

observe that the culture of higher education in the United States is leading to an immense oversupply of persons with advanced education and no marketable skills. Many of these professionals find employment at jobs that are far from "professional" in the classic sense.

A second is the use of *professional* as a means of distinguishing a person employed in a given field from one who participates as an amateur or volunteer. A common use of this distinction occurs between professional and amateur athletics in this country or between professional theater and community playhouses in which local citizens participate "for the fun of it." Although one seldom sees the term *amateur nurse,* there are many who nurse families, friends, and the downtrodden and who are, by implication, contrasted with those who receive a paycheck for performing the duties of professional nursing. In this sense *professional* may have the connotation of commercialism, the sense that the individual engages in the activity because it pays well in money or status. The amateur, in contrast, is truly dedicated, feeling a definite call to the tasks at hand. The term *professional politician* carries this weight.

Another use of the word *professional* is one that has certainly affected nursing because it calls for the distinction between technical and professional aspects of any activity. In general usage the terms are used to distinguish between one whose standing in a given field is primarily related to the performance of specific repeatable tasks that could be learned by apprenticeship and one whose standing is based on a wider, more theoretical understanding of the goals of the work. The latter is usually recognized by the granting of higher status, title, and pay. An example of such recognition is that bestowed on and associated with the "professional engineer" as contrasted with numerous "engineers" who have learned their jobs the hard way. Many in the nursing profession have urged the delineation of nursing into these two categories, using the type of initial educational program as the distinguishing feature.

Such categorization also involves the separation of those tasks that can be standardized (technical) from those functions that must remain nonstandardized (professional). It is argued by some that no nursing tasks are amenable to standardization, since the nurse deals with people and must, in the performance of any task, consider the idiosyncrasies of the individual. As a result, professional judgment is always required.

Some nurses seem to believe that it is possible not only to identify some nursing tasks as standardized but also to identify attitudinal correlates of professional and technical practice. This distinction, to the general public, appears to be a manufactured one, since patients and families seem to believe that "a nurse is a nurse is a nurse" as long as she wears white and makes them feel better. This distinction has some bearing in the legal world, however, because it would affect the granting of differing employment benefits (such as workmen's compensation) to persons in the category of professional nurse or technical nurse. In addition, it is becoming increasingly significant, since those designated as professional employees may be held liable in court of law for malpractice or negligence, whereas technical employees rarely are. The professional/technical distinction is also important to nurses in relation to military service because graduates of associate degree nursing programs have been classified as technical and have been ranked as enlisted personnel rather than granted officer rank. The latest move has been to rank them as junior officers but to deny them promotion unless they show evidence that they are moving toward a professional degree.

Professional is also used as an adjective to describe a certain attitude or approach to one's occupation. This use of the term is usually found in descriptions of individuals who are precise, businesslike, and organized and who are objective, scientific, and even cold in their approach to the task at hand. When applied to nurses by the general public, *professional* generally means one who is cold and impersonal in patient care, even to the

point of regarding patients as objects rather than people. Two widely disseminated research studies[2,2a] legitimized the use of the term *professionalizing nurse* to refer to one concerned with efficient institutional and personnel management. This identity is contrasted with that of the traditionalizing nurse, who cares for patients as people and wants to be with them. These connotations have remained in the minds of many nurses and probably affect their responses to those who urge nursing to move toward professional activity, professional organization, and professional performance. This connotation does disservice to the word *professional* since the root means *to profess,* a form of commitment that is far from impersonal or noninvolved. Students may be exposed to the mechanistic attitude understanding of the word *professional* in required courses on nursing identity and history. Such courses, in the past at any rate, have utilized texts that discussed professional attitudes, good manners, and proper dress as if these were what made a nurse rather than the knowledge that could be brought to bear to alleviate human suffering.

A final connotation of *professional* would rarely come to mind unless one were familiar with sociology, since the term *profession* is used by sociologists to describe a highly specific and limited type of social group.[3] These groups are marked by a devotion to a particular field of learning and science, the nonstandardized utilization of knowledge in the achievement of acknowledged social goals, a code of ethics, and the granting of permission (license) to practice only to those who have demonstrated competence. Most discussions have identified theology, medicine, and law as "The Professions," although some have indicated that other occupational groups, including nursing, have the potential for becoming professions. Etzioni[4] has extensively discussed nursing, teaching, and social work as semiprofessions. They remain in this ambiguous status by having become trapped in bureaucratic systems that smother individual thought, by having a variety of entrance routes, and by having been seen as "women's fields," within which "ladies" could function without having access to power sufficient to cause an excess difficulty to the remainder of the social system. In addition, large numbers of persons prepared to practice those semiprofessions have been expected to leave active practice to rear families, thus being less likely to rise into the higher administrative ranks.

The failure of nursing to achieve truly professional status is documented by a study of health professions reported in the *American Sociological Review*.[5] The discussion of the study procedure indicates that the five health professions studied were chiropractic, dentistry, medicine, optometry, and pharmacy. The paradigm for study contained a ranking on the basis of resources and structure (including cohesion in orientation) in the professional group and the professional organization. The first item is size—the larger the group, the higher will be its rank. By this criterion nursing should top the scale, yet it was not even considered in the study.

Figures on the costs of health education add to an understanding of this phenomenon.

People value what is rare and costly. Not only are there far fewer physicians than nurses, but also recent studies document that a medical education costs over three times as much as even the most expensive beginning nursing preparation. Whereas nurses should not necessarily aspire to cost the public more, they should not delude themselves concerning the existence of some real bases for the public's attitudes.

Although the first four connotations of professionalism justly receive some attention, it is the sociological understanding of professionalization that seems to be most strongly represented in the socialization process through which nurses move, particularly in baccalaureate and higher degree programs. Perhaps the popularity of internurse discussions on the professional status of nursing is due to the minimal conflict they stimulate. Many nurses would like to see themselves ranked with physicians, lawyers, and ministers. They often have been grouped together, of course, as appropriate matchmaking material, but that is scarcely the same as being considered professional

Table 5. Average annual education costs per student, 1972-1973 (offsetting research and patient care revenues and net education expenditures)*

Profession	Education costs	Offsetting research revenues	Offsetting patient care revenues	Net education expenditures
Medicine	$13,100	$2,100	$1,300	$9,700
Osteopathy	8,950	100	1,850	7,000
Dentistry	9,050	700	950	7,400
Optometry	4,250	50	1,050	3,100†
Pharmacy	3,550	450	50	3,050
Podiatry	5,750	0	800	4,900†
Veterinary medicine	7,500	600	1,350	5,550
Nursing				
Baccalaureate	2,500	50	0	2,450
Associate	1,650	0	0	1,650
Diploma	3,300	0	1,800‡	1,500

*American Journal of Nursing **74**:600, April, 1974.
†Totals do not equal sum of components due to rounding.
‡Cost reimbursement by third-party payers to parent hospitals.
NOTE: Dollars are rounded to nearest $50.

peers and colleagues. At any rate the professional discussions do not arouse the type of angry feelings stimulated when the possibility is raised of calling some nurses technicians rather than professionals, thereby implying a significant demotion. Especially if the conversation on professional status is kept entirely within the occupational group, it can lead to many positive attitudes. Unfortunately, unless students and faculty discuss professionalization with nonnurses, they never realize how futile such an internal label can be in the cross-system debate or conflict.

By the sociological definition a profession is developed to meet a societal need. Nursing would certainly appear to fulfill this qualification, especially in modern, urbanized society where there is a need for someone prepared to nurse those who are ill or injured as was done by extended family members in other times and cultures. As a profession, nursing was not legitimized because it described this need and then sold itself to the public. Rather, some persons began caring for others and called themselves nurses. As they became known, others in need of care sought such nurses for assistance. Eventually the group of nurses did some selling through individuals such as Nightingale and movements such as the economic security push of the last decade. The goal was to convince the public that nursing ought to be given certain freedoms or rights to better fulfill its assumed and assigned role. It is important to realize, however, that if professionals only participate in political activity when their own status or rights are threatened, they will lose societal support. If professionals participate in political activity when the issue is the resolution of the societal need for which they were created, they will be recognized by the public as helpful, concerned, and valuable and will thus probably increase their status at the same time. Organized American medicine failed to realize this principle and lost much general respect and support through the campaign against Medicare, since the public was able to see this as antagonistic to the goal for which medicine was supposed to exist. There

are those who would comment by saying, "But nursing never got anything until nurses stood up for their rights and demanded recognition." These people might remember that nurses had not only been silent regarding their own rights but had also often been nonparticipants in conflict regarding community health needs. It is not surprising that the community did not grant more recognition to a group which did not seem particularly aware or concerned with the political aspects of meeting health needs. This is not to ignore the contributions of many nurses, but the crusaders have not often been openly allied with groups of nurses.

Nurses are the second largest membership group in the American Public Health Association and have provided its president more than once, including the late Margaret Dolan. This organization in recent years has done much to change its image to one of public advocacy and activism for the general welfare. Perhaps such a program does best come from an interdisciplinary body like the American Public Health Association; there is less danger of it becoming the platform of one profession. The range of issues covered in the resolutions and position papers accepted at the 1973 convention illustrate the breadth of concerns that can be encompassed, including personal health services (medical devices, current scope of maternal health services, foot health, abortion as a personal health service, need for a national blood resources policy, injury control and emergency health services, personal health services research, home health services, comprehensive planning), environment (milk and food sanitation, conservation of energy, elimination of non-health-related x-ray exposure, environmental quality), manpower training (reimbursement affecting the utilization of health care extenders, minority health care manpower), and social factors (cooperative system for health statistics, standardization of birth and death certificates, impoundment of funds, substance abuse, health care in jails and prisons, Professional Standards Review Organizations, involuntary sterilization, treatment of Soviet scientists, lives and safety of public health colleagues in Chile, increased efforts in health education).[6] The next step is the identification of routes of action that will communicate these identified concerns to the public and appropriate political bodies so they have the desired impact. Neither nurses nor the American Public Health Association has mastered that step as yet.

One example of health professions and the political units coming together to work toward a healthier society is illustrated in the movement to reduce cigarette smoking. Health officials in general agreed that smoking was (and is, for that matter) bad, although not immediately fatal. Argument regarding interpretation and application of constitutional provisions became extremely complex in the enforcement of the Public Health Cigarette Smoking Act, which became law on April 1, 1970. It provided for a ban of all cigarette commercials on radio and television the following year, based on a belief that the rate of cigarette consumption was directly related to the quantity and quality of the advertising about smoking. Beside the unhappiness created by the loss of millions of dollars that the industry provided broadcasters, there was another issue that the media made public. The ban might be construed as a violation of the first amendment, which guarantees freedom of the press, or alternately the fifth and fourteenth amendments, which guarantee equal protection under the laws. In regard to the first amendment it was argued that since cigarettes, advertising, television, or radio were not illegal, the ban could not be enforced. In regard to the later amendments it was argued that equal protection would be provided only if cigarette advertising were also banned in all other advertising media. Beyond providing the data that the smoking of cigarettes is unhealthy, most health professionals were not prepared for the constitutional and economic aspects of involvement in public issues pertinent to their publicly given professional mandate.

It must be recognized that in today's culture no problem as complex as the need for health can be resolved completely outside the political structure, including government. Any group that is involved with societal needs becomes open to public scrutiny and can act only in concordance with other parts of society. Yet such groups are composed of individuals who are entitled to privacy regarding their action, opinions, and way of life. It is appropriate to believe both statements: "that is my private attitude" and "I am a health professional and as such should have a public forum." No one has yet discovered any easy method of determining the dividing line between the public/professional and private aspects of life of those persons who, through their occupation or profession, serve society's needs. The struggles of physicians with the federal requirements to organize Professional Standards Review Organizations (PSROs) provide an excellent example. The high cost of health care and increasing number of complaints regarding the quality of health care available stimulated the demand for regular, thorough, critical review of the practices of physicians. Their response was that all professionals regularly review themselves and each other and that there was no need for any external regulation on the peer review process. Counter response involved multiple examples of how such review had failed to ensure quality and how the review process would continue to preserve the integrity of the individual practitioner and the profession. The same conflict is arising around mandatory continuing education for relicensure or recertification in a specialty. The rate of obsolescence of medical and health knowledge is rapid, yet self-discipline was not enough to keep health professionals involved in reeducation as their information became inadequate. The public is now forcing the issue in their support of new licensing regulations in several states. Such laws are also receiving support from those within the profession who see this as an enforceable means of policing the deadwood that has accumulated, particularly in rural and inner city areas.

A profession, as defined by sociologists,

will have a code of ethics that governs the actions of its members. This is related to the implicit assumption that professionals are highly moral, dedicated humanitarians who are more concerned with the good of everyone else than of themselves. There is almost a religious flavor to this expected dedication, and in fact many medical and nursing institutions are owned by or closely related to organized religions. This was even more common in earlier periods, and the medical or nursing missionary has played an important role in history. The professional, in this sense, is contrasted with the average employee or working person, who is expected to be concerned mainly with wages, benefits, holidays, and work hours. In fact it has shocked many people that nurses should concern themselves with economic matters to the extent that they have even gone "on strike" in some cases. The high percentage of nurses who are members of religious orders or who were educated under the influence of such has meant a confusing overlap of religious vocation, or calling, and intellectual and personal commitment. One carries out a religious calling regardless of martyrdom; one is more concerned with nurturing a spiritual family than feeding an earthly one. It seems strange to some that although commitment to medicine is held to be akin to such a call, it is only recently that the culture has questioned the income bracket of the dedicated physician.

An overlaying confusion for nurses and nursing is that despite their purported dedication of a supposedly religious nature, they are also open to suspicion regarding their morality. Older orientation texts for nursing students consumed valuable educational time warning delicate students of the potential sexual stimuli and advances to which they would be exposed. Popular literature and even television and movies continue the myths that nurses arouse to passion comatose patients and are highly likely to be carted off to bed by the handiest male (usually a physician in training). Given the changing social customs, it is likely that young nursing students, male

and female, are changing with their peers. It is true that some practicing health professionals, like those of any profession, may have the problem of frequent attacks. It is also true that some health professionals may take advantage of their intimate contacts with patients. However, it is not something unique to nurses or the health field. Both physicians and nurses, because of their intimacy with others necessitated by the nature of their role and the necessary violation of taboos such as those regarding bodily exposure, do have to learn to handle some inappropriate advances from their patients and clients. If one reads the magazines directed at other helping professions, such as ministers, one can find documentation of the same issues. Probably the myths surrounding the morality of nursing will end only when the mythology regarding the role and position of women in the social system is changed as well.

Although one of the professions, law, has been extremely involved in political matters, members of the other professions are generally expected to be apolitical, especially if one puts politics into the more common negative light. Although professionals should be good citizens and vote, they have often been expected to remain silent about their personal political convictions and to abstain from any public statements that would indicate a position. This view received a rather resounding blow during the massive upheaval over the Vietnam conflict. Many health professionals became active campaigners against a specific political activity, which they saw as endangering the health of many. Although, indeed, it may seem "unprofessional" to use one's professional status to advantage in partisan politics, it does appear to be clearly within professional boundaries to express views on whether one decision or another would better meet the societal need to which the profession was created. This matter is complicated by the fact that many nurses are civil servants within some governmental unit. A hallmark of government service, as idealized in the United States at least, has been the merit system and the nonpolitical nature of those in the public employ. Much careful thought is necessary to distinguish professionally appropriate involvement in the political scene on vital health issues, while avoiding inappropriate misuse of professional position in partisan politics.

Another of the identifying features of a profession is the possession of a specialized body of knowledge that is utilized in the meeting of societal need but that is not available to or shared with the general public. Whereas nursing may have a limited body of unique knowledge, it certainly does share in the understanding and application of the knowledge held by all health professionals and has a unique slant on that material. Part of the motivation behind increasing the number of nurses holding doctoral degrees is the desire to have such nurses add to the body of specialized nursing knowledge. In recent years there has been increasing debate as to the amount of knowledge physicians or nurses may or must share with their patients. Public journalism and a generally higher level of education has made much previously private information public. Certainly in regard to medical research the professions have been forced by the public to share more than they seemed readily willing to share. Beyond even the results of any research, hypotheses and potential results must be shared with research participants to ensure the protection of their rights. Extensive publicity of poorly policed research activities has led to tightening of regulations governing disbursement of funds for studies. Since the disclosure in 1972 of the Tuskegee study, in which poor black patients were deprived of treatment of syphilis for up to forty years and were made aware of neither their condition nor the implications of the research, the degree of scrutiny has increased. Some states have considered legislation that would add state regulation onto the existing United States Department of Health, Education and Welfare review process.

On the whole nurses have barely confronted these issues. Most nurses participate in research only incidentally, that is, if their patients become part of a study by some other profession. If nurses were accepting the professional mandate of concern for individual health, they would probably insist on their right to review research protocols and assurances regarding safety and privacy before consenting to supply data or give the researcher access to the patient. One might wonder, for example, about the presence of moral conflicts, if any, in the nurses who had contact with the Tuskegee study during its forty years. Other professions have turned to animal research (despite occasionally loud protests from antivivisectionists) as the way to obtain preliminary data safely. Whereas nursing may eventually do more of this, it is wise to remember that much of what is nursing depends on verbal interaction, and this is difficult to replicate with nonhumans. One must also be aware that there can be other than intended consequences of the more careful protection of civil and human rights. One may be the limitation or slower rate of production of new health knowledge. Another may occur in eventual treatment, where, for example, the intensive efforts to prevent inappropriate confinement in mental institutions has led to a considerable increase in the nontreatment of those who really want and need it.

Dewey[7] suggested that "no scientific inquirer can keep what he finds to himself or turn to merely private account without losing his scientific stand. Everything discovered belongs to the community of workers." This sharing might even be extended to the concept that everything discovered belongs to the entire community. In regard to the dynamics of political decision making it would seem appropriate for professionals to share their knowledge when such knowledge would have an effect on the public's understanding of the issue in question. Nursing has consistently failed to share with the public the existence of knowledge relevant to health that might increase the public's positive awareness of the profession. Physicians often get press coverage for their "discoveries" such as learning that a presurgery interview and psychological support can decrease the need for sedation and shorten the hospital stay. Nursing studies at Yale University and elsewhere support the same conclusions and have been available for at least a decade. Alternatively nurses have been involved in public education for childbirth. Many of those teaching the Lamaze and other methods are professional nurses. Public action to obtain such information has increased. Community colleges offer consumer education courses on health and nutrition, especially aimed at the poor and elderly. One problem with openness is that information provided by several health professionals may prove conflicting, and thus confusing to the public, which has been falsely supported in beliefs regarding the existence of "right" answers within professional fields. It will take some time for this view to be altered.

A concomitant of the professional's special knowledge is the professional's right to prescribe for those who turn to him. Although the word *prescription* is most often associated with physicians, the response of the public to the directions of other professionals closely resembles the response to a physician's medication directives. The attitude involved is expressed in phrases such as "the doctor knows best" or "I'll do what the doctor tells me." Only recently have the professionals become aware of the degree of noncompliance and independent behavior masked by such words and an appropriately thankful attitude. People at times wish to prescribe for themselves. Canada has been plagued with controversy over whether it takes a dentist to prescribe and fit dentures or whether a toothless person can identify his own problem and go directly to the denturist, who actually makes the teeth, for his prosthesis. Whereas nursing does not have the same professional standing as medicine, the orders, advice, or suggestion of nurses, even given over the back fence, are often taken seriously. This complicates the participation of professionals in public political activity.

If one accepts the philosophical bases of American democracy, one believes that each person has the right to share in decision making and that each person's voice should be equally heard. Although the professional may indeed be justified in prescribing solutions to problems within his jurisdiction, he must be aware that he cannot prescribe the outcome of political issues. Certainly an example which has aroused many people is that of Benjamin Spock. It was appropriate for a man with his credentials to prescribe approaches to child rearing (although many feminists have even challenged that), but many believed that it was erroneous for him to prescribe the national policy. He may have seen this, however, as merely a natural and acceptable outgrowth of pediatrics, as a means of creating the appropriate atmosphere for the development of his ideal child. A less political example is that of chemist Linus Pauling's campaigns for the ingestion of vitamins C and A. The limits of professional jurisdiction and professional expertise are indeed difficult to identify. As was stated earlier, it is appropriate for the professional to make public factual information that may have a bearing on public issues. However, once the facts are presented, the professional's opinion as to the actions that should follow the fact should have no more political weight than the opinion of any other informed, concerned individual.

The use of the word *prescribe* in the preceding paragraph leads to the following example of professional/social/economic conflict. Some companies and organizations utilize mail-order approaches to fill prescriptions. The opposition to this practice is led by the retail pharmacy industry. Although the druggists are arguing public protection issues, such as prevention of drug abuse, it would be hard for an informed public to ignore the economic reality that the Veterans Administration mail-order drugs averaged $2.67 for each prescription (in 1973) and retail filling of the same drug prescriptions ran $7.03. The presence of economics in so many seemingly ethical issues is often overlooked by those new to the political scene. The hotly debated issue of how to present creation and evolution to schoolchildren may be religion to some, but it is a living to others because the decision affects the routing of millions of dollars of textbook money across the country. One can readily imagine or recall similar issues in health care, even to the extreme example of the economic upheaval that could follow reducing hospital occupancy time and income by encouraging terminally ill patients to insist on the right to die quietly, with dignity, and at home instead of in intensive care units. Former Secretary of Health, Education and Welfare Elliot Richardson highlighted the alternate overconcern with numbers and economics by proposing the development of a unit of measure called a HEW. In this system for measuring the relative cost effectiveness of projects under his jurisdiction, the HEW would work as follows.[8] If a child-year of preschool education is worth one HEW, how many HEWs is it worth to avoid one traffic accident? To rehabilitate one disabled worker? To cure one drug addict? It would be expected that if such a system could be implemented, it would indicate at least some areas where large numbers of HEWs are being expended without much measurable benefit. It would also indicate the extreme immeasurability of so many things in a social system.

The closed nature of a professional group can work to the detriment of its members as well as the public. Medical groups have investigated the supposedly high rates of suicide, drug abuse, and alcohol abuse among physicians. Indications are that this is indeed the case and that it is difficult for the troubled physician to receive help. Perhaps the same social factors that prevent physicians from being open with the public regarding difficulties in health care delivery prevent physicians from being open with and helpful to one another.

Nursing is currently expending much energy in attempts to delineate the professional boundaries within the health field. Other nurses are as exceedingly concerned with justifying nursing as a profession. Nursing appears to be a profession by most common definitions of the term. It is an occupation more complex than manual labor; it is not amateur; its practitioners are capable of more judgment than technicians; it involves certain attitudes; and it meets many of the rigid sociological specifications. Nursing fails in being a profession primarily because a large percentage of its members are not practicing up to their potential, have become cogs in an industrialized health system, or have completely ceased to practice at all. Until a majority of persons who enter the system seeking health care encounter caring, compassionate nurses who creatively aid them in adapting to the problems of overcoming disease or maintaining health, nursing has no constituency and no right to demand societal help. What support there is may well be directed at maintaining the status quo: a woman's occupation that fits the classic, submissive female stereotype to an almost-too-perfect "T."

If one can grant, however, that nursing is or should become a health profession, it clearly has a societal mandate to concern itself with meeting society's need for health and health care. It would seem logical therefore that nurses should be involved in political activity when health is the issue. They should neither avoid politics nor limit their activity to those occasions when the status or rights of nursing are at stake. John Stuart Mill[9] says, "When a person . . . has encouraged another to rely upon his continuing to act in a certain way . . . a new series of moral obligations arises on his part towards that person, which may possibly be overruled, but cannot be ignored." We would say that nursing has encouraged such a public reliance and thus has incurred a moral obligation to society to be concerned about health care needs. That nurses continue to form professional associations (when they join organizations at all) and have only minimal involvement with self-serving labor organizations supports the view that nursing is accepting that public obligation, at least at a minimal level.

References

1. Wall Street Journal, Jan. 12, 1972.
2. Habenstein, R. W., and Christ, E. W.: Professionalizer, traditionalizer and utilizer, Columbia, Mo., 1963, University of Missouri.
2a. Vaillot, Sister M. C.: Commitment to nursing, Philadelphia, 1962, J. B. Lippincott Co.
3. Kurtz, R. A. and Fleming, K. H.: Professionalism: the case of nurses, American Journal of Nursing **63:**75-79, Jan., 1963.
4. Etzioni, A., editor: The semi-professions and their organization: teachers, nurses, social workers, New York, 1969, The Free Press.
5. Akers, R., and Quinney, R.: Differential organization of health professions, American Sociological Review **33:**104-121, Fall, 1968.
6. News, American Journal of Public Health **64:**173-174, Feb., 1974.
7. Dewey, J.: Individualism old and new, New York; 1962, Capricorn Books.
8. An embraceable HEW, Wall Street Journal, Feb. 24, 1972.
9. Mill, J. S.: On liberty. In Castell, A., editor: Selections from the essays, New York; 1947, Appleton-Century-Crofts, p. 105.

10

THE NURSE AS TENSION REDUCER

It is seldom disputed that anger is a normal, natural emotion. Students of human nature recognize that unfortunate consequences, including increased risk of some illnesses and increased potential for social upheaval, can occur when the healthy expression of anger is not permitted or possible. When unaware of anger, a person can often feel anxiety instead. When movement toward goals is thwarted, frustration and anger readily build up. Nurses have traditionally not allowed themselves or have not been allowed healthy expression of anger. They have been inhibited from consciously acknowledging the true sources of their frustrations and resultant anger. At the level of patient care, this inhibition begins if students of nursing are not taught healthy recognition and acceptance of emotional experiences. Experiences cited by colleagues and friends include being told that one would fail nursing for crying at the death of a patient, being urged to read library books on death after expressing shock the first time

one discovered that a patient had died, or being exhorted not to react at all when viewing a colostomy stoma for the first time. It is difficult to imagine how nurses can assist persons to adapt in the face of emotional experiences unless nurses themselves are prepared to openly acknowledge that they *have* emotional reactions, that some of them are negative, and that it takes work to live with them. The work expended to deny emotions can be greater and more devastating in the long run than that involved, for example, in talking openly with a patient who agrees with you that his stoma is ugly or than that of a family broken apart by grief and crying with the nurse.

Too often nurses have withdrawn in hostile silence instead of openly confronting situations and verbalizing their anger to both gain personal relief and begin movement toward resolution. Without anger, which is a form of conflict, there would be less action taken than at present against the injustices

146

that individuals experience. Growing annoyances can eventually drive people to active involvement toward the forming of pressure groups and toward action. When direct outlets and action are impossible, indirect means such as involvement in energy-consuming paper work or hobbies not related to the job are utilized to work off tension and restore one's perspective. Given the stereotyped image of the nonemotional nurse, it is a wonder that the typical nurse is not also pictured as a mountain climber, boxer, or miracle worker, as a means of converting the amassed unexpressed tension of a usual day.

Many of the descriptions of the nursing role or the unique function of nursing are concerned with the nurse as expressive,[1,2] or tension reducing, or as the maintainer of equilibrium. All of these are usually contrasted with the idea that the nurse might be "instrumental," that is, seeking to achieve some specific goal by whatever means are available. This latter concern is usually assigned to physicians. The function of the nurse is described as the enhancing of the physician's curative efforts by assisting the patient to remain comfortable and, if possible, content at all times. In the more elaborate theories of nursing practice this function is described in technical detail as a process of maintaining a delicate balance among the components of the individual's physical, psychological, and sociological being so that the stress of illness does not overbalance him in one direction or another. In some presentations the vagueness of the discussion can be interpreted to mean that no direct, discrete, identifiable units of activity, which might be seen as instrumental or powerful, are needed to accomplish the goals. It must be admitted that discussions of this latter variety appear seldom in today's journals. The current explorations of roles that greatly overlap with those of medicine, such as the pediatric nurse practitioner, the nurse-midwife, or the family nurse practitioner, plus the many changes in traditional nursing situations make it easier to see that the nurse clearly contribute instrumentally as well as expressively toward achieving the goal of health. In addition, current medical interest in the need for personal or family physicians would indicate that physicians are more concerned with the expressive aspects of their role than previously.

A person normally utilizes a certain level of energy to maintain homeostasis. The presence of an illness can certainly necessitate the expenditure of additional energy in attempting to regain that homeostasis. It is appropriate therefore for nurses or others to use expressive, tension reducing techniques to control or prevent an overexpenditure of the patient's energy supply. An obvious physiological example is the use of cooling measures for the patient with a high temperature, not because it will cure his illness but because it will maintain life so that the illness may be cured. On the other hand, the physical law of entropy states that all systems tend toward chaos, since that state requires the lowest expenditure of organized energy. Too much tension reduction in a patient might encourage regression to a much more inefficient level of functioning than is necessary for the curative process to occur. An excess of opiate to relieve the stress of pain can lead to respiratory depression and death. In sociological language this would be equivalent to sustaining and encouraging the sick role beyond the present stage of critical illness. Some individuals, it must be remembered, even question the utility of such a sick role at any point in time. It is the balance between useful tension reduction and unhealthy biological, psychological, or sociological regression that is of importance to the nurse.

It appears to some observers that nurses rarely think before they act and that a nurse seldom raises questions before deciding to comfort a patient to relieve stress or tension. The overall rarity of nurses doing adequate assessment of patients prior to making judgments and planning care supports this. Tension reduction can become a bad habit. It is easy to recall instances of nurses saying, "there, there, dear" or "it will all be all right" when those phrases had little relevance to the immediate situation. First-person accounts by former patients indicate such phrases may even erroneously serve to raise the level of tension. Perhaps nursing educators and supervisors sustain this approach. It is much easier to evaluate someone as being successful if everyone is at least quiet, and a ward on which patients are encouraged to cry if they wish, or be angry when they need to be, or pace the floor with relatives, presents far from a showplace image.

Away from the patient's side the role of the nurse as tension reducer is certainly open to question. Even superficial observation can show that nurses expend much of their own energy attempting to comfort and reduce tension in families, visitors, other nurses, physicians, and administrators. The reader should recall how often the nurse disrupts a care regimen to keep radiology personnel, the dietary department, or the bookkeeper from becoming upset. The philosophy can appear to be based on the premise that any disagreement between individuals is wrong and that continuous agreement that all are sharing identical goals and preferences is essential. Especially in relationships with members of other health disciplines the nurse may well be eliminating opportunities for useful interaction by a preoccupation with maintaining a calm, nonstressful atmosphere. It is important to remember that growth and change cannot occur in the complete absence of tension.

We would raise the question of why nurses are apparently so unwilling to tolerate the existence of stress or tension if it is at all possible to alleviate it. This is especially true when the tension takes the form of conflict among individuals. In some cases it would appear that this is done as a means of self-protection. The automatic focus on others' comfort or reactions may be a way of removing attention from the self. When one recalls the many nurses whose professional commitments are mingled with religious ones, such self-effacement is not surprising. It even allows the development of a protective pseudo-professional shield. There may also be some

influence from the societal expectation of women. There have been few social opportunities for females to learn appropriate use of interpersonal tension. The men go out each day to do battle; the women keep the home fires burning. Publications on the role of women in business[3] indicate that the process of learning how to react appropriately to arguments and conflict is most difficult for the woman emerging into leadership and management roles.

Perhaps some of the tension reduction and nonemotionalism is necessary because of the nature of nursing; the stress of contact with the ill or dying might be overwhelming if it were allowed to become too real or come too close to the nurse's own core. However, some evidence of the personality or personal aspects of the individual nurse may be far more effective as a meaningful tension reducer than all the comforting words or touches from a closely guarded professional (in the cold sense) nurse. It is interesting to note that the currently popular idealized health giver whom everyone wishes they knew as a child could scarcely have been impersonal, although he might have reduced tension by being a friend as well as a physician and by being willing to share some of himself as well as his knowledge. Whether nurses are concerned about tension reduction in the interest of themselves or in the interest of their patients remains a question. It is crucial to become aware, however, that some tension is essential to the continuity of the human system.

One wonders whether this desire to be a tension reducer is an innate quality of those who elect nursing as a career or whether it is a characteristic that is communicated to neophyte nurses during the process of educating and socializing them into the profession. It is probably not clearly one or the other. There is a large connection with the feminine nature of nursing, with the cultural norm that women are soothing, nonaggressive, and noncombatant. Associated with this is the perpetuated myth that each woman harbors an unstable, dangerously emotional core which must be kept under strict control at all times, especially in public places. It should be the task of nursing, however, to explore what levels of interest in tension reduction are more useful for nurses in various settings and to adapt the education and socialization process so that it enhances appropriate stress reduction but does no more than that.

In contrast to the reduction of tension the presence of dissonance contributes to the amount of stress or tension experienced by the individual. It is one possible form of conflict but is usually internal to the individual. Dissonance, meaning disagreement or incongruity, may seem to have a negative connotation; yet cognitive dissonance,[4] the simultaneous recognition of two or more incongruous concepts, is what leads to a great deal of learning. Politically it is the process of resolving the conflict between dissonant viewpoints that leads to public policy. The question can be raised therefore whether or not there are occasions when it would be wiser for the nurse to allow or even foster dissonance or conflict rather than to function as a tension reducer. Clinical examples are possible. A person who has learned a way of life that is incompatible with existence as a diabetic will go through a period of great conflct before making life-style changes. If the patient is to have an opportunity to make such changes, the nurse will have to contribute to his discomfort by calling to his attention the necessary changes and the consequences of not making them. The nurse also has to learn to cope with the tension and potential internal distress that are associated with caring for the patient who decides that the potential harmful consequences will cause less stress than making the suggested changes.

Some sociologists distinguish between the concepts of competition and conflict. These are neither mutually exclusive nor consistently positive or negative; both are forms of struggle. As frequently defined, competition is continuous and impersonal in nature, whereas conflict is intermittent and personal. Both kinds of struggle occur in nursing. Competition seems to be illustrated by nurses' perpetual concern with the neatest beds, the cleanest ward, the fastest meal service, or the earliest hour when daily bath routines can be complete. Few nurses appear to do much to eliminate or reduce this form of competition, which is consistent with viewing health care as an industry and measuring one's success or failure on a numerical scale such as bodies handled per hour or something of that nature. In hospitals where inspections or audits for such measures are conducted, the nursing staff have apparently learned to compete, and display proudly their achievements, and work to correct their flaws, even if they failed to measure up because of heavy commitment to something more directly relevant to human health.

Nurses' tension-reducing behaviors seem to be stimulated by the desire to avoid conflict. Indeed the reward system within nursing and the systems that employ nurses seem to have become heavily preoccupied with identifying and promoting those nurses who can most successfully avoid any form of personal controversy. By personal controversy we mean face-to-face encounters with persons of differing viewpoints, not quarrels with colleagues over personality factors. Even in those institutions in which reward systems are now being designed for nurses who do not wish to move further away from patients, it would be interesting to study the characteristics of those nurses being rewarded. Following up on an interest in baccalaureate graduates and why they leave nursing, Kramer[5] discovered that nursing directors were able to identify some nurses who would engage in conflict, who were disruptive to the social system, and who were significant contributors to patient care. The study explored with those nurses how they would behave in a wide range of different situations. From those discussions examples for use in the educational setting were abstracted, and they have been employed with upper-division nursing students in an effort to keep them from believing that the only way to survive the system is to keep it calm or get out. A long-range goal would appear to be the development of a larger pool of nurses who are not content blindly to reduce tension and who are capable of surviving long enough to reach the powerful positions in nursing organizations, thus enhancing nursing's contribution to total health care.

The preceding paragraphs have presented somewhat of a dichotomy. We have indicated the value of tension reduction as a part of nursing and health care, and we have also indicated that conflict or other forms of dissonance contribute to learning, growth, and change. The question for nurses is whether they can tolerate or participate in both. If they are to fulfill their societal position, they must continue to perform their role in relation to those in need of health care, including some tension reduction. Yet we have also posed the proposition that nursing has an obligation as a profession to participate in political activities as they relate to health or health care. This may mean creating or adding to tension. It would be unfortunate if one or the other of these aspects of nursing would be eliminated. Historically there has been a division. Most nurses have focused on the tension-reduction role; yet there have always been some nurses who were willing to participate in conflict, whether with patients, other health workers, or "the system." Those who are remembered well for the latter activities and who are successful at them tend to be persons who had outstanding records in the patient-care area, through which they developed a constituency who could proclaim accurately that others should listen to the nurse in question. The realm of conflict is not a place for an adage like that adapted from students' complaints about teachers: those who can, nurse; those who can't, agitate. Perhaps more nurses are needed who can both reduce tension and raise tension at different times. Again we will remind the reader that conflict does not mean a fight for the sake of fighting or a blindly negative attack on the remainder of the world. It is the essential process of combining divergent viewpoints into a solution sufficiently representative of the original viewpoints that

it can serve at least some of the purposes of all concerned.

In the past, nurses were cautious to stay out of areas that might infringe on what might be considered personal or family territory. Unwed mothers were taught the necessary aspects of nutrition, personal health, and care of the baby. The feelings and concerns of the mother were often considered outside the role of the nurse. The same might be said of the nurse's role with regard to abused children. Observations of signs and symptoms were noted, often not recorded, and quietly reported to the school principal or someone else not in a position to intervene. Others, including professionals, became concerned to the point of establishing a pressure group that successfully stirred legislators until bills were negotiated to establish and fund demonstration programs under a National Center on Child Abuse and Neglect for the prevention, identification, and treatment of abused or neglected children. At about the same time the bills were brought before Congress, the Executive Committee of the American Nurses' Association Division on Maternal and Child Health Nursing Practice published a statement in support of the legislation. By that time a good deal of the controversy surrounding the wisdom of such legislation had been drained off or handled by other groups.

During recent sessions of Congress, nursing educational program funds have been drastically cut in comparison with those of other health professions. The National League for Nursing brought and won a suit that ordered the release of other nursing funds that had been impounded. Several points should be made. First, the nursing profession did show muscle, and resentment regarding apparent discrimination did lead to effective action. Second, the professional status and equality aspects superseded the broader issue of whether the funds to be appropriated overall were rightly and legally administered and whether the direction of additional dollars into nursing would lead to an appropriately useful increase in the national health manpower pool. Third, the entry of nursing into conflict regarding the wording and regulation of health maintenance organization legislation and the proposed national health insurance measures should be considered from the same viewpoints. The multiple conflicts here involve not only who will pay the bills but what the practice patterns will be. If none of the major payers will pay for nursing, what then? It has been clear to many that the heavy burden on emergency rooms at the present time is only partly caused by the unavailability of other ambulatory health facilities. It is mostly because the insurers will pay the bill.

One development in modern nursing that has received much attention is the role of the clinical nurse specialist or the master nurse clinician. The courses of study developed for such an individual include both the clinical nursing studies and study of concepts such as role development and the process of change. It would appear that nurses are being taught more and better ways of tolerating or participating in conflict. This role originated partly from the perceived need to reinstate the nurse at the patient's side as the person most concerned with his adjustment to the process of getting well. Yet it also originated in a need to have nurses who are better able to interact with all professionals in the resolution of conflicts regarding health and health care. Since most clinical specialists or nurse clinicians hold master's degrees, they are more likely to be perceived as colleagues by other professionals, many of whom hold the doctorate as their first professional degree. Despite the clamor within nursing, it is probably somewhat unreal to expect a person with eight years of higher education and some postdoctoral training to accept as an intellectual equal and professional collaborator an individual with twenty months of study after high school and an associate of arts degree. Even if the two can establish a mutuality of goals, the comprehension of what the other is about is extremely difficult.

Participation in conflict situations is made more difficult if one or more of the participants perceives no way out, that is, if there is no option of leaving the situation entirely if the resolution of the conflict becomes intolerable. For many nurses who are tied to one locale by spouse and family, a willingness to risk angering a large portion of the professional community is understandably lower than might be ideally desirable. From our observations, even clinical specialists have a difficult time in fulfilling their dual roles in patient care and system change. These nurses appear to be making the same choices as nurses have historically. They focus on practice or system change, perhaps at a higher level in the system than they did before assuming the new role. These nurses take the alternative of leaving the profession entirely less often than their colleagues at the baccalaureate level, perhaps because of their greater investment. Many do, however, become involved in teaching and do both their practice and organizational work indirectly, through students. The frequency of such occurrences should be considered by any nurse who is considering becoming involved in political dynamics.

Nurses are unable to escape societal stereotype. It may be somewhat compared to that of the Afro-American, or black, previously labeled "nigger." Whereas the black members of society were stereotyped as lazy, dirty, and smelly, eating chicken and sliced watermelon, a natural-born irresponsible citizen, and so on, nurses have been depicted as willing to work twenty-four hours a day with little if any remuneration, being totally responsible for meeting patient's needs, yet following the physician's orders unquestioningly. Which of these stereotypes are at all similar to the real human experience of either group? The black revolution has taken place; is there any question that a revolution by nurses may take place "for real"? How prevalent is the prayer for physician wisdom and healing without mention even in a sophisticated sanctuary of the nurses' functions to that same end. It may be innocent oversight or commercial gimmick. Awareness of the stereotype may well be fuel to the fire of nurses who are desiring change. They should know clearly that it can only be done with tension creation instead of tension reduction.

References

1. Bettelheim, B.: To nurse and to nurture, Nursing Forum 1:61-76, Summer, 1962.
2. Johnson, M., and Martin, H.: Sociological analysis of the nurse role, American Journal of Nursing 58:373-377, March, 1958.
3. Korda, M.: Male chauvinism; how it works, New York, 1973, Random House, Inc.
4. Festinger, J.: Conflict, decision and dissonance, Stanford, Calif., 1964, Stanford University Press.
5. Kramer, M.: Reality shock; why nurses leave nursing, St. Louis, 1974, The C. V. Mosby Co.

11

THE IMPACT OF HEALTH CARE ORGANIZATIONS

Power in bureaucracies, among them health care organizations, was discussed earlier in the book. There have been several studies, some of them excellent, that analyzed the structure of health care organizations from multiple viewpoints, including analysis of the environment in which most nurses work. It is not our intention to duplicate those analyses but to discuss some aspects of health care organization that can affect the involvement of nurses in political activity.

Whether public or private, most health care organizations are bureaucracies. More than that, however, they have grown more or less directly out of the traditions of two classic examples of bureaucratic organization—military service and organized religion. These have left their mark on many of the day-to-day activities in which nurses are involved. The most striking feature of any bureaucracy is its structure. As in a pyramid, at each

higher level there are fewer individuals, until one reaches the peak at which the leader, or a very few leaders, be they generals or hospital administrators, have ultimate authority. At any level an individual has authority only over those below him and can be held responsible to all those above him. By far the largest employers of registered nurses are hospitals, and it does not take any great calculation to realize that the majority of those employed would have to be somewhere well below the top of the pyramid. In actual practice large numbers of nurses have authority over no one and are frequently held accountable to everyone. Nurses may also easily become the scapegoats in such cases. Although not proved, this appeared to be the case, for example, in a Los Angeles County coroner's jury decision that cleared the physician involved in an abortion death but referred vaguely to "some evidence of negligence"

153

(unspecified) on the part of the nursing staff. Apparently there was a need to have someone to whom to attribute the death.

The bureaucratic structure tends to emphasize the position on the organizational chart rather than the individual who fills it. Specific nurses as identifiable human beings can become lost in the shuffle. The emphasis on uniform dress, as relaxed as this is by older standards, contributes to the blurring among individuals. Additionally the structure is often such that only one or two nurses high on the nursing pyramid are given access to other members of the system. For example, whereas medical records committees include many physicians and seldom the chief of staff, it is usually the (one) director of nursing who serves. This means diverse nursing viewpoints seldom develop interprofessionally, and others blur nurses into a mass behind the one or two faces they learn to recognize.

The multitude of constraints tends to inhibit the willingness of nurses to become actively involved in the political world, since it could so readily invite conflict with so many. This inhibition is probably fostered by the fact that most of those at the top of the pyramid are men, and nurses are generally women. Such a situation makes it easy for all those control measures pervading the business world, and being fought by today's active feminists, to be perpetuated. It is also easy to see how nurses in higher positions than the staff nurse could retain the hesitancy to action as they move up the pyramid. In fact they may well have moved up because they have not been noted for involvement with conflict or political dynamics, but rather for their ability to maintain tight control.

The lines of communication in a bureaucratic structure are rigid, at least when viewed from the formal side of the organization. People tend to form work companionships (and to continue them away from the job) with others on their own level, to be differentiated from those above them, and to avoid the company of those perceived as below them. Even the clinical nurse specialist, who is better prepared than many to cross bureaucratic lines and work with people from all levels, may be placed in an organizational box that limits effective communication. When it comes to the political sphere, however, one's interest does not necessarily depend on where one is in the bureaucratic structure. In the political world, group activity is more and more effective. In the community at large, people have a free opportunity to gather themselves into various groups around their similar interests. If those within a bureaucracy wish to find such a group, however, they may not be able to cross the rigid structural lines to locate any other persons with similar concerns. What is most likely is that after several unsuccessful solo attempts, the person will withdraw from political activity.

The grouping of persons around a political interest does not mean locating everybody on the job who will vote for Joe Doe. Although campaigning is one political activity, it may well lead to an untoward personal conflict. In the fostering of involvement in decision making it would be more important to identify all those concerned with a current public issue and to encourage activity in the community. As an example, in many communities the fluoridation decision was made on the basis of information that was far from accurate and pertinent. If more health professionals had been comfortable with involvement in some conflict, there might have been more attempts to make more complete data, for and against, available to the public. The same might be true regarding other issues such as health-related bond decisions or health services reorganization considerations.

One usually unspoken assumption of a bureaucratic organization is that its members have congruent ideologies (the exceptions are prisons and drafted armies, into which those at the bottom are clearly coerced). Certainly in the historical models of voluntary military and religious nursing orders, this was a realistic assumption. However, it does not seem possible for the same to be the case in a modern health care organization that employs many persons from a variety of educational and experiential backgrounds. The various definitions of health or the alternate philosophies of health as a privilege or a right lead to disagreement. Bohr and Kaplan say the following:

Many health care organizations are public bureaucracies, and their professional administrators are middlemen, caught between employees and government. As public officials, health care administrators share some of the vested interests of employees, particularly the need for more money and improved patient care facilities; however, as salaried functionaries they lack the power base from which to press effectively to meet inadequacies of which they often are painfully aware.*

Although it is possible for administrators to maintain a public illusion of agreement, they would do so at the expense of the healthy, enthusiastic involvement in and commitment of their employees to the task at hand. This does not mean that the employees may not share some or all goals. In fact most of them are striving, at least in part, toward the goal of promoting the health of individuals, families, and the community. The variety of beliefs about the best approach toward achieving this goal is probably infinite. If the organizational structure can recognize and allow this variety, it will stimulate interactions that will probably lead to action that is more acceptable to a wide range of employees and increasingly effective in improving patient care. This issue might certainly arise in a private health care institution such as a small hospital, which may operate on the assumption that its continued growth and prosperity as currently structured are the only ways to achieve optimal health in the community that it serves. Some major alterations in the standard economic commitment would be necessary to change this attitude. But the employees, including nurses, could be much more valuable, comfortable participants in political activity if they could work within a framework that acknowledges their employment by or association with one

*Bohr, R., and Kaplan, H.: Employee protest and social change in the health care organization, American Journal of Public Health **61**:2229-2235, Nov., 1971.

of many contributors to the solution of a given societal problem, rather than expecting them to support the status quo whether it meets the goal or not. It is not intended to imply that such a major shift in the orientation of an institution is easy or probable. In the shift of the National Foundation from controlling poliomyelitis to stopping birth defects, one of the basic features remained the same—the involvement of many people raising a lot of money.

The involvement of group activities around societal issues is certainly a problem for employees of governmental health units who are, by law, constrained from open participation in partisan politics. Nonetheless, even public employees should have the freedom to participate in discussions of political (in the broad sense) issues. This is so particularly in the case of health workers who are involved in the provision of services to the public. The dissemination of relevant factual data seems appropriate and necessary, even as the use of a civil service position to further a personal campaign seems inappropriate. We are aware, of course, that "facts" can say many things. If the reader is moved to begin a public education campaign regarding some health-related issue, much advance research is indicated. The professional should provide complete, accurate, understandable data and present them in such a way that the readers can safely draw their own conclusions. Anyone can probably recall campaigns in which data were so presented that from one perspective the material was perfectly clear and obvious, the alternative view was obscure and threatening, and the truth of the matter was known to lie somewhere in between. The current campaigns for and against the passage of the Equal Rights Amendment in the several states resemble such an instance. On the one hand, femininity is doomed to complete extinction unless the measure is stopped at once, and on the other hand, there is no hope for equal opportunity unless the measure becomes law instantly. In fact many equal rights are protected under existing law, but this amendment reinforces the protection and probably would serve to speed up the equalization process. It is doubtful whether legal equality will deprive women of the features that embrace the essence of femininity, since this is, at least in large part, derived from physical fact and such facts are not changed by law.

The response of many nurses and much of the public to the nursing profession's economic security program illustrates a common misconception. Again, probably because of nursing's religious roots, some people believe that nurses have no strong feelings or concerns beyond the public good (vaguely defined) and that they are willing to accept whatever is given them in return for service. Alternatively, since most nurses are women, others may believe that their income is merely supplemental to a family income and, if increased, would only serve to purchase more needless extras. Like any members of society, nurses have both personal and professional goals that may be affected by political decisions. They ought to speak out regarding these real or potential effects. At the same time, they must continue to separate their personal and private interests from their professional interests and to act appropriately on each. As the 1974 convention of the American Nurses' Association assembled in San Francisco, nurses at forty northern California hospitals began picketing to emphasize their views in a dispute with hospital administrators. Both economic issues and patient care issues were involved, one of which was the desired use of only properly prepared staff in specialty units such as coronary care divisions. Said one picketer,[1] "We are a new breed of nurses, fighting for our rights and those of our patients." A convention goer commented to one of us "I wish I could support them [but] I'm an old-fashioned nurse." The conflict involved in changing interests and approaches to issues will be with nurses for a long time. There is much concern presently over changes in federal laws (the Taft-Hartley amendments) that facilitate the use of collective bargaining in nonprofit institutions. Many professional nurses are employed by community hospitals and have not yet had access to group action such as collective bargaining regarding working conditions. Nurses are also hesitant about using such a method should it become available. It is important to remember that for a professional in the health field, working conditions include the existence of a system that truly promotes health and well-being of the public. With this in mind individuals who feel constrained from using powerful tactics for their own economic advancement may well see their way clear to engage in mass action for the public good.

The adherence to policy and the acceptance of orders are two characteristics of bureaucratic organizations that may affect the nurse's involvement in political activities. Both of these seem closely related to the issues discussed in the preceding chapter on tension reduction and are intimately related to the traditional socialization process through which the professional nurse is put. If one follows the policies, written and unwritten, and obeys whatever commands are issued, one will not be contributing to the amount of tension present in an organization. If one can accept the concept that some tension and conflict are useful and even necessary, one can also see that there may be times for breaking or changing policy or for refusing to follow orders. This may happen in the case of a nurse who becomes involved in the resolution of political conflicts relevant to health. Nurses are not the only professionals (or would-be professionals) caught in the bind of bureaucracy without the necessary knowledge, skill, or experience to get out. The following anecdote was shared by a registered record librarian at an informal meeting recently. She said, "If my boss, the admininstrator, tells me to release a record without proper consent, I won't do it. . . . I hand it to him so that he can." In the web of bureaucracy this individual has apparently come to believe that an approach which keeps the system going, avoids confrontation with the boss, and does not risk one's employment status discharges a professed obligation to guard the privacy of health data.

The development of policy that relieves one

of decision-making power and freedom of choice can become extremely restraining. The popular novel *Catch 22* elaborates in tragicomic detail on the hazards to individual sanity inherent in the military bureaucracy. The use of quotas for the inclusion of various minority groups has a similar stifling result. The intent was to ensure that members of groups frequently underrepresented have assured openings should they wish to engage in a given activity, such as higher education or employment. The impact has been to set rigid quota specifications, which remove choice from both the majority and minority groups and severely limit all freedom. T. H. White[2] discusses this phenomenon as it affects school integration and the reorganization of the Democratic Party. The health parallel might be response to Joint Commission on Accreditation requirements: the institutions might respond to guidelines as laws without considering their relevance or engaging in dialogue regarding possible alternatives. Nursing personnel have frequently become trapped in this kind of system. The acceptance of responsibility for maintaining a Kardex as a nursing contribution, yet using it only as a means of communicating medical and administrative data and not recognizing the lack of substantive nursing content may be an example. It might be better to reject the policy of maintaining the Kardex until the substantive nursing diagnostic terminology that can make the Kardex a real nursing tool has been developed.

The slow rate of change within bureaucratic structures may contribute to nursing's limited involvement in political activity. As in the case with birth and death, change is sure but often slow. The individual nurse so frequently encounters the fact that one's activities do little to hasten or retard such eventualities that it is easy to cease trying. Suggestions and ideas have so little observable impact on the bureaucratic pyramid that one fails to consider any possibility of impact on the political system. Here a sense of historical perspective can be most useful. We might point out that not all political systems are bureaucracies and that there are

undoubtedly some organizations which are more susceptible to change in observable increments. It is essential that nurses both locate these other systems and consider changing the structure of traditional systems.

It is also important in the process of change that nurses who leave the bureaucracy and those who remain and keep it functioning not lose each other. Although it may well be true that many nurses are not living up to the level of knowledge they have or potential impact they could have on health care, at each moment each nurse is doing what seems possible and what seems to be most effective to achieving progress. If a nurse does a little private duty and spends most of the week in a counterculture clinic or campaigning on local issues, it does not necessarily imply more or less commitment to health care than the behavior of the nurse who organizes and supervises a fifty-bed unit in a large hospital and helps out on the Red Cross bloodmobile once a year. It is too easy to see the supposedly bad (anticommunity or antiestablishment) actions of the others and to overlook the healthy contributions of each: "We need each other, not to be the same but to be different."*

The history of American nursing has been greatly influenced by a group of nurses who have remained outside the traditional organizational structure—the private duty nurse or private nurse practitioner. The number of such nurses has decreased in recent years because of the proliferation of intensive care units in hospitals, yet many remain in practice. Conversation with a private nurse practitioner indicates that one attraction to this field is the relative absence of organizational constraints and existence of greater freedom to exercise independent judgment in the care of patients. Some of these nurses have readily bridged the dichotomy between the traditional role of tension reducer and the more active role of involvement in political activity. Many of the new clinical nurse specialists and clinicians seem to be interested

---

*Sermon by John Sherer, St. Mark's Lutheran Church, Spokane, Washington, on January 27, 1973.

in a variety of community-based practices rather than employment in a bureaucratic organization. If they are making the decision on a logical deduction that they can better fulfill their professional responsibilities in that way, it would seem also that they might be able to affect the course of political decisions related to health. On the other hand, if they are merely fleeing bureaucracy or seeking to imitate the apparent independence of the physician, they may remain as constrained as if they were in a small organizational "box." This is also an area in which a word can be most devastating to a goal—*private practice* describes an economic approach and *independent practice* can imply an attitude of disdain for others. The nurse calling a practice independent may alienate some potential allies.

Although buildings and bureaucracies may go together, the nurse who is not confined geographically may well be held by the same constraints as the hospital-based practitioner. The rigid lines of communication, the administrator-physician-male—dominated powerful board, and the struggle with policy and rules can exist as well in any physical plant. The public health or visiting nurse may feel as bound to the system and be as constrained from free activity as the ward head nurse.

As long as most health care organizations remain bureaucracies confined for the most part to hospitals, the limited contact between the nurses and the community may serve to limit the nurse's involvement in political activity. Even if the typical structure of a health care organization remains bureaucratic, the move toward providing health care to people through new types of community clinics and centers should make nurses more aware of the variety of political issues and conflicts related to health. This may, in turn, stimulate more nurses to participate in political activity when the health needs of society are involved. The truth of this potential is borne out by observation of the public health or community health nurse who, although working for a system as rigid as any hospital, more readily becomes involved in a range of community activities and issues.

References

1. Bay nurses strike hospitals, San Francisco Chronicle, June 8, 1974.
2. White, T. H.: The making of the president 1972, New York, 1973, Atheneum Publishers.

12

THE IMPACT OF PERSONAL BELIEFS

Because each nurse is an individual human being, each will have an individual outlook on life. Despite the tendency for congruence in belief among the members of identified social groups such as a profession, there remains a great deal of diversity. This will probably increase rather than decrease as societal stereotypes lessen and a wider range of individuals avail themselves of more diverse occupational choices. The personal opinions and beliefs of an individual nurse will affect both the decision to enter or avoid political conflicts and the stand on the issues that might eventually be taken. Several publications have dealt with this issue and have served as stimulus to our thinking; among them are Ujhely's *Determinants of the Nurse-Patient Relationship*[1] and Storlie's *Nursing and the Social Conscience.*[2] Although there are many that could be discussed, the personal beliefs most pertinent to participation in political dynamics would be one's philosophy of man, one's religious beliefs, and one's political stance. That does not imply that these three are mutually exclusive. One's political stance depends on one's interests and position on various controversial issues such as the view of man and beliefs about immortality and God or gods. The way in which individuals will vote or attempt to influence policy depends on their viewpoints about what they have, what they want, and to what extent they are willing to share with other people either that which they have or that which they want. This pertains to multiple factors, including economic and religious ones.

What one inherits, the amount of money one earns, at what type of job one makes a living, and the promotions and bonuses one anticipates are only a few of the economic influences. Rich people tend to see things differently from poor people. Urban workers tend to think differently from farm dwellers. Those who make their living through national or international affairs tend to think differently from those making a living in small towns. Women who are socialized to think of their earnings as less important, insignificant, or frivolous see the world differently from men who perceive themselves as the pivot of the economic wheel. Few nurses have come from the extremes of the income range. The acceptance of nursing as a "woman's field" has made it an acknowledged career for the daughter of an upward-striving family, and the relatively low cost of the diploma school made nursing feasible for many. The association of nursing with domestic functions has probably been a deterrent to recruits from upper middle and upper class groups. The same association may make nursing distasteful to families at the lower end of the economic spectrum, since it appears too much like the domestic labor cycle from which they might like to escape. Thus economically, nursing's interests are those of the broad middle portion of the system. Some nurses may have a tendency to remain cold to the economic issues in health care because of their remote nature. When the patient's fee is actually paid to an employee benefit fund, thence to an insurer and the hospital, and finally to the nurse, the concept of cost of health differs from what it might be if the dollar came (or was unable to come) from the patient's pocket to the nurse's hand directly. While arguments regarding complete removal of the fee for service mechanism from health care rage, it may be difficult for many nurses, if they have not had to pay out for much personal health care, to grasp the issue.

There is also an overlap between economic and geographical factors. *Regional politics* is a phrase that is applied to a geographical area in which a powerful common interest links the residents across local or state political boundaries. The link may be more than economic and reflect a common history, hero, or current problem. Nurses who have grown up in the Southwest, faced with a regional concern for water, will differ greatly from those whose eastern megalopolis origins orient them toward overpopulation and mass transportation issues.

Population mobility has altered the pattern of regional homogeneity, and identification of the regional tendency has not eliminated it. The distinction between one geographical area and another may be made on the basis of ethnic or racial identity. One need only mention the Yankee-Puritan of New England, the Irish of Boston, Italians of New Haven, the blacks in Harlem, or the Mexican-Americans of Los Angeles, to name a few. Nursing is composed of individuals from all these groups and others in varying quantities, although their impact as singular groups on the profession is difficult to evaluate. Recent evaluations have indicated that all the health professions had assimilated the supposedly dominant WASP (white Anglo-Saxon Protestant) values and were ignorant of and nonresponsive to other groups and their concerns.

One's personal political conviction usually does not dictate whether or not one will participate in conflict resolution but, rather, which position one will take on any given issue. The effect of a political stand which seems most pertinent to the involvement of nurses in conflict is that which is reflected to such an extent in the so-called younger generation—the view that the system is hopeless and participation in its machinations on any level is merely an exercise in futility. A much-debated work that describes this viewpoint is Reich's *The Greening of America*.[3] It is unclear to what extent this attitude is prevalent in nurses, but there have been research studies that point out the withdrawal of new graduates from efforts at changing nursing practice because they seem to perceive the bureaucratic system as beyond hope of changing (Kramer[4]). It would also seem that older nurses might be influenced in their willingness to engage in conflict by their perception of the effectiveness of such activities. By their age many nurses are eligible to be labeled part of the silent generation, which did not supposedly actively work toward the resolution of common problems. If this is true, that generation may find it impossible to change its whole identity and engage in the type of conflict resolution to which acceptance of the premises of a book such as this might lead.

Philosophy and religion

Ujhely[1] summarized the various viewpoints concerning man into four major categories. Although this is an oversimplification that hardly does justice to the heritage of philosophy, it does provide one with a swift overview. The four possibilities are the following: (1) humankind is basically good and rational; (2) humankind is basically bad and irrational; (3) humankind is basically the product of its environment; and (4) humankind is a combination of the first three. Although most people do not articulate a philosophy of humankind on which they consciously base their interactions, all individuals interact with those around them in ways that reflect one or another of these possible viewpoints. Nurses' professional behaviors would be no exception. If one looks carefully at the patient care given by any nurse, one could probably distinguish the major components of the view of humanity on which it is based. In addition, one might be able to predict the direction of the responses that would be elicited in the face of political conflicts.

If one sees humankind as basically good and rational, it is probably easy to accept the right of all persons to participate in decision making concerning their own destiny. The nurse with such an outlook will probably be more concerned with the inclusion of co-workers, patients, community members, or others in decision making regarding the health care system. They would be seen as having the ability to think through the issues and make a positive contribution to the outcome. Such ideation is behind the push to attend to patient's rights at all times during the provision of health care.

If one sees humankind as basically bad and irrational, it is more difficult to justify the involvement of many persons in decision making. One would be more likely to attempt to limit power to a few who would be labeled as capable of controlling their natures and mak-

ing correct choices. A nurse with such a view would most likely be comfortable with the role of prescriber in relation to community-wide health problems. That person might also be able to accept the placement of relatively few persons in positions of power, since this is a way of controlling the bad side of human nature. The use of patient education and community education would be minimized, unless it was used to increase conformity to a plan designed by the nurse-teacher.

If one sees humans as basically a product of their environment, one is probably less concerned with the involvement of individuals in any change process. A nurse with this viewpoint would most likely become involved in the planning and organization of health service systems on an impersonal level or in the problems of community environment, believing that the only way to change people and improve their health situation is to change the total situation. Experiences with the futility of individual effort and preoccupation with the suprapersonal aspects of the social and political scene indicate that this view is increasingly prevalent, especially among the younger adult group.

The person who does not hold rigidly to one view of human nature but sees that people are composed of both good and bad and are influenced by their environment is probably in agreement with most nurses. A nurse who has this eclectic view would shift in various settings, such as upholding the right of professionals to prescribe in the face of an identifiable disease entity, promoting the involvement of all in decision making regarding the ongoing provision of service, and working toward the management of the environment so that it does not have an adverse effect on individuals. Alternately such a nurse might force prescriptions on patients for their own good with no explanation, and yet might articulately complain about health care received personally because people "treated me like an idiot for trying to make my child ill" by erring in medications because the prescriber did not explain it.

Ethnic and racial categories blend and correlate with philosophical and religious beliefs, and these in turn become identified with the other characteristics of regions and geographical areas. For example, the Mormon religion greatly influences political policies in Utah—to the extent of affecting individuals, some of whom are nurses—because those who hold religious power overlap with those who hold the political power. Another example is moderate Lutheranism in Minnesota and Wisconsin, which influences political decisions and affects individuals, including nurses, because many of the most powerful persons (socially and economically) are also Lutheran. The various organized religious groups teach moral and social codes that go far beyond a narrow conception of group interest. Rather they develop within the individual, in addition to commitment to that religion, a mode of thinking about all aspects of living and about man himself, including his political side. Alternate views on abortion laws and practices have been directly linked to religious commitment. The provision of articles on safe nursing care for the woman seeking an abortion has been soundly attacked by nurses identifying with the anti-abortion (or pro-life) lobbies. They see the publication of information as condoning what is held to be immoral. Others argue that the professional is ethically bound to know how to care for each patient regardless of personal preferences. With the great decrease in membership in organized religious groups, only partially compensated for by the rise in so-called Jesus people and the interest of the young in various faiths, it might be hypothesized that articles of religious belief will have a decreasing impact on the attitudes and actions of the next generation.

As was mentioned briefly before, an individual's religious beliefs can strongly influence choice of approach to situations involving political conflict or dynamics. Many nurses see their profession as a religious vocation, particularly the many nursing nuns and deaconesses. Others at least relate their practice of nursing to duties incurred within their faith; the faith held has an impact. At the level of one-to-one patient care, the response to the dying patient is probably the best illustration of this. The meaning of death to individual nurses will be reflected in the kind of care, comfort, or assistance offered or withheld from the dying person, regardless of that person's beliefs. The fact that the dead person cannot later complain about the care limits the times the nurse may be directly challenged about specific practices.

On a broader level one's religion may set limits on those issues that are considered open to debate or conflict. A timely example that was mentioned earlier is the availability of abortion to the woman who desires one. Those whose religion declares this to be sinful in every way have had a more difficult time seeing this as a debatable question with many facets such as individual freedom, community integrity, medical care, legal precedent, and moral integrity. The issue of providing health care to disadvantaged populations is also one that lies close to religious views. In many places the only health care available to the disadvantaged has been provided by charitable religious groups as an outcome of their religious conviction. The care giver may come to believe that charity patients should take what they are given and like it. The availability of payment, such as from Medicare and Medicaid, is having a major impact on their charity system, the extent of which is not yet known. Those giving the care may still harbor the same attitudes, yet the charitable system may be operating with a reimbursable budget far larger than could have been imagined prior to the funding. The current movement defining the access to medical care as a right has precipitated many health care personnel into conflict over the provision of such care; those having ethical foundation for their involvement may have had greater difficulty in identifying their position.

The influence of religious belief on one's participation in "political" conflict can be seen in the traditional American separation of church and state. Most questions of conflict are seen as related to the governmental structure, and in fact many of them are related. If one sees one's profession as related to religion or if one treats the profession itself as a quasireligious group, as many professionals do, it is obvious that this would limit one's ability to participate in conflict situations. One illustration can be found in the responses to the economic security program of the American Nurses' Association. A great many nurses, and many of the public as well, believe that nurses practice their profession for the intrinsic rewards of helping people get well and not because it should also pay for the amenities of life. In fact the many nurses who are members of religious communities do practice out of such a commitment. Those who feel this way have seen it as extremely inappropriate for nurses to actively engage in conflict over the issue of salary. Even members of religious orders are changing attitudes on economic matters. The cost of supporting a community that includes many elderly, nonworking members is becoming prohibitive. For some nurses this view is carried even further. Not only is it inappropriate to engage in conflict for one's own betterment, even if such betterment might eventually result in better patient care, but it is inappropriate to engage in any conflict. The nurse should keep attention focused on the individual patient and care for him in any situation that society should dictate.

The brief discussion in this chapter has by no means exhausted the possible effects of personal beliefs on the nurse's participation in conflict resolution. Opinions or attitudes resulting from a person's strong commitment to a specific position in regard to any of these factors are not usually conscious. One need only cite the difficulty in altering the impact of Dixie attitudes in a nurse who grew up in the Deep South even long after she has moved to an area where significantly different attitudes predominate. The neglect of health problems of drug addicts, such as failure to identify and treat addicted newborns, may be another example. Beliefs about the willfully evil behavior of the parents have unintended consequences for the children.

Identification of beliefs and the tracing of their origin are essential to a nurse's rational behavior, since it is only in this way that decisions which nurses make will be based on more than opinion, underlying attitudes, or pseudocompassion used to mask underlying self-interest and motivations and unresolved intrapersonal conflicts. An examination of one's personal beliefs about the nature of humankind seems an appropriate starting point. From the discussion presented the reader may be better able to examine possible viewpoints regarding involvement in conflict resolution and develop a framework for the understanding of other nurses when confronted with their behavior in conflict situations.

The women's movement

A final area of personality that must be considered is the nurse's identity as a woman. We are delighted that changes in attitudes toward women have freed women to enter many fields; it may mean fewer women forced into nursing as the only way they could go and more men and women in the field who are committed to the professional goal and willing to work actively toward it. Both men and women in nursing are or should be acutely aware of how the female stereotype affects their achievement of professional goals. Although nurses are the largest group of professional women in the United States, they have been slow to join the feminist movement and apparently even slower to grasp its essential message of self-determination. This is the accumulative effect of being the classic handmaiden stereotype and being insulated in pseudoreligious bureaucracies. Aggressive wooing by advocates of the feminist movement may change this in the near future. The American Nurses' Association 1974 convention included a program called Women's Rights and The Nurse. One speaker was Wilma Scott Heide, past president of the National Organization for Women.

Nurses who challenge the stereotype that their education is more than an excellent stepping-stone to marriage and child rearing probably resemble women in the more classic professions. (See *Women in Medicine*[5] in which Lopate states that a woman seeking eligible bachelor physicians would better enter nursing and not work as hard as she might in medicine.) Such challenging nurses make career decisions earlier, tend to resist standard women's life-style pressures, and believe that professional career and personal life-style including family are compatible.

The society-wide nature of the issues relating to women are illustrated in the fact that schools such as the fashionable Katherine Gibbs School in Boston attract executive secretary students seeking to learn how to behave in all the ways that please the boss (always embodied as a HIM).[6] Despite talk regarding expanding job opportunities for women, college preparation, and the feminist movement, enrollment in the Katherine Gibbs chain of schools has increased since 1911 to the point where there are now six schools and 2,500 students. Students learn how to free the boss's valuable time by secretarial techniques such as never letting him into the files. Graduates from college have turned to the Gibbs' chain to learn a salable skill and become employables in the male-dominated business world. They are taught grooming perfection and adaptation to rigorous schedules. The owners and managers of the schools have been under attack for teaching women to be subservient. Although some students protest the details they are taught, others proclaim that it is great and that they have no interest in the women's movement. Gibbs' administrators point out that in spite of their old-fashioned approach, many women graduates move up to higher positions in management from their secretarial beginning.

Nurses who work in educational institutions are perhaps more conscious of the "equal pay for equal work" impact of the women's movement. It is difficult to justify paying a female assistant or associate professor much less than a male at the same rank, although arguments are put forth based on the lack of direct comparison if there are no men teaching in the same department, the lack of a truly competitive marketplace (on which the extremely high salaries paid medical and law school faculties are based), or the incomparability of teaching nursing and English. With this in mind it is easier to see how difficult it is to discover and validate if indeed nurses in general are being compensated at a generally lower rate than men with comparable responsibilities and education. For general duty nurses discriminatory rules such as those requiring women to wear outdated caps (or any old cap if she comes from a school that requires none) are easier to spot.

Nurses have fostered the male-dominant stereotype within nursing also. Men in nursing have moved toward higher paying, more powerful positions much more rapidly than women. This push is apparently based on the arguments used in business—that the men are more committed to their work, will stay in the job longer, and need more income to support a family. All these fantasies are being dispelled, albeit slowly, and it would behoove a female-dominated profession to examine whether or not it does a disservice to the majority of its members through traditional attitudes toward males. The low visibility of nursing as a responsible, responsive profession adds to the failure of nonnurses to identify the same issue. It may not be difficult to agree that $10,000 a year is too much to pay a person who says "ask your doctor" to every question—if you can get her to stand still long enough to give an answer at all. Nurses have remained relatively quiet also in such aspects of the women's movement as increasing women's knowledge about their own bodies, particularly the sexual aspects. Other women could be a powerful force behind nursing if they saw the point of perpetuating and improving it as a helping profession.

There has been little consideration of the relationships between those women who choose medicine and those who choose nursing. The medical profession is still male turf. In the health field a woman's place is predominantly to nurse the ailing, be sympathetic to those who complain, and slap surgical instruments into the physician's hand at his demand. Approximately 15% of medical students in the United States today are women, but it seems that little is done to prepare them for the problems they will face as they enter a male-dominated profession. One documentary[7] has been written detailing women's encounters with sex discrimination in forty-one medical schools across the United States. It does not aim at discouraging women from entering medical school but rather forewarns them of the heckling and belittlement they can expect. Offhand remarks about female anatomy, livening up lectures with pin-up pictures, ill-disguised contempt for women's bodies, and dismissal of many problems as being of "typical female origin" put female medical students in confusing situations and can further add to a desire never to be the female patient. This treatment of women in medicine does several things for nurses, generally negative. It drives some women into nursing as a way to avoid discrimination or as a result of it, but the associated frustration with not being in medicine can lower productivity. It also can promote an attitude of nonfeminism in any women who succeed in medicine, so that they are unable to recognize their feminine nursing colleagues as women and work with them to promote the cause of women in general. Many individuals responding positively to the doctor-dominated physician assistant programs indicate that they see this as a way to get even closer to their thwarted goal of medicine.

The pervasive male chauvinistic attitude of at least some physicians is not difficult to identify. In an attempt to open communications between physicians and nurses, Shirley Smoyak, R.N., Vice-Chairman of the National Joint Practice Commission, addressed an open letter to physicians by way of the letters column of the *American Medical News*.[8] The answers in response[9] were marginally relevant to the issues raised. One answer covered the superiority of medicine because of its masculinity and correspondingly lower status of nursing because it is composed of persons who are less bright, less educated, and women. Another invoked the sacred status of the family, indicating that maintenance of one masculine head was the foundation of stability. Yet a third reply referred several times to the law of God as if He spoke only to physicians and they conveyed the message of truth to the remainder of the world.

The effect of the traditional use of nursing as a time filler before marriage is well illustrated in this story from Europe. Somewhat in the style of Florence Nightingale, more than fifty years later a nurse was the youngest and almost the first woman to land on the beach of Normandy during that historic battle of World War II. She was a fully trained nurse and a member of the Queen Alexandria Imperial Nursing Service, with the assignment of quickly setting up a tent hospital on the beach. As the dead and wounded became visible, the guns and noises became real. She described the feeling as if it were a nightmare, as though the world had gone mad. It led to a feeling that the closer one was to danger the closer one was to people—anybody and everybody. She had been raised in a conservative family and had been a member of the Conservative Party. After the war she became a more active member of another party and felt that she had more sympathy for others and greater ability to help them. On the beach at Normandy, she met the man she later married, and when she was assigned to establish a proper hospital at Antwerp at the end of the war, she ended her nursing career and returned to Britain. As she adopted a traditional woman's life-style, the power potential she had attained through experience went with her, of no further direct value to the profession of nursing. It should be remembered that she may well have actively contributed to the advancement of health care through continuing some traditional woman's community activity such as volunteer work, as have many other nurses. However, current evidence shows that this is not as effective in achieving goals as direct professional involvement.

Equality in economic opportunity for women as a principle is sound. For the issue to be resolved there must be examination of specifics as they relate to public policy. The United States Department of Labor is proposing that disabilities associated with pregnancy and childbirth be treated like other temporary disabilities. Some would assert that economic protection for childbirth is to the female the same as economic protection for the loss of limb is to a male. One problem with that assertion is that childbirth can generally be anticipated, unlike accidents, and that it is at least in principle a healthy, happy process. Should the employer be allowed to discriminate against women by not paying this expense? For single women bearing children outside of marriage the economic protection factor is a different public issue. Some would argue that because of moral standards such women should not be supported; others claim that their need for support is as great or greater. If one upholds the principle of some compensation for the working woman who is temporarily away from the job because of childbearing, the question must be answered as to how the cost will be covered. It is most certain that eventually the price will be passed on through raises in the cost of consumer goods and services.

Despite the arguments that such practices will encourage more women to work and weaken the family structure, there is an alternate viewpoint. Social and organizational consideration for the childbearing woman might in fact strengthen the family. Young couples who depend on the wife's income often develop deep conflict over the postponement of pregnancy, or the rearing of children who were conceived ahead of schedule, or the sharing of traditional child-rearing and homemaking tasks. As such strains persist, the strengths of marriage are threatened. Rather than a sex discrimination issue, the relationship of childbearing women to the job situation represents the tip of an iceberg of change in the social order.

The dehumanization elements of bureaucratic systems come to mind in various ways. One is through the frequently used "statistics" from the Bureau of Labor Statistics, as though statistics in themselves are useful in helping to improve the condition of life. The number of working mothers (many undoubtedly nurses) has increased significantly over the past few years. More than 57% of all women with children between 6 and 17 years old worked during 1972 as compared with 45% of the women with children under 6 years old. The proportion of black working wives rose from 26% in 1969 to 41% in 1972. Economic pressures and social and cultural factors such as divorce and declining birthrates have their influence. As these factors act to pressure mothers to work, another need becomes inevitable—day care centers. Can day care centers actually replace maternal fostering of youngsters or are they a substitute implemented because of pressures from an inhuman power structure?

Not only are rather drastic changes in laws, expectations, and on a lesser scale attitudes in process regarding heterosexual interactions and relative male/female positions but homosexuality has also come under a great deal of scrutiny, and many including some homosexuals have pushed to make open practices more acceptable. This may have been stimulated in some measure by the 1969 recommendation of the National Institute of Mental Health encouraging a revision of the laws and employment practices as they concern persons who admit to homosexuality; this was later backed by the American Psychiatric Association, which removed homosexuality from the list of mental disorders. Although the focus has been on change in societal response and acceptance, the original National Institute of Mental Health task force has stressed that the greatest need is for health professionals and others to learn more about the whole phenomenon and potentially focus on preventive aspects. Whereas it is difficult to draw any impressive or meaningful conclusions, this material does form a part of the necessary awareness of the place of nursing in the total social picture, with the subsequent effects of responses to individual nurses. Certainly in the minds of a portion of the society a woman's profession, in the classic sense of nursing, is a place that harbors both female homosexuals looking for partners and male homosexuals who are unable to make it in the traditional men's fields. Opening awareness of the multiplicity of reasons for which one chooses a profession may decrease the prevalence of both erroneous views.

At any rate it is hoped that the woman's movement will reduce the probability of the following case ever occurring again:

A 38-year-old woman came for therapy following what was apparently a suicide attempt with an overdose of barbiturates and alcohol. . . . After high school she matriculated at a school of nursing where again dates were plentiful and she excelled in her work.

She met and subsequently fell in love with a young law student, quite handsome, with a promising future. . . . They were married while he was attending law school and she was completing her nursing training. Completing her education first, she was able to obtain immediate work at the University hospital, where again she was both accepted and praised. She was there for two years. When her husband completed law school they moved to another city. . . .

Thereafter she was to attend to her new family. . . . She was contented at home; in a short time there were two children.

When she openly wondered about the possibility of "keeping her hand in" nursing, her husband, as well as her parents, indicated that there was really no need for it and it might be an embarrassment to the husband. After all, the wife of a successful man shouldn't be handling bed pans. She offered no resistance—there was too much going for them.

She made friends easily and in her own right ascended the social ladder. . . . She was known not only as the wife of a successful young man but as a person in her own right.

It was in this setting and circumstance that he was sought out as a full partner in a metropolitan law firm. . . .

The move was made, a new home purchased, children placed in the right schools, proper country club and church joined. . . . She tried to make the social contacts expected of her, but she was now new-low person on the totem pole. . . .

She became increasingly withdrawn. . . .As she withdrew, she used alcohol and barbiturates increasingly. . . . She became determined to return to nursing despite the feelings of her husband. But then the problem of licensing in a different state arose. Refresher courses became a requirement, but her drinking made this impossible. . . .

The husband in the situation above cannot be blamed, since he was acting within the legal and societal rights of his role; precedent dictates that the wife follow the husband in his need for achievement. . . .

There is a fear that the development of woman will make her less of a wife, a mate, that [he] might lose her. . . .

If one must discover the tragic flaw in this patient, she must be faulted for leaving her profession in the beginning, thus depriving herself of residual power for changes that had to be made later. . . .

Charles Reich in "The Greening of America" reflects on what is perhaps the inordinate importance placed on credentials in our society: "In a world where men are recognized only by their credentials, to lose credentials is to cease being a human being."

Agreeing with this statement in general, some however, would substitute the word "persons" for men.*

The reader may not have been pleased with the title of this unit, particularly with the use of the word *dilemma.* Many nurses have not consciously felt pulled or divided between various choices in regard to political issues. At least in the current situation, however, it is the rare individual who has not begun to look at many issues as debatable, even if he or she is not prepared to take a stand on one side or the other. It is our goal that this discussion make the reader more conscious of the various factors which may be pulling the individual nurse into or out of participation in conflict or into one side or the other of an ongoing debate. It is hoped that reflection on being a professional, functioning as a tension reducer within health care organization, being an individual with certain beliefs, and constrained by societal sexual expectations will facilitate the integration of new theoretical material in such a way that it can be put to use both for the good of the communities that nurses serve and with an increase in their own satisfaction with their behaviors.

---

*Seidenberg, R. S.: Dear Mr. Success: Consider your wife, Wall Street Journal, Feb. 7, 1972. Reprinted with the permission of The Wall Street Journal, copyright Dow Jones & Company, Inc., 1972.

References

1. Ujhely, G. B.: Determinants of the nurse-patient relationship, New York, 1968, Springer Publishing Co.; Inc.
2. Storlie, F.: Nursing and the social conscience, New York, 1970, Appleton-Century-Crofts.

3. Reich, C. A.: The Greening of America, New York, 1971, Bantam Books, Inc.

4. Kramer, M.: Reality shock; why nurses leave nursing, St. Louis, 1974, The C. V. Mosby Co.

5. Lopate, C.: Women in medicine, New York, 1968, Josiah Macy, Jr. Foundation.

6. Gumpert, D.: Women's liberation has all but bypassed the Katy Gibbs chain, Wall Street Journal, March 15, 1974.

7. Why would a girl go into medicine: medical education in the United States, a guide for women, Old Westbury, N. Y., 1973, Feminist Press.

8. Smoyak, S.: My opinion, American Medical News, p. 13, Feb. 11, 1974.

9. Letters, American Medical News, p. 6, March 4, 1974.

UNIT FOUR

PREPARATION FOR ACTION

13

ANALYSIS OF SYSTEMS AND ORGANIZATIONS

The slowness with which change occurs discourages many nurses, especially those who are poorly endowed with patience. In 1915 Margaret Sanger was indicted for using the mail to provide information to people about birth control.[2] Ten years ago nurses were not allowed to discuss the matter with patients, or did so only under certain conditions. Fifty years after the Margaret Sanger incident the United States government was supporting a birth control program. Health insurance was discussed for at least thirty years before Medicare legislation was adopted in 1966. A more comprehensive national program of health insurance is still under discussion. Nurses have historically worked among the indigent, in both urban and rural areas, and have been only too well aware of the needs and conditions of a large segment of the public. President Johnson's "war on poverty" in 1964 was not a new idea. It had only taken thirty-six years to develop from 1928, when

President Hoover campaigned to abolish poverty.[2] Vaccination became widely practiced in spite of early hostility, and health officials have now gone so far as to question its relevancy. Many cities are still arguing the issue of fluoridation and refusing to implement changes in the public water supply after fifteen to twenty years of professionally recognized effectiveness. One reason for slowness in change relates to the turnover in population and the loss of much from the past with the turnover. People die and their memory of events and conditions die with them. Those born at the same time are born without benefit of memory.

Despite being a technologically advanced nation, Americans have been described as "borne back into our past" by nostalgia. The fondness for the "good old days" has been present throughout American history and is manifested in many ways. At present the yearning for those romanticized days is es-

171

pecially strong. It is brought out in films such as "The Great Gatsby" and "American Graffiti" and can be noted in the market of old-time articles of glass and clothing, a return of 1920-1930 hair styles, and the demand for early model cars. The New England Puritans looked back on their ancestors as a special breed who left good homes in England to establish a pure, godly community in America but contended that their descendants were poisoned with materialistic devices, immorality, and conflicts. The past seemed better. In the early 1800s began the development of industry and a new financial system. It resulted in a serious depression, and the growth profits made through speculation seemed to undermine and invalidate the traditional American philosophy about work. People wished for the earlier days when finance was simple and they could depend almost exclusively on the labors of their own hands. During the 1900s, industry sprang up everywhere and the society of independent farmers was replaced by a society of underfed, underpaid factory workers who probably longed to be back in the days when America was new and men were their own masters.

Today history repeats itself again. The early twentieth century now is thought of nostalgically because its crime, pollution, and congestion were minor in comparison with those of today. These problems are well known and could be listed. Perhaps two problems stand out above others—the confrontation of Congress and the public with the Office of the President, and the threat of political blackmail in the rise in kidnapping and terrorism.

The aftermath of the Watergate affair will undoubtedly be traumatic, and a considerable length of time will be consumed in the shaping and reshaping of the basic underpinning of institutions along with the political processes and all of government. The institution of the Presidency must be reaffirmed. Congress must regain strength lost over past decades. Distraught with personal issues, former President Nixon was unable to portray a clear picture of who was in charge as it related to big issues. With Secretary of State Kissinger's efforts some triumphs could be claimed by former President Nixon in foreign affairs. On some matters such as national health insurance and further revenue sharing he was able to maintain an image of leadership. At a time when Congress might regain increased control, it is having difficulty coming to grips with its internal problems or preempting more aggressively while the opportunity is present to fill the void.

The 1974 elections allowed the Democrats to capture increasing elected power. This would seem a logical time for Democrats to meet and shape alternatives for the future. The elders in the Democratic Party would be the logical movers to that end. The extent to which they have been able to move is for the twelve of them to form two task groups, one on foreign affairs and one on domestic affairs. Eighty-one-year-old Averell Harriman could have been expected to be a "natural" for the position of the central figure in the area of foreign affairs. For lack of another to head it the economist Walter Heller consented to serve as advisor on domestic affairs, but no task force has yet been made operational, even on an interim basis. The Republicans are likewise unable to present a united front. Some of the stronger members are attempting to rebuild the Republican Party by denouncing any responsibility by the party for the Watergate affair and claiming that Nixon is totally to blame. At other times they were obliged to seek support for and from him so it resulted in a Dr. Jekyll and Mr. Hyde image to the citizenry. The effect was a deepening public disillusionment with all of government and politics; this is supported by results obtained from public polls. The irony of it all is that people generally are becoming more alienated from participation in the political process.

So was the past better? Man and nature were seemingly closer then. Perhaps man was closer to other men because there were no automobiles or televisions to separate them. They entertained themselves and each other.

Husbands and wives made their marriages work somehow, so that divorces were few. Perhaps men and women enjoyed their work more when they could derive satisfaction from creating a whole product with their own hand; that is, the cobbler made the entire pair of shoes and the housewife cooked meals from unprepared components. If people continue to look at the bright side of earlier years, the natural tendency is to become discouraged with their lives, since why should one strive to create anything new only for it to be buried in a better past.

It becomes necessary, however, to consider alternative views to the brighter side. The brighter yesterdays are often greatly exaggerated, and its serious problems ignored. The lives of human beings have indeed been improved over past centuries. Perhaps the success of marriages was caused by the unavailability of divorce. A toothache no longer creates anguish as it did in years past but is now quickly treated by a dentist, and the tooth need not be extracted painfully without anesthesia. One hundred years ago mothers and infants died early, whereas women today look forward with some confidence to having and enjoying their children who will not die or be crippled by disease before reaching adulthood.

Political, economic, and social discrimination created a highly unequal sharing of life's benefits, although admittedly there remains yet much to be desired. Perhaps there were fewer tensions of the nature people experience today, and many uncertainties that afflicted men and women then are no longer as serious. Indian warfare, destruction of total food supplies by insects and weather, and political issues were no less uncertain or troublesome. Not all people were agreed as to the fighting of wars or believed in certain religious doctrines. Early medical handbooks contained remedies for nervous stomachs.

Organizational change

The democratic process itself is slow. It is more than the formal process of election but is a process affecting people every day, in school and outside. People debate, hear, report, argue, protest, petition, investigate, and associate with one another. Congress is addressed with a problem. Investigation is begun by committees that seek support and comments. Bills are revised and passed into statute through the whole system of pressure groups and the public, committees, Congress, and the President. Public debate, criticism, and review and new data eventually lead to a revised version of the statute, which was somehow the outgrowth of the original perceived problem.

The problems are identified by private individuals, people anywhere, and do not come to the attention of politicians until they have created significant discomfort. Matters of private concern remain so for a long time before they become public concerns, and it is at that point that government becomes involved. Government through its structure can do things that nobody else can. The slowness of the process has the effect of developing more support because the problem continues to nag on and public attention is drawn to it. Solutions or projects to deal with it seek more creative approaches, and the public is moved to action Schattschneider states:

> We ought to try to get accustomed to thinking about the future of government for several reasons. Government is the most successful idea in the world, but for all its success and importance it is something imperfect. There is no ideal state. After thousands of years it is still a mixture of good and evil. The flaw in the idea is that government, the basis of the social order, is itself disorderly. About the best that can be said for government is that it solves one problem by creating another, and that therefore, we get the bitter with the sweet.*

Our conviction holds that the changes necessary in the current system must be brought about through a process that is consistent with democracy and visible to those of the public who are or should be interested. Decisions in a true democracy are not made behind closed doors, neither should a profession exist except to serve society. More-

*Schattschneider, E. E.: Two hundred million Americans in search of a government, New York, 1969, Holt, Rinehart & Winston, Inc.

over, the process of change must be carefully deliberated. Within the professional organizations things must be thought through. Their goals should be stated, premises viewed openly, alternatives explored, and conclusions questioned. A professional organization has the opportunity of filling the unique function of providing a forum for debate of issues and for direction of accountability for action taken, which means therefore that it is here where credit or blame can be affixed. This responsibility is vital to any professional organization, especially when, at this time, not only the public but professionals as well have lost faith in such organizations.

Representation of the interest affected by professional organizations and health care institutions must exist so that there is opportunity to be heard. Neither health professional organizations nor health care institutions should operate without hearing those who want to be heard as they have done in the past. Representation means that administrators and staff must listen to those on whom their actions have an impact. Although this may sound blatantly obvious, it is difficult to accomplish in actuality. Responsiveness to needs is a further requirement for democratic functioning and service. Responsiveness is difficult to measure because people perceive problems and solutions in various ways. However, careful attention must be given to what seems generally to be the real problem, and the organizational structure should not prevent the overall body from working toward its goals.

In addition, two other aspects might serve as guidelines in improving or in some ways reorganizing existing professional structures. First, a relative equality of all members should be maintained. Some members should not be pushed to feel like a barely tolerated fringe group, since every member is important. Second, although leadership is necessary and differences in personality cause some to be more influential than others, organizations should be structured so that all are given an opportunity for participation. Then those who opt to remain silent or neutral have clearly done so at their own choice.

Questions arise about how best to structure the health system to serve the public, the nursing profession, the other professional organizations, and health care agencies. Several questions come to mind. Should establishment of financial appropriation and authorization functions be separate? Is a ceiling to be placed on the budget? Where in the organizational level should debate occur regarding priorities? What mechanism(s) guarantee coordination between collection of fees and how they are spent? How is compliance to mandates to be assured?

As to the professional organization, should it be divided into broad interest areas or into areas of subspecialty? Are multiple disciplinary groupings the best approach toward development of greatest overall expertise? Do single interest divisions respond better to input from the outside? If the organization is divided into multiple-interest or disciplinary groupings, should they be related or deliberately different?

Monitoring of the executive level is basic, whether in a professional organization or any health service organization that employs nurses. The decision must be made as to what activities are subject to monitoring. Is the monitoring of fund acquisition and expenditure the only really essential area requiring oversight? If internal jurisdiction and procedure must be optimally carried out, what committees or system encourages efficiency and economy yet guarantees maximum participation? Well-known examples of the complexity of factors that protect organizations from outside interruption are multiple standing committees (with duplications) and committees so large that they are immobilized when expediency of response is necessary. Are subcommittees meaningful in carrying out necessary work or is establishment and maintenance of a system of subcommittees a method to guarantee continuation of the status quo?

Three alternative schemes for reorganization are proposed. Perhaps no one is a panacea to all circumstances or types of organization. Each should be explored carefully before a system is changed or retained. One system provides for multiple-interest committees or sectioning of subject matter that is similar. All such divisions would be exclusive and have equal significance, power, and responsibility. The second system provides for a drastic reduction in the number of committees, sections, or divisions; each, like its counterpart in the first system, would consist of multiple interests and be exclusive. This second system, however, would deal with a greater diversity of subject matter. The third scheme provides for a combination of single- and multiple-interest divisions, committees, or sections. In the three systems the budgetary or economic aspects differ. In the first, groups, committees, or sections would determine a budget ceiling for acquisition and allocation; authorization and appropriation would be separate. In the second, some groups, committees, or sections would have the combined function of collecting monies (fees or funds), but others would acquire, appropriate, and authorize expenditure of monies. The third proposal establishes a separate body to deal with budget. It would combine the acquisition (appropriation) responsibility with that of authorization of expenditures. It might not include the power to establish and spend fees and charges, however, and the budget group might not represent the entire range of interests present in the organization.

Any reorganization requires a search and examination of concepts underlying the divisions within a larger system. Health care would be the larger system, and the nursing profession would be a division of the system. Changing the divisions within systems is a difficult undertaking, both intellectually and practically taxing. From experiences such as reorganizations at governmental levels, it is possible to see the inherent risks. Reorganization at the conceptual level is not synonymous with the reality of reform. What seems like a sparkling new organizational approach today becomes the out-of-date inadequate organization of tomorrow.

Questions such as those that plague government plague organizations of all kinds. How many standing committees are necessary to expedite accomplishing what must be done and to sufficiently spread the work load? Special committees are probably always necessary at some point, but there are diminishing returns as the numbers are increased. Public interest can become diffused too broadly, or alternately joining committees within only one specific organization may weaken the benefits that are created by difference.

To stimulate beginning consideration of one possible change, the reader is urged to apply the preceding discussion to the following example taken from the economic and social realm. Changing a major institution, such as the health care system of private enterprise, can be an overwhelming task. There are requirements of analysis and consideration of consequences that must precede any action, and they may provoke a number of reactions, desired or not. The private enterprise system, particularly as related to large corporations, has come under scrutiny of late and indeed may be headed for change.

Bauer[3] provides a suitable analysis of what one suggested direction for change, increasing social responsibility, might produce. If a firm determines to assume social responsibility, it should do so within some context of its usual activities before the change. Even so, the added cost of social programs may be a form of taxation without representation on the investor, the customer, and the employer. Firms could become subject to a social audit to ascertain performance criteria for the socially responsible behavior. Any change in the usual mode of operation will necessitate a great deal of education—for executives, employees, stockholders, and the consumer. Basic business techniques will also be subjected to change. How can minority struggles, costs and gains from antipollution devices, and job retraining be shown in a usual profit-and-loss accounting system? The bare beginnings of this are present in the Securities and Exchange Commission's requirement that relationships between compliance with environmental laws and projected earnings be determined. This must be done only if the impact of the controls on the earnings is significant.

Health systems

In many instances nurses retain the concept that each person must exist by his or her own strength and ability to play a shrewd game. Our philosophy of group interaction, which is consistent with most stated philosophies of nursing, is that the nurse's role is to help people to become the best they are capable of being in domains related to health. How can nurses who hold to the latter philosophy survive and produce change in a world prevalent with the all-too-frequent inhumanity of the former? It is somewhat parallel to the novel *From Here to Eternity*,[3a] in which the boy from the poverty of a rural Kentucky setting joined the army in the hopes of being a bugler. The organization wanted him to box and to continue even after he accidentally blinded someone whom he considered his friend. In his conflict with the organization he is like the young nurse who has a patient needing nursing care that no one else on the nursing team possesses. The nurse may be a woman who "wants to help people" and learned to give such care but who is in an organization that wants her to assume responsibility for Ward 15A from 8 A.M. to 3 P.M. and is caught in the position of keeping patient records and keeping the administration happy. To do so, the crucial bedside care of patients is delegated to much less skilled personnel. If a patient dies because of the action of such an unprepared person and the nurse's conscience finally leads her to seek advice from other professionals, the advice may well be to "do it the hospital's way," despite knowing that the aide could not do the job and she should have taken care of that patient because that is what she was trained for. There is the risk of finally being labeled a rebellious staff nurse, demoted, and discouraged; soon leaving to assume another job in another field. At one point the nurse sees the distress of the profession and the public. She wants to return to resume nursing patients but has learned that although the profession might give lip service to consumer participation, the administration structures can continue to destroy attempts of nurses to be independent in their judgment regarding who should take care of the patient needing clinical skills that no one else on the nursing team possessed.

Many nurses are caught in versions of this same trap. As a beginning, one necessary lesson for the nurse is a realization that there is no ideal government, no ideal program, no ideal organization. After many years health agencies and programs are a mixture of good and bad. Even after thousands of years governments also provide a picture of a similar mixture. Government, which is the basis of an orderly society, is disorderly in and of itself. Health agencies, which are the providers of health services, are equally disorderly. Goals and roles, communication and responsibilities, gaps and overlaps are only some of the problems. Most accurately it might be said that government at all levels and health agencies and programs of all kinds solve problems by creating others so that society must accept the undesirable with the good. Questions are raised by this type of awareness as well.

Some lying and deception may have been inherent in government from the beginning; it may be necessary and/or possibly justifiable. The decision as to whether it is within acceptable limits is a complex one. Harvard University political science students were presented with several case studies[4] and asked by their professors whether the officials were right or wrong. Their responses indicated that they overwhelmingly supported deceptive techniques when used on behalf of something in which they believed. That was less surprising than the students' acceptance of the widespread deceit and lying surrounding the Watergate situation. The decisions were made based on cost-benefit, chances of getting caught, and if caught, how much would it hurt? The Harvard University study pointed out that greater emphasis is necessary on acceptable and unacceptable behavior. It suggested that the Watergate affair may not negatively affect future American leaders. Although a case can be made by the optimist that the recent scandals may have such an impact on the nation that there will be a return to some widely accepted ethical standards, an equally strong case can perhaps be made that the lowered moral standards in areas of business, labor, and other areas as well as within government have set the standard acceptable in society generally. If it is true that society either lives up or down to the standards of its leaders, perhaps there will be a tightening of expectations, with lying and deception becoming more risky and unexcused by others.

Where to begin

In learning how to approach any system or organization that one desires to change, cookbook approaches are not always helpful. Specifically nurses who have become involved in a struggle to drop such recipes for patient care might well be inhibited by a rigid formula from the development of more appropriate sophistication. There are some general points to bear in mind, however, and the first is that knowledge from multiple sources of data and increasing consultation with more sources will increase the completeness of the picture.

Data regarding any organization should include its offical publications, including charter or founding document, and any current commentary regarding its role or position. Thus with the United States political system one contemplates essays by founding fathers, state and federal constitutions, and current public documents. Human data sources are at least as important and should include representatives of the following: (1) those who belong to the organization and are committed to it; (2) those who are outside the organization and are opposed to it; (3) those in either group who remain neutral; (4) those who receive services from the organization; and (5) neutral students of the area in which the organization operates. In all cases each item of information should be evaluated critically for important factors such as the potential good or harm to the organization done by sharing the material, the degree of freedom within which the information was shared (or coercion applied to obtain it), and the consistency of information among various sources. It is helpful if some time can elapse between data collection and the need for action based on those data. Reflection can aid one in making the most of even inadequate data. There is also a need for constant interaction with those in a system about which one is concerned. After a problem has arisen is too late to begin learning what went on.

One example of how the passage of time and advent of new ways of handling data can lead to the development of a radically new perspective is that of attempts to quantify historical data on social problems. Every issue has controversial aspects inherent in it. The argument often utilized to support behavior, actions, and expenditures is that certain areas cannot be quantified and that only qualitative data are available as evidence. One example indirectly related to health has been discussed by Fogel and Engerman,[5] who refute the argument that slavery in America was really not as bad as historians have made it appear. The authors contend that in the computer age, historians can use an econometric approach to compile more reliable information. The authors fed into a computer 1850 and 1860 census data for individual plantations, invoices of the New Orleans slave market, account books, wills, and other plantation records filed in state historical societies, and they showed that traditional historians drew broad conclusions from fragmentary weak evidence. Some "racist" historians described the biological inferiority of blacks, whereas some antislavery historians pointed out that the Sambo stereotype of blacks was caused by an inhuman, destructive system. The data used by Fogel and Engerman, however, indicate that treatment of slaves was not as cruel as commonly accepted literature paints it, that the diet of most slaves on plantations was nutritionally adequate, and that relatively few slave families were broken up by their owners (most of those sold were unmarried or were sold with their mates). Using an elaborate productivity index, the data refute the notion that slavery was detrimental to the economy of the South and indicate that the overall per capita income in the South exceeded that in the North and all of Europe except England. One conclusion, startling to some, was that on a majority of plantations the top non-ownership management was black. Rather than rationalizing slavery, this new use of computers and complex mathematical techniques to treat historical data breaks down old images, builds history on quantitative data, and reveals to both blacks and whites black achievement under adverse conditions and the efficiency and special skills of black labor and management. The new approach can also be used to say that 350 years on the cross is long enough for whites to be held accountable for supposed atrocities—debts to humanity that they were made to feel responsible to repay, but which may never have occurred.

With the danger of sounding repetitive the reader is again warned not to take to a sudden new view wholeheartedly without first raising the questions: who is saying it, when, where, and why. A further area for consideration concerns the validity of the approach. Can social data ever be quantified? If not, what is demonstrated by the preceding example? A mental health example is that of the widely circulated data on the reduction of occupied mental hospital beds. They were regrettably equated by many with a drop in the morbidity rate for mental illness where actually they were only evidence that a proposed shift in treatment site had occurred. Since many of the mental health programs included in this shift were funded by federal dollars, most mental health centers were subjected to review and visit by outsiders. Such federal site-visit teams are composed of officers who are charged with the review of programs, to provide federal administrators and legislators with a guarantee that programs funded over a given mandate are meeting the terms agreed on when funds were granted to them. From observations and experience with programs mandated under the Community Mental Health Centers Act we have become aware of

the impact that timing can have on the observations made by site-visit teams. Like groups such as those from the Joint Commission on Accreditation of Hospitals, a site-visit team schedules a day and establishes a protocol with the agency for routine review of its program. Scheduling the review in advance allows the agency time to establish a neat file of seemingly objective, self-evident support and statistics and to make provisions for persons to be present who will testify to the fine job that the agency is doing. Such review by site-visit teams may fail to locate evidence of violations such as the agency's denial of services to eligible persons, blatant co-optation, and other practices not in keeping with federal program criteria developed from the legislation.

Assuming the mandate's intent is, in fact, to meet an expressed societal need, the question follows as to whether the local program evolved in a manner congruent with the original idea and the legislative intent. From our experience in the area of community mental health, undoubtedly not unique among governmentally mandated programs, grant projects were written and funded to meet community needs. However, a few individuals here and there saw it as a chance to receive tax funds to support their already established programs. The only strings attached, in the view of the agencies, were "having to put up with" a site-visit team now and then. Although such a program was supposedly established in response to a community-expressed need, it was in reality a proposal written by one or a few individuals to address what they defined as "need" for additional funding and which they were able to "sell" to a sufficient number of community people to be worthy of government support. An assumption seemingly made in error by review committees or site teams is that the individuals proposing the program are truly speaking for their community and that their presentation is on behalf of that community's needs. In actual fact, however, it may have evolved with little if any community commitment. Even though a list of names appear as community supporters, it is necessary to be aware that individuals will provide their signatures in support of a social improvement program without following through by demanding action and accountability in terms of tangible services.

Reflection on the process

Some public figures are considered by others to be "troublemakers" by virtue of their reflective stance. When social activists would have an instant social program, an individual legislator or administrator often stands back and persists with the question: "Wait, how did we get to this point?" These individuals are often labeled as sticklers, conservatives, or holders of the status quo. However something must be said for that approach. As an example, in meetings of a county's supervisors one person may frequently be skeptical of views presented by his colleagues. Although it may not appear so, the perceived lack of cooperation in council meetings may well be in the best interest of people, taxpayers, and potential recipients alike. Perhaps society is changing in such a way that it is expecting people to realize that they must always raise questions about the

how, why, and wherefore. One indicator of this may be what is occurring in the American educational system. Students are demanding "relevancy," and they want to be interactive and question rather than memorize and absorb that which is taught. After they graduate from such an educational program, it seems unrealistic to expect them to be less than reflective and questioning. It seems therefore that reflection and questioning of dynamics are developing spontaneously. Not only should society avoid restraining such questioners, but reflective observation should also be consciously developed and nurtured.

References

1. Wall Street Journal, June 8, 1971.
2. Schattschneider, E. E.: Two hundred million Americans in search of a government, New York, 1969. Holt, Rinehart & Winston, Inc.
3. Bauer, R.: A free market for responsibility, The Center Magazine, pp. 51-60, Jan.-Feb., 1972.
3a. Jones, J.: From here to eternity, New York, 1951, Charles Scribner's Sons.
4. Otten, A. L.: Politics and people: means and ends, Wall Street Journal, April 11, 1974.
5. Fogel, W., and Engerman, S. L., editors: The reinterpretation of American economic history, New York, 1971, Harper & Row, Publishers.

At last it's seen that someone must
Attack this problem now, not just
Sit back and hope (while washers' slosh)
That it will all come out in the wash.

Y. Sterling Leiby[1]

14

PRESENTATION OF
A PROBLEM

Any matter that becomes a public issue, whether within an organization or a larger political body, is one that appears to be a problem to at least some portion of that group's membership. The analysis and presentation of a problem for one's own consideration or for use by the final decision-making body is no simple matter. A brief look at two problems pertinent to health care can provide multiple examples.

Group practice, as some have proposed, may be the answer to the lack of health care integration and may serve as a means of simplifying the system from the client-patient standpoint. There may well be no way in which a bureaucratic model can be totally eliminated, but if not, it must be organized efficiently and tailored to the human person who enters it. Patients usually decide when they need care. Garfield[2] categorized them as "well," "worried well," "early sick," and

"sick." In the past it has been the fee that kept persons from entering the system and thus it was the sick, early sick, and worried well who sought care. Unless the fee barrier is removed, the well will not seek service. If the barrier is removed, a flood of additional people can be expected. The system must thus be designed to utilize all personnel, including paraprofessionals, in a systematic manner that allows for the best utilization of all skills and for the most costly skills to be concentrated where none less will suffice. One suggested approach to humanizing and creating responsive health care is to develop a medical ombudsman[2a] who is sufficiently technically trained to know the way around medical settings and specifically trained to be sensitive to social and behavioral aspects of care, establish coordination among persons providing health care, contribute to the education of patients concerning their health

180

and care, and above all, function as a person responsible for unifying all medical, rehabilitation, and social services provided for the individual.

Professionals from minority groups describe their difficulties in dealing with the inequities in the health care system, both with respect to their own participation in professional organizations and improving health care for minority peoples. Racism is charged as pervasive in the health care system. Sanders[3] says that in professional organizations social workers are more concerned with achieving a strong black base and building coalitions among blacks, whereas health administrators stress the development of white coalitions or alliances with the power structure. Greater efforts, he continues, are made by social workers to build and strengthen their home communities and to obtain consumer input, and they are more receptive to taking members lacking professional credentials into their ranks. Meanwhile, health administrators are generally of older age and indicate greater concern about their jobs, their profession, and white health professional associations. The administrators do not perceive racism with such intensity as the social workers. Institutional racism is described by Sanders[3] in areas of staffing, role and function, organizational values, membership pattern, programs, publications, recruitment, training, evaluation, formal positions taken on social issues, and alliances to deal with minority group problems.

The principal caveat to anyone encountering a problem such as these is that of not assuming that the person summarizing the issue has covered all aspects. In regard to the health care example there is only a brief reference to "removing the fee barrier"—what would there be in its place? How would fee or cost be handled? Only physicians and the new ombudsman are discussed—how do others concerned view the issue? The well are apparently to start seeking service—what services? Do they know when to come in? Do health care personnel have anything to offer when they arrive? The minority group professional example necessitates broad questions regarding the entire social system. How is racism to be identified? Could any *one* group such as social workers succeed in combatting it without a total cultural agreement on the issues? Should the issue be presented from the viewpoint of the damage done the black or other minority professional or from the viewpoint of the damage a racist profession does to its clients or patients?

The presentation of ideas in legislation reflects the power of those involved and affected. In the proposed rules for the Health Maintenance Organization Act of 1974 there were several references to the "licensed health professionals" who would be involved in developing the intended new approaches to health care. There was much juggling over how specific the identification of those professionals would be. No group mentioned by name could be kept out of the money, and any group not mentioned might have difficulty getting at funds directly. Few would deny that professional nursing is needed to provide complete health care, and by definition a registered professional nurse is a licensed health professional. Yet nursing was listed only among those groups that could be subcontracted with for services, not among those that would be part of the primary organization. They are not specifically excluded but would have a difficult time getting in. There is a problem in stating this issue so that it reflects the belief of nurses that they are essential to the primary provision of health maintenance services rather than jealous of others, if this is indeed the case.

Medicine is currently engaging in massive efforts to re-create the family physician of an idealized earlier era, while continuing to develop the scientific base for more and more specialization. Studies have shown that medical students enter school with an interest in general or family practice and leave to become specialists. This shift has been blamed on the socialization process through which the student goes. Some observers might challenge the interest in family health care as not being a return to the true goal of medicine but as an attempt to control and limit the moves of other health professions into the void. The nurse practitioner and nurse clinician being prepared today come close to being what the supposedly ideal health worker of the past was. There is an interest in persons and families in both health and illness and a capacity to support and nurture as well as beginning to cure. Medicine's move out of family practice may have been appropriate to its goal of curing illness; the move into family care may be appropriate to nursing's mission. But the real battle over the shift involves not only philosophy and expertise but power and prerogatives, economics, and politics. Nurses caught in conflict with physicians over new roles should remember this well.

The assumption is usually made that when an individual presents an idea for the purpose of stimulating social legislation, the idea is born out of his or her altruistic and humanistic concern for the improvement of humankind. After the idea is presented and has generated a sufficient number of supporters, it develops into a mandate. However, the mandate often differs in quality and content from the original idea. The variance is the product of at least two areas of difference, one of which occurs as a result of difference in individual supporter's interpretation of the idea and the second of which occurs between supporters and nonsupporters of the idea. It is possible that supporters and nonsupporters alike maintain their respective positions with the assumption that the development of the special legislation in point (or other social legislation) is altruistic. Their agreement or disagreement with it, however, is based on various personal philosophies regarding what each believes is an individual's and society's responsibility for being "his brother's keeper." We suggest the possibility that a question may never arise as to who in the particular case is the brother. The proponent of an idea for the establishment of some social legislation may indeed be successful in efforts to achieve a goal on the merits of the assumption by others that it is based on a concern for

fellow human beings and others' conviction that the proponent is willing to assume at least an equitable share of responsibility toward improving that aspect of life among those for whom he has expressed concern. Little suspected is the possibility that he/she (or some supporters) may be opportunistically perceiving that sufficient social concern at the appropriate time will cause a mandate to pass but that it will ultimately result in the proposer being the brother being kept.

Culture and health

Both the pervasive nature of problems and the slow rate at which problems are dealt with are described in this section. It was originally prepared by one of the authors as a discussion of educational problems ten years ago. It is a brief look at disadvantaged children from the lower socioeconomic groups and their personal development during their early years of life. The question that should bother each individual is whether the children of poverty in the United States today will have an optimal opportunity to develop into functioning citizens and will "get the most out of life" in American society. One is quick to see that such an optimal opportunity does not exist for all children today. Thus it behooves society to gain a better understanding of the nature of the problem and to move toward a better tomorrow in this area. So closely related are the problems of health, education, and welfare that by looking at one aspect one cannot avoid the others. These problems are a concern of all those working in any of the areas, and it is difficult to separate out responsibilities that belong to one area and not another. For example, to improve the health standards of the culturally handicapped, a great deal of education must be done. In moving a person toward intellectual maturity, one cannot ignore his health and well-being.

Health is one of the means, if not the chief means, through which an individual may improve himself and his social status. Goals for those disadvantaged in health care are the same as those for other children, on the basis of the assumption that the disadvantaged have as much innate ability as the advantaged. The potential of most disadvantaged children has not been realized because of adverse environmental and family circumstances. Ideally the family provides for the physical and emotional well-being of children and raises them to levels of understanding, expectation, and aspirations that support the societal effort to promote health. These foundations are often lacking in children who fall into the disadvantaged group.

Although the term *disadvantaged* is the general category, other categories or groupings may fit under this term. *Educationally disadvantaged, culturally disadvantaged, socioeconomically disadvantaged* are all overlapping, but the terms are not interchangeable and must be used carefully.

The health system is concerned with these variables, since largely the net result is below average development, low aspiration to healthy status, and lowered self-concept—all of which affect the ability to stay healthy. Current efforts to help the disadvantaged American child are inadequate. The health system and society must find ways to help him overcome his handicaps and to find the opportunities that the American tradition promises him. The problem is (1) to identify the abilities, interests, and needs of disadvantaged children and (2) to raise the levels of aspiration of these youngsters and simultaneously to improve their ideal self-concepts.

One of the most pressing problems facing urban hospitals and health agencies today is the disadvantaged child. In 1950 approximately one child out of every ten in the fourteen largest cities in the United States was "culturally" deprived. In 1960 the figure had risen to one in three. This ever-increasing trend has largely been attributed to the rapid migrations of the families of those children to urban centers. In the 1970s it is assumed that this proportion is not falling and that it may even continue to rise. In the attempt to understand a culture it is important to see how customs are transmitted through the family to the child. Early identification of deprived children will better enable the health system to understand their needs, abilities, and interests and thereby to make recommendations that will stimulate them to achieve high or more realistic levels of development and health.

Culture may be interpreted as meaning a selective, man-made way of reacting to an experience. The term *culturally deprived* is frequently used to refer to those formal aspects of middle class culture, such as education, books, and formal language, from which some groups have not benefited. Ideal self-concept is the conceptual pattern of characteristics and emotional states that the individual consciously holds desirable (and undesirable) for himself. The assumption is that the individual can order self-perception along a continuum of value from "what I would like to be" to "what I would least like to be," or from "like my ideal" to "unlike my ideal." Cultures impose on individuals a basic set of values and social habits for controlling everyday life activities.

All children bring to the health care setting a collection of values, beliefs, and attitudes plus behavior patterns through which their values and meanings are expressed. Children have little control over these cultural factors that play such an important role in making them what they are. Social classes differ materially in approving or stigmatizing certain beliefs, values, and behaviors, particularly in the using and benefiting from health care. Middle and upper socioeconomic classes particularly stigmatize conduct in the lower classes, which the upper classes call laziness, shiftlessness, irresponsibility, ignorance, and immorality. However, some of these are accepted ways of behavior ensuing from the background and rationale of the lower classes. The lower classes may resent what they call snootiness or snobbery, good manners, proper language, lack of aggressiveness, or unwillingness to fight in the upper classes.

The terms *lower class* and *middle class* may

refer at least as much to systems of behavior and interests, concerns, and values as to the amount of money that an individual has, as is often assumed. However, it appears that the lower class people, in terms of behavior, interests, and so on, are also usually those with fewer material things, and children from this group may be identified by their interests, behavior, and values. They might show minimal interest in their health. Their clothing may be soiled and worn, and their appearance generally unkempt. They come from homes with "poor" addresses. Many live with step-siblings. Their mothers may do day work, and their father's occupation is listed as "laborer." They tend to speak grammatically poor English, do not comply with prescriptions, and often are seen in the emergency rooms with a variety of problems.

Their health care experiences are handicapped by factors that characterize their home and family experiences, such as poverty, disease, instability, and conflict. Therefore the children remain tired, hungry, and emotionally unstable and lack motivation. In situations where physical punishment is common, as it is in many disadvantaged homes, the children may learn that violence is their best weapon and often their only defense. It is understandable that they have difficulty in participating effectively in a health care regimen.

Culturally disadvantaged children are believed not to be satisfied with their lot in life. They want genuine understanding and respect, not love; they do not want a handout. The only way to give them respect is to comprehend their way of life and their efforts to overcome the negative aspects of their environment. Without such understanding the demand for respect simply has no meaning. Children need security in their environment and a sense of belonging. They cannot learn mores, social drives, and values—their basic culture—from books. They learn a particular culture and moral system only from those individuals with whom they have frequent relationships. If they associate only with slum-cultured persons, they will learn only slum culture, since the immediate environment or social class provides the "maze" in which children learn various controls and patterns of behavior.

In the biography of Ishi, the last "wild American Indian,"[4] one realizes that when an environment is provided in which close relationships are encouraged with a limited number of persons initially, even older adults can make a relatively good adjustment to an extremely foreign set of customs, mores, and system of communication.

In physical and intellectual developmental tests, disadvantaged children tend to obtain lower scores than their ability actually indicates. Reasons for this are various. They lack meaningful, directed practice and motivation, and they show fear and distance toward the person examining. The intelligence tests have been much criticized, since they tend to measure the aspects of intelligence that are especially emphasized in middle class life—verbal fluency, reading comprehension, and substantive knowledge derived from conventional middle class interests. The lower scores that the culturally underprivileged children obtain are not due to lesser potential for learning but to conditions under which they live. Because children in culturally deprived homes often have had difficulty in developing a conversational kind of relationship with their parents, they have difficulty interacting when they come to a health care facility.

Riesman[5] listed the following characteristics that are typical of the deprived child's style:

1. Physical and visual rather than aural
2. Content centered rather than form centered
3. Externally oriented rather than form centered
4. Problem centered rather than abstract centered
5. Inductive rather than deductive
6. Spatial rather than temporal
7. Slow, careful, patient, persevering (in areas of importance) rather than quick, clever, facile; flexible

It can be seen that many of these characteristics overlap. They seem to form a pattern that is similar to that found among one type of highly creative person. But the creative ability of the underprivileged child fails to materialize for various reasons, the most important of which perhaps are verbal difficulties.

Mobility is a prime factor in displacing former inhabitants, spreading decay, and multiplying the problems of a community. The trend seems to be increasing mobility, but a tremendous lag exists in the ability of large cities to aid the disadvantaged to participate constructively in their society. One facet of the problem is that group, which, either voluntarily or involuntarily, remains apart. When members of the group are brought in direct contact with the rest of America, many are unable to adjust because their ways of living are not attuned to modern methods. The South, for example, is an area that experienced industrialization late. Many Spanish-speaking Americans and American Indians on reservations remained isolated from the major changes in American life simply because these cultures were less challenged to change.

There is a vicious cycle. The people have low socioeconomic resources, so they live in a ghetto. There is no ready access to health care and health achievement in the child is low; as a result, his or her status as an adult will be low, with shorter life-span and achievement. So the cycle is repeated from parent to child. The autobiography of Carolina Maria DeJesus,[6] although in a South American setting, illustrates this. The trend is upward from one generation to another, but with a definite lagging effect.

Movement from one health facility to another is a characteristic common among all groups of underprivileged children. This really multiplies problems for the child. A nurse or physician may have accomplished a good relationship with such a child and is about at the point where it becomes a helping relationship, but the child suddenly moves. After several such unsuccessful relationships the child will probably be counted among those who avoid health care. Parents may value or support what the health system does in terms of its teaching their child to practice sound health habits but separate this from what they expect of the child at home. In other words the child learns to live in two different worlds in terms of behavior expectation from adults. It does little good to teach a child what to eat if there is no possibility of changing the family's dietary habits.

Interestingly the urban health system is managed by boards that draw largely from upper class circles, is staffed by professionals who come mainly from middle class backgrounds, and is attended mainly by children from working class homes. These three groups have difficulties in communication because of the difference in their manners, power, and value systems.

Most lower class children are well adjusted in terms of *their own society*. It is the factor of the "known" to the "unknown" that causes the difficulty. This is sometimes a phenomenon prolonged into the years after high school. The educational director of a three-year nursing program in a North Dakota wheat-growing community related this consideration. The curriculum was programed to include three months of psychiatric training in a large hospital in Chicago. The program of study had to be altered because the young nursing students were getting into a wide range of problems, and the school of nursing could not accept the responsibility. Because the students came from a highly homogeneous environment and had learned controls and patterns of response in terms of that environment, their experiences were limited, and when the restrictions that had kept them in line were suddenly gone, they were not prepared.

All children are engaged in a quest for identity. They need emotional support and respect from significant adults and their peers. If they must get along without one or the other, they can get along less without support of their peers. The health system plays an extremely important role here, but it can depend on how the staff inculcates the principles on which their practice is based—not only in what they teach and say but also *how* they do it. By encouraging children to respect one another's opinions, to listen, and to show that each has a right to individual feelings, thus granting them the security of knowing that others understand their opinions and feelings, health personnel generally can give immeasurable emotional support.

Health centers must cease to think of themselves as only centers that are preparing individual children for healthy future life. They have gradually recognized their role as a part of the process by which society renews itself as a society. Health must be a part of the community. In turn the community, the life of the society, must be a part of the health setting. Each renews and stimulates the other. If nurses aspire to work in such a setting, with individuals having equal human value (but unequal intellectual capacity and personality resources), they must, indeed, be self-critical.

Any health problem must be stated in its total societal context, not only as a health issue.

Vested interest

Any social legislation has the potential of empire building and financial misdirection. This includes every law with any degree of significance and leads to some necessary observations. It requires directing effort toward questioning the *actual* basis underlying the proposal of any new program. The importance of such questioning is extremely important because (1) large amounts of funds can be potentially diverted by those individuals bent toward the establishment of personal empires and (2) a great deal of time often passes before it becomes evident to a sufficiently large proportion of the society that such bilking is occurring and that it must be stopped. At that point perhaps the chance for affecting compliance is so remote and the interim costs so high that the only alternative which remains is to repeal the mandate. From reviewing history, one can see that actions which repeal an existing law are met with in-

creased resistance from those with vested interests in the empire. The results are not only frustration in the members of society but also the contribution to a loss of commitment to moral standards, since the apparent wrongdoers are seen to have made out successfully. The cycle is one that establishes and perpetuates alienation of people from their government. It can only be broken by a long, intensive process which aims at eliminating a widely accepted assumption among people that the intent of any mandate is automatically good, that any mandate will measure up to that automatically good intent, and that those charged with administration of the program at the citizen level are unquestionably moral rather than possible opportunists seeking to divert funds for personal gain.

This entire chapter may appear to be a course in suspicion. It is impossible to overstate how crucial to effective participation in political activity it is that one be constantly reflective and concerned that critical attitudes are maintained. Legislation that is aimed toward the improvement of the human condition proceeds through a conflict resolution process and results in a compromise. The compromise tends to be a single one. Individuals and groups holding conflicting views seem to find it easier to accept one compromise rather than several alternative measures. It is difficult (1) to determine which proposals among a number of alternative ones hold the greatest promise, particularly when implemented simultaneously, and (2) to determine the unanticipated impact that one alternative proposal may have on another.

One might consider, for example, the present child advocacy legislation. This provides for a program that actually may not be feasible to implement in a particular community because of the sociocultural patterns. It is ridiculous to make the generalization that a large ghetto area such as Watts in south central Los Angeles is one community. To make the further assumption that a child advocacy mandate will be interpreted in the same manner throughout the entire area of Watts is equally absurd. If there are seven different places where interpretation must occur, the potential number of different interpretations is seven multiplied by the number of people in each place. One countermeasure to the implementation of a program in isolation from its community setting, such as in the instance just mentioned, might be the use of the geographical block and an extended family approach. Rather than a single compromise being accepted in the enactment of legislation to resolve a given social problem, provisions should be made for alternative solutions to the problem in legislation, and compliance measures must reflect these possible alternatives.

If one's profession is health, one must learn to consider all public issues from the view of potential health concerns. The fuel shortage is a case in point because of its potential impact on the delivery of health care and the health of the population if heating fuel becomes too scarce or costly. A recent study was conducted by the American Public Health Association and National League for Nursing in cooperation with the Association of State and Territorial Health Officers and United States Conference of City Health Officers. It showed the following:

1. Difficulty in obtaining heating oil was experienced by 32.6 per cent of the 65 responding agencies.

2. An increase in the cost of oil—of as much as 110 per cent over the cost during the same time period in the previous year—was experienced by 67.3 per cent of the respondents.

3. The gasoline shortage had a negative effect on 89 per cent of the state health departments, 60 per cent of the county health departments, 59 per cent of the city health departments, and 80 per cent of the visiting nurse associations, of 155 respondents.

4. The crisis had an effect on overall costs of 71 per cent of the state health departments responding, 47 per cent of the county departments, 49 per cent of the city departments, and 83 per cent of the visiting nurse associations.*

A lack of availability of gas, combined with the higher price of that fuel, plus the in-

*Better fuel allocation urged to avert potential tragedy, The Nation's Health, May, 1974.

creased costs of heating oil and petrochemical products, can greatly impede these agencies that already lack sufficient funds to provide services. The curtailment of a public health worker's ability to reach a patient and maintain his health status could lead to a detrimental change in that status and possibly to a life-threatening situation, particularly for those individuals who rely entirely on a community agency to provide home health care services. Looking toward the future, the report also calls for formation of a coalition of organizations to seek a mandated priority for public health in the event of another fuel shortage. The coalition would act as a liaison to aid both public health agencies and government offices responsible for fuel allocation in reorganizing priorities for the distribution of resources. A major objective of the group, in addition to the formulation of such priorities, would be the exposure of existing discrepancies in fuel distribution.

This broad approach on the part of a health group can be used to limit the push applied by the vested interest groups usually associated with fuel.

Making a point

At times a problem may be analyzed and solutions discussed with an eye not to the essential solution of the problem as discussed, but for the effect a new or alternate view will have on existing perspectives. For example, several times it has been proposed that to create more homogeneous, logical "communities" of people in the United States the present fifty states would be divided in different ways. Pearcy[7] proposed a thirty-eight state United States of America. All state boundaries and names would be changed to better reflect physical and cultural environments of the areas. In addition, eliminating twelve state governments would theoretically be an economy measure. Under this proposal state capitals would be located more in the center of each state. Other advantages discussed include those of facilitating sales distribution and addressing the energy crisis by controlling natural resources.

Another proposal has been made to redesign the United States along population lines. There would be ten states, each with a capital and regional centers.[8]

It is unlikely that either of these plans would ever be passed because of lack of public support. Equally or more important, the sparsely populated areas now receive greater voice in national affairs with the fifty state division under the Constitution than they would if as many as seven or eight such states were cut to having two senators only, as opposed to their present fourteen or sixteen. The discussion stimulated by proposals such as these, however, may well lead those whose position would be most threatened by such a change to review actions more carefully and to develop a power base more congruent with the actual needs and desires of their constituencies.

There are conditions that favor application of new ideas in organizations. The ideas that fit into the general scheme of things or into the decision-making process will be more easily accepted if (1) there is a systematic search for innovation and (2) a buildup of vested interests is avoided so that new ideas can be applied. By the same token there are ways to prevent innovation or the conceptualization of new ideas in organizations. These include (1) keeping employees too busy to entertain new ideas and read reports and bulletins; (2) denying innovators the resources (funds, etc.) to develop new ideas; and (3) installing "deadheads" at critical points within the communication system. Even if new ideas have been conceptualized, there are ways to prevent their eventual application. These include (1) assignment of low priority and consideration to the new idea; (2) setting up a system of pluses and minuses to make it possible to underestimate the benefits and overestimate the costs (may include a demand for absolutely certain and short-run results); (3) rigging up a feedback or evaluation process of new ideas through the use of wrong indicators or misinterpretation of proper ones, perhaps requiring evaluation before the results are complete; and (4) lining up a network of difficulties so that resources and their awards will be granted to the wrong people.

Knowing the preceding dynamics makes it possible to distinguish among those organizations that are innovative and those that are not, with all organizations falling on some point in the wide spectrum between essentially no creativity and high creativity. On one end of the spectrum are those organizations that are about to "go under." Innovation tends to be short run, is geared merely toward survival, and is satisfying instead of maximizing. At the other end are those organizations with resources to spare, that is, personnel, and money, so that they can develop new ideas whenever they come up. Moreover there is less centralized control of resources in this type of organization.

Essential to the presentation of a problem is the knowledge of the system in which the problem exists. If the problems are not viewed in relation to societal expectations—goals, dreams, understanding—their presentation may do more damage than good. The long fight for the passage of a constitutional amendment clearly forbidding discrimination on the basis of sex highlights this. Among the many assumptions made by various proponents of the Equal Rights Amendment are that all people want to be equal under the law, all women are aware of their second-class citizen status, and men are aware of how absence of equality hurts them. On an issue as emotionally charged as this it may be impossible to state the problem in such a way that the need for solution is evident to all. In that case the complete analysis done can highlight which presentation would be the most likely to affect the necessary powerful people and thus most likely to lead to the desired attention and action.

The various approaches to presentation of a given problem may not be necessarily problematical. Just as it seems proper to have solutions with multiple possibilities, the complexity of current social issues leads to the belief that no one description of the problem could be presented adequately. In regard to health, issues have been raised regarding cost, organization of services, education of providers, policy-making personnel, and definition of the term. Various discussions at times appear to imply that if one tackles any one item from that list, all other aspects of the issue will fall into place and need not receive consideration. In fact it is probably healthiest to keep all the issues before various portions of the community, but with each group aware of the activities going on elsewhere. So in regard to nursing's contribution to health care it is appropriate that this problem be defined and discussed within the profession. However, those concerned with review of financing and organizational issues must know what is being done, or their definitions of the problem may leave no space for alternative nursing roles and contributions.

Privacy, as a human right guaranteed under the Constitution, requires constant definition. A study is currently being conducted by a medical center in Chicago to find all persons having thyroid cancer in an attempt to learn how many cases may be directly related to x-ray treatment of enlarged tonsils many years earlier. This was a painless treatment approach used by various physicians to avoid performing tonsillectomies. This study may well stimulate increased demands to establish a national medical records system so that patients can be readily located and followed over the years and to encourage giving serious consideration to long-term consequences in any medical treatment regimen. The rationale for such a system seems valid on the surface from a medical point of view but may have serious inherent problems relative to revealing personal data of a strictly confidential nature, particularly as records of other treatments such as medications, surgical procedures, and diagnoses are started. It takes a great deal of discipline to master the art of always restating a question into its negative possibilities. As in the preceding, for many the restatement from "Shouldn't we have a way to locate those who have possibly been harmed by obsolete care methods?" to "Is it ethical to risk exposing publicly a person's total past health history?" is impossible to make.

Use of theory

Any study of a problem or problems must take into account available theoretical resources. Such abstract materials have value in several ways. They serve to decrease the direct emotional response to the data of the specific issue, which perspective is essential to coherent political activity. They give weight to one's eventual discussion of issues, since they become not only a personal concern but also an appropriately acknowledged matter. Particular evidence of the latter can be drawn from the Inter-University Case Program study[9] of the Ancker Hospital site controversy in St. Paul a number of years ago. Several groups with economic and social concerns had advance commitments to specific placement of the new hospital plant. Serious, open consideration of the best possible site to solve the problem of good health care for the citizenry was almost entirely averted. One of the more distinguished participants in the planning presented the site decision as appropriately based on a rating scale that he presented and that validated his site choice. Only determined effort showed that the apparently theoretically sound scale was not based on any widely accepted theory and that a more appropriate scale utilized similarly yielded different results.

In the development of arguments and problems based on theory it is important to consider the appropriate limits of each concept encountered. The idea of "therapy" in psychiatric care has been stretched so far as to make it appear that there is no human problem not amenable to therapy of some kind. Indeed there may be no area of human life not of concern to mental health professionals, but that is different from sounding as if therapists have technical skills necessary to do everything. When the more expansive view is expressed, it can sound much like that of the health quack or faddist who proclaims loudly that "X," the new wonder drug, exercise, or treatment, can heal any human woe. How much easier it is to see the flaw in another's argument! There are several potential issues in the use of theory in practice settings. Nurses as a whole have not been accustomed to making broad use of abstractions as a basis for decision making, and many need to be particularly alert to criticizing the theoretical base for a problem presentation.

The person who uses theory must first of all make a distinction as to whether the theory selected is from a basic or applied science. Theories used by nurses have come from many fields including physiology, psychology, education, administration, and sociology. The reason for questioning the original source of a theory should be obvious. If a theory originated from one of the basic sciences, it is "pure" in that it represents the conceptualization of a certain set of phenomena by individuals who hold in common a symbolic language understood by each individual. The theory probably came about as relationships among sets of phenomena were observed and found to be valid. In the case of theory from some area of applied science one must acknowledge that it may not necessarily be valid. Instead, it is likely to represent a translation and synthesis of material from several basic sciences, formed into a symbolic language of the particular applied science to fulfill some societal need. In addition to describing relationships among a set of phenomena, a theory from an applied science area may include certain guidelines for action that are accepted by the discipline that developed it.

If the theory under consideration came from an applied science, it is necessary to review (1) whether the relationships among the phenomena described and the actions suggested for use by members of the discipline that developed the theory are actually applicable to the solution of the present problem and the achievement of the desired social ends and (2) whether the features of the theory that made it seem applicable to the present situation are transposed from a basic discipline to an applied discipline. If the theory is useful and has undergone a transposition, it would seem advantageous to go back to the basic discipline from which the theory came and to make the translation directly into the symbolic language of the problem-solving situation. By doing this, chances of distortion of the original theory are minimized as well as the potential gains for action being maximized. Rather than utilizing only selected components, one is allowed access to the basic science theory in its entirety.

Another major area for consideration in relation to the use of theory is in those situations wherein two or more theories from different disciplines might be applied. In such cases one might have at least three possible methods by which a selection of one is made, as follows:

1. Of the theories which seem appropriate, it is found on further examination that only one is actually valid for describing the phenomena at hand and contributing to understanding the situation which exists. In this instance the valid theory would be retained.

2. Two or more theories may be advanced that deal with the same phenomena and describe the same relationships among them. The difference lies in the fact that the theories describe the phenomena in the symbolic languages of the different disciplines which developed their use. When this situation occurs, it becomes necessary to select one theory for use, with the decision being based on the familiarity of the individual with one of the symbolic languages (patients, clients, audience) or the public's familiarity with one or the other of them. It is not appropriate to mix symbolic languages from two or more disciplines haphazardly, even though the same relationships are described in their theories.

3. Although two theories do actually describe the same phenomena, frequently they describe different relationships among phenomena. The planner may do one of two things in translating these theories for use. The decision may be that for particular purposes it is necessary to be concerned with only one of the possible relationships among the phenomena. One would then select the theory

which best describes that relationship and eliminate the others, at least for the moment. For purposes of sound theory it might be determined, however, that aspects of the two or more theories can be appropriately combined to describe different relationships among the phenomena. If this is done, care must be taken to relate the symbolism of the original theories accurately to the symbolic language of those concerned with the current problem, thereby combining them in a manner that is intelligible and consistent.

Thus a critique of changes in life-style may be presented from several viewpoints.

If it is acknowledged that loss of a sense of community is a current problem, one asks whether a concrete multicomplex medical center will restore the sense of belonging to a community and freedom from loneliness. Perhaps it can be paralleled somewhat with the hippie community phenomenon.

For several generations western cultures have rebelled against the restrictions of family, church, and town (community) to find freedom. This is easily seen among the present generation whose members sought freedom but finding it intolerably lonely, banned together in a sort of communion (a description of their attempts is the commune). The commune seems to satisfy simultaneously their desire for freedom and their sense of belonging. The problem, however, is that the commune lacks stability, which is a basic human value. As a result, it might be predicted that the communal style of living will fail, and a way must be found to reconcile the individualism that has taken the form of a continuous struggle for freedom with the community in which human bonds and interdependence abide. In earlier eras the basic community was the family, which was held together for purposes of obtaining material goods sufficient for survival.

Community is encountered at the levels of family, neighborhood, and city. Individuals gain from love of family, participation in activities within a neighborhood, and progress of the city where they live. What they gain in each of these communities is balanced against the freedom they lose. This loss has been significant in postindustrial America. As the large majority of people have moved into urban areas, they have done so without having a clear awareness of a need to cooperate with (or in some cases even tolerate) others. The bonds created by cooperating have failed, and pride in the city or home town in which they live has gone. The sense of community has decreased with modern communication by telephone and travel by car, making it unnecessary for people to continue living in one place for economic reasons. As the city or home town itself became less meaningful, it also became easier to destroy through crime, pollution, and bombings rather than to restore.

The neighborhood or home town as a "community" for many people today has been replaced by their joining a community of interest. This also has been stimulated by modern communication systems, which make it easier to identify and be with such communities in which people hold interest. With the extended family gone, persons who previously found consolation from their immediate family have a dilemma. How they choose to state the problems will in large measure dictate the range of solutions available and the final selection of a course of action.

References

1. Wall Street Journal, April 8, 1971.
2. Garfield, S. R.: The delivery of medical care, Scientific American **222**:19-20, April, 1970.
2a Mechanic, D.: Human problems and the organization of health care, Annals of the American Academy of Political and Social Science **399**:10-11, Jan., 1972.
3. Sanders, C. G.: Black professionals' perceptions of institutional racism in health and welfare organizations, Fairlawn, N. J., 1973, R. E. Burdick.
4. Kroeber, T.: Biography of Ishi in two worlds: a biography of the last wild Indian in North America, Berkeley, 1961, University of California Press.
5. Riesman, D.: Individualism reconsidered, and other essays, Glencoe, Ill., 1954, Free Press.
6. DeJesus, C. M.: Child of the dark, New York, 1962, E. P. Dutton & Co.
7. Harris, L.: The proposed 38 states of America, Mainliner Magazine, pp. 34-37, April, 1974.
8. Or should we redesign the states by population, Mainliner Magazine, p. 37, April, 1974.
9. Ancker Hospital controversy, ICP Series Case Study, University, Ala., 1964, University of Alabama Press.

It's hard to believe
But it's true, I vow,
That the time will arrive
For those still alive
When the Good Old Days
Will be now.

R ICHARD A RMOUR[1]

15

CHANGE*

It is hardly possible for a week to pass without hearing of some new training program designed to expand or alter the nurse's performance in a given setting or of some agency reclassifying positions and changing administrative lines to give nurses some new degree of freedom and responsibility. As nurses individually hear about these changes, they may be alternately delighted or horrified, since the concepts presented appear to be "exactly what nurses and nursing should have been doing for years" or "something which nurses and nursing shouldn't touch with a ten-foot pole."

The reader may react with delight or horror to the example of a program initiated by Samuel Shukert, a physician in Denver.[2] While working profitably for about five years in a poor run-down area south of downtown Denver, Shukert grossed a comfortable $130,000, with $73,000 of that coming from Medicare and Medicaid. Then he reportedly initiated a "total health care" package for a cost of $20 to $40 a month, providing unrestricted visits to or from the physician and free hospital and dental care. He moved his family temporarily into a one-room apartment while the modular facility where he could house patients was under construction. From the beginning of his plan he was plagued with problems from bureaucratic agencies. The State Insurance Commissioner claimed he was selling insurance illegally; to evade the many state and federal hospital regulations he called his modular facility a "home-pital." Patients lauded his plan; he

---

*Portions of this material were originally developed by K. Gebbie for a speech given at Faculty Agency Day, St. Louis University School of Nursing, 1972, and subsequently published in the *Missouri Nurse.* Other portions comprise unpublished materials prepared by G. Deloughery during doctoral study at Claremont Graduate School or subsequently for unpublished speeches or presentations.

was apparently happy but getting poorer by the day, and professionals did not like to believe he could succeed. The immensity of the change that Shukert designed is its principal feature, and the one that probably stimulates the major response in observers.

The sudden interest in change may appear to be a fad. Books such as *Future Shock*[2] have hit the best-selling popular press market, telling the public about the problems and dangers of rapid change in the environment and social system. For several years there have been various predictions that economic growth in the United States would soon end, and there is now some concrete evidence in that direction. Energy and food shortages have lent support to those who painted gloomy pictures of industrial and food supplies necessary to cope with the population booms and those focusing on the resultant pollution. This has called attention to wasteful habits and energy-resource uses that serve no economic good. Some people began to reject the ethic of growth for growth's sake. Although it is neither better nor possible to return to the rural agrarian outlook, it is important to look at those aspects of the gross national product that simply indicate increased output or actual progress. The process of eliminating waste must be sufficiently thought out so that the cost of the bureaucracy policing the cut will not be larger than the original investment.

Social change can never be accomplished through simply changing the political structure or law or through balancing power differently; it can only come about through change in the consciousness or internal philosophy and behavior of the people. Change involves change in values. Value change, according to Weinstein and Platt,[3] "alters the meaning of life for individuals in society, and also the character of society itself. It should be clear, however, that social change as such need not occur at the expense of inherited values."

Americans have become accustomed to a life of plenty. With Keynesian economics they were encouraged to spend, buy on time-payment plans, and give less thought to savings accounts. The first response to an attempt to bring about the behavior changes necessary to cope simultaneously with money that buys less and higher price tags has been an overwhelming cry for relief. When realities of fuel shortage, unemployment, and the scarcity of various other supplies are faced, people will adjust to what might then become an economics of scarcity. This, although unpalatable, will change the character of life in America, but not necessarily at the expense of inherited values. The final change in the energy situation should probably be one that supports as many as possible of the "comforts" associated with the materialism explosion, but in a more energy-economic (energy of all resources) manner—an integration of changes in several spheres.

In recent years several areas indirectly related to nursing have raised the question regarding the worth of a human life. When speed limits were decreased to 55 miles an hour, the National Safety Council predicted a significant reduction in traffic deaths. If speeds were reduced further, it seems that even more lives would be saved. However, what is the point at which speed as a convenience becomes of greater import than the additional lives that might be saved? War has been fought with the intent to kill. Killing is done at the risk of being killed. Long ago man indicated by assuming the risk of being killed that such risk was preferable to rule by maniacs and tyrants. There was nothing glorious about Dachau, only to mention one example.

One question must be considered seriously today after increasing concern has been shown for respecting human and other animal life. The Supreme Court has virtually eliminated the death penalty for crimes in the United States, and before that it was a long time since anyone, especially someone of status, was executed. Many sociologists, meanwhile, held to the theory that threat of execution does not deter anyone from carrying out his crime. Yet since execution is hardly a possibility, regardless of the seriousness of a crime, police are more frequent targets; murders, rapes, and kidnaping continue to become more frequent and ruthless. If it is true that crime is encouraged by rewards, America must be paying a costly price for its softened attitude toward the criminal. The Bible reminds people that (according to Deuteronomy) to the Lord only belongs vengeance, taking from the hands and minds of men the power to punish other humans for wronging them. The end of ever-increasing tolerance can be chaos, exemplified in such crimes as the Patricia Hearst kidnaping. The good of the Symbionese Liberation Army that kidnaped her was put forth as one step toward redistributing wealth, and it was pointed out that the alleged graft of the wealthy, such as profited the Hearst family, was no longer tolerated anywhere in this society. The larger quantities of food demanded by the Symbionese Liberation Army benefited others as well as being distributed only to the poor, so that actually society then participated in the fruits of crime.

Throughout time the life of the criminal was valued at no more than that of the criminal's victim. Now value judgments have created general confusion in this country. It is presumed by many that criminal acts are done by individuals not in possession of their faculties. The criminal no longer gets blamed; rather the nebulous concept of "society" is blamed. Has society's reasoning gone too far? Who is to blame? What is the answer to such a present state of affairs?

Adequate food supplies have historically been lacking for many. Waste on the one hand and starvation on the other have existed throughout time. For several years the United Nations and experts in various fields have publicized concern that unless population growth in various parts of the world were curbed, famine and starvation would become such a serious problem that the present energy crisis and increased prices of food should be considered insignificant. To this supposed nation of plenty, however, sharing of resources with the presently less fortunate peoples of the world has become somewhat questionable for ultimate survival. Who will share with the United States when its resources are gone? Will international kidnaping for a food ransom then be undertaken, and who will benefit?

In the professional literature the phrase "process of planned change" has been used ad nauseam. Awareness of the constancy of change is not new—an ancient philosopher built his entire understanding of the world on the sentence, "You cannot step into the same stream twice." The upsurge of interest in change is related to a growing societal awareness that it is indeed possible and desirable to have *control* over the multiple changes which occur. Prior to the industrial age man was in large measure in the control of natural forces beyond himself. Health has long seemed a state beyond the complete control of man, although gradually this is being altered. As years pass, the ability to control and plan has increased; health strategies for identifying potential victims of disease have led to decreases in many formerly fatal conditions, and interest in preventive health care hit an all-time high. A sense of power over the physical and natural world has led to interest in the changes that occur in social and human systems. Perhaps society is not so helpless here, either. It may be possible to cure societal ills. The actual use of change and the study of planned and unplanned change in the social system seem to date from the 1940s—events reported as the "Hawthorne effect." In a manufacturing plant an attempt was made to improve work output by increasing lighting. Small groups were put into private rooms, and the amount of light was varied according to schedule. The work of *all* groups improved, regardless of the amount of light. The ultimate conclusion was that the interest shown in the workers and the provision of privacy was the causal factor—change could be induced in a human system by human means.

An honest approach to change would be one that acknowledged the ultimate association between change processes and power.

The various change strategies reviewed represent greater or lesser degrees of power over others; that is, one who is extremely powerful can more readily succeed in a coercive propaganda and compulsion campaign than one who is not, since the powerful person has more direct access to means of communication and to other influential (powerful) individuals. Several thinkers have developed considerations of the continuous power relationships present in community mental health practice, from the individual patient-therapist relationship to the mental health center—community encounter. They see the responses of the individual and group as a continuum, whether they are observed in a one-to-one session or a neighborhood and points out the need for the therapist to be honest that power concerns do not enter until one moves beyond the office.[4] Nurses, too, should develop this awareness. Although nurses may perceive themselves collectively as having little power in the health system, they do retain a great deal of power over their individual patients and often over other health workers. Continued unconscious abuse of that power (as in overmedicating a talkative patient rather than carefully assessing the reason for restlessness) does not well fit nurses for healthy participation in power on a larger scale.

Nursing has come on the idea of change perhaps a bit later than other groups, but it has made up for the delay with energetic devotion. There is hardly a nurse who has been a graduate student in nursing anywhere in the United States in the last ten years who has avoided the issue, and many undergraduate students are also learning about change and planned change. Kramer[5] of the University of California is extensively involved in delineating change approaches and system-survival techniques appropriate to the new graduate in the hospital setting.

Rush-Presbyterian-St. Luke's Medical Center, Chicago, is an example of one new approach to providing health care for the aged and a prototype medical care program similar to the one proposed by the Nixon administration. It reopened as a merger among Rush Medical College, the Central Free Dispensary, and Presbyterian-St. Luke's Hospital. The first two mentioned were opened in the 1800s, and each is historical in its own way. As they move toward anticipated completion in 1976, the merger, extensive enlargement, the model itself, and their ultimate functioning together thereafter will be watched with interest. The organization combines a prepaid employee medical care plan and planned health park for chronically ill elderly persons, including housing accommodations with a program for training medical and allied health professionals for long-term care of the elderly. In the long-range planning, a network of fifteen to twenty community hospitals are to send problem patients to the Rush-Presbyterian-St. Luke's Medical Center. Various sources of funding for the plan include the funds from building depreciation, government, equipment leases, endowments, personal contributions, and loans.

The physical arrangement is in itself unique in that walkways and tunnels connect the various areas for protection from the weather. The base of the new high-rise hospital was planned to be over and around the Chicago Transit Authority's north-south elevated tracks, which run through the medical center property. A plan was set forth to construct a station inside the building—a new stop for trains on their route.

At the same time more Americans are turning to emergency rooms to receive the care that is not readily accessible to them outside. Emergency rooms are flooded with patients, and poor care is given because of lack of staff and equipment. A study[6] in 1971 at Johns Hopkins University School of Hygiene and Public Health showed that more than half of a group of automobile accident victims who died of abdominal injuries should have had a reasonable chance for survival if errors had not been made in diagnosis and treatment in the emergency rooms. Another study showed that one third of persons with nonemergency problems coming into a big city hospital emergency facility received adequate treatment. From 1965 to 1970 hospital admissions increased by 10%, whereas emergency room visits increased by an overwhelming 49.2%. Several factors may be accountable, which will be discussed in greater detail later. Added to this, it has become a frequently heard statement that some of the least experienced physicians and nurses work in emergency rooms, including interns and nurse and physician graduates of foreign schools where preparation (or lack of it) and a language barrier confound an already stressful situation. One area of weakness among these persons is that of understanding the emotional, mental health, or psychiatric aspects; Canadian professionals might serve as a case in point, since they frequently do not have such content included in their preparation for practice. The trend has been toward eliminating moonlighting medical interns from emergency rooms; it is not known how true that is of nurse students receiving clinical experience, although nursing students working as practical nurses or nurse aids are frequently expected to carry responsibilities beyond their titles in many situations.

The solution is not simply to develop an emergency room nurse or physician specialist. The issue is a broad one that points to the emergency room crisis as a symptom of a malfunctioning total health care delivery system. Is the approach taken by the Rush-Presbyterian-St. Luke's model an appropriate means toward resolution? Unless the nurses at Rush-Presbyterian-St. Luke's were an unusually active group, they participated in the change planning after the politics had been set and within broad boundaries set by others.

The greater the understanding people have of change and the human responses to change, the better people will be able to understand what is going on in the world, and the better they will be able to assume some active control over those events rather than just reacting to them after the fact.

Conflict and change

The close relationship between conflict and change has been discussed elsewhere in this book. Without conflict (or tension or differences) there would be no change or even human life as people know it. The situation in which the human race finds itself today is the result of the constant resolution of conflict between individuals and groups and between human beings and the environment. Nurses have a great deal of difficulty being honest about conflict and tension. Nurses play the expressive roles of tension reduction among the participants in health care.[7] Some brief observations of any nursing situation quickly confirm this. It is nurses who soothe and comfort—not only their distressed patients but also harried staff, angry physicians, and distraught personnel from other departments who telephone or enter the scene. The nurse *must* learn to distinguish between useful and nonuseful tension or conflict. The nonuseful tension must be reduced, or all suffer. The useful tension or conflict must be consciously utilized to ensure meaningful progress toward better health care for patients. The more comfortable nurses become with allowing multiple options for achieving common goals, the more likely they are to perceive tension among differing viewpoints as a healthy option rather than a hazard.

The process of change, whether it is planned or not, follows a certain pattern wherever it occurs: (1) introduction of a new idea, (2) tension between the new and the old, (3) probable compromise and alteration, (4) a decision, plan for action, and then actual implementation, and (5) feedback, which may in turn become the idea for a new cycle of change. There are those who imply that there is only one model for planned change, or at least one current model.

Ideas for change may be stimulated in any number of ways and may occur to a wide variety of individuals. People have threatened agency red tape creatively, including the woman who put her dog on Medicaid, seeking to call attention to the need for reform. While change occurred (face-to-face interviews were quickly required for enrollment), the woman, like many others, was prosecuted for fraud. The system's response to change was to punish her as strictly or more so than the person seeking personal gain. The history of science is full of incidents in which the same idea occurred to several persons in different locations at approximately the same time. In some instances a single person with an idea is labeled as "ahead of his time" because there is little prompt action to implement the idea. In fact the person may be exactly on time; there is often a period of apparent rejection of an idea while it is considered by persons who might be affected were the idea implemented.

Any idea has a greater opportunity to be acted on, positively or negatively, the more often it is heard in more places. The speed of communications possible today increases the opportunity for an idea to gain widespread exposure rapidly. Often this dissemination process distributes the preliminary findings of what appears to be a major discovery, but the process of other happenings tends to suppress the report of later findings that led nowhere. Anyone who follows the popular press can recall the multiple "New Cancer Cure Near" leads of recent years, most of which have led directly nowhere. Indirectly, of course, they contribute to the bulk of knowledge about cancer, and their time may come later.

Another current problem is coping with multiple conflicting new ideas. A brief review of news coming close together indicates that one should (1) avoid raw potatoes so as not to give birth to anomalous babies, (2) eat raw vegetables so as not to contract gastric cancer, and (3) time both processes by biorhythms!

The common reaction to an idea for change is some form of resistance. There will be alternative ideas proposed or some changes in the ideas presented. In response to these suggestions the person with the original concept may experience strong feelings of defensiveness. If the idea is to continue, this tension

is necessary. The gradual resolution of conflicting viewpoints means that the final concept will represent something of value to several persons or interest groups and will enhance the possibilities of success in implementation. The change in funding mechanisms reflected in revenue sharing provides illustrative data. One highly publicized goal was to give local units more control over local programs. Funds to programs controlled in Washington, D. C., were cut to provide the dollars. In many instances the discontinued programs remain that way, and "frills" are purchased with the windfall. Only gradually will the tension between "continue the same programs" and "buy for fun" be resolved. It is necessary to recall also that the quantity of resistance to change is reduced if the alterations are directed toward clearly acceptable goals, with the conflicting viewpoints being related to how to reach those goals. On occasions where the goals are also in conflict, two conflicting ideas will clash more directly.

The plan for action and implementation may be either formal or informal. Changes in attitude and vocabulary are more often informal, with the change becoming evident over a period of time. Other changes such as those in organizational policy are more formal, being made by official vote in group meetings. When change is formal, it is usually possible to identify the point where it began and perhaps a point at which it became final. Changes of the informal type are less readily identified, but they occur as certainly. One example is the gradual resocialization that follows a move to a new city or state. It is sometimes difficult to pinpoint a change as being of one type. There have been some indications that there is an increase in the use of child labor, a violation of labor laws. One reason given was economy. Was it planned? The employers knew they were doing it. Was it unplanned? The social complications do not seem to have been considered. Was it formal? The child labor laws are not being changed but are being reinforced. Was it informal? If it still occurred within a highly organized segment of the society, it was informal.

After any change there will be feedback—comments, facial reactions, and patterns of behavior. Taken all together, they can signify approval or disapproval, acceptance or rejection, happiness or unhappiness. In some few instances these responses have no effect; generally they lead to modifications and further alterations in the original change. In many cases the feedback regarding one change is transformed into an idea that is the germ of a new change. As one person says, "What I really like now is . . . ," another person says "Aha" and shares a "new" brainstorm, and so the cycle continues.

Changing legislation provided compensatory funds for those injured on the job. The struggle to identify this as an obligation of the employer and the state was a long one, but it was finally won. It has triggered another struggle, however—that of defining or redefining injury. The original cases involved were those of gross bodily harm such as limb loss on the assembly line. Current areas of debate relate to compensation for carcinoma developing forty years after industrial exposure to asbestos and death from myocardial infarction after unusual exertion on the job. The latter area is involved with stimulating additional medical research to determine the immediate triggering event in heart disease.

The feedback cycle, in regard to the social and political sphere at least, has derived some exciting new aspects through the citizen's movement. Whether working toward consumer protection, environmental protection, peace, or social justice, these groups have grasped the fact that the availability of adequate data can have an impact on political decisions. With the data presented in a holistic manner rather than as fragments, the groups are having significant effects on multiple social and economic changes.[8]

In some cases the feedback is so negative that there is an attempt made to cancel the change after it has begun. This is impossible. At times the visible remnants of a change can be removed—forms torn up, offices remodeled, and so on, but things can never be exactly as they were before the change occurred.

At one time the United States willingly recruited numbers of foreign students and encouraged the immigration of foreign professionals. This was formalized to the extent that foreign nurses, for example, were given preferred immigration status. Alterations in the educational system and economic structure of this country have led to reservations and changes of mind about those policies. One individual contends that foreign physicians and nurses are not adequately prepared to provide quality care. Another individual disagrees, saying that foreign graduates must pass rigorous examinations in their area before being permitted to practice in the United States. Still another individual raises the question of whether the examinations that any graduate, American or foreign, must take really provide a measure of the skill and knowledge necessary to provide good health care or if they really only reveal those who are good "test takers." Further study of the issue leads to consideration of how the United States can continue absorbing foreign physicians, since the American medical community had been contending that there was no need for additional medical schools or larger classes at those schools. At any rate the numbers of individuals already in the country cannot be ignored, and they are in a position, albeit a weak one, to protest the changing rules and to prevent the public from simply erasing the prior events from memory. It is a common mistake to think that things will be "just as they were before." Even if the only trace is in the memory of the emotional reaction to the change, this will continue and will affect the subsequent actions of those who participated. Indeed, every person can recall instances when, perhaps in an organizational meeting, a newcomer presents a fairly neutral idea, and all respond with criticism and negation. After such sifting and sorting it became apparent the reactions were triggered by some similarity and that the members were reliving their emotional reaction to some change that was suggested or attempted in the past. Being aware that this can happen is often useful when reacting to ideas for change.

Planned change is basically the same as the process of general change that was outlined. The implications are that the person who introduces the new plan had the basic idea, has anticipated the possible responses to the idea, and thus has planned the introduction in some way.

Community development is one form of planned change. Social scientists have identified three change models in common use.[11] One model focuses on the prescription of social cures by professional panels such as planning boards and consulting firms. Health and welfare council proposals are often of this type. Another model is concerned with the radical redistribution of power, as in revolutionary upheavals. The third model is based on a self-help philosophy in which professionals aid a social group to set priorities and then make plans to achieve the determined goals. Equally as planned are the types of change processes often rejected out of hand as immoral—co-opting a group into the power structure to silence it, using propaganda to alter opinion, or giving small visible privileges to agitators to distract them from major issues. This planning may be identifying the people to whom the idea is to be presented, selecting carefully the time and place for presentation, anticipating with some alternate proposals the resistance that will arise, and having some concrete suggestions for implementation, should that be possible.

One author[10] distinguishes traditional approaches to change from planned change. By implication, exposition and propagation, elite corps, psychoanalytic insight, staff and strategy, scholarly consultation, and circulation of ideas are not planned. This is obviously not necessarily the case—each approach can be carefully mapped or can "just happen." Choice of each approach depends on philosophical commitments and social system dynamics. The alternative, so-called

planned change, is an approach that may be closer to what is being presented throughout this book—the participation of persons in decisions that affect their destiny. All nurses have had some experience of introducing a planned change—we make out assignments for students or staff, time the presentation of it carefully, have a list of counterresponses for the inevitable complaints, and are prepared for two or three small changes that will make the plan mutually acceptable. Then we sit back and wait for changes to go at least reasonably the way we planned them.

Planned change (as a technical term) differs in the implication that the person planning it has learned, not by trial and error but out of a textbook,[11] what the proper approaches might be. It is not necessarily bad; people can waste a long time on trial-and-error learning. On the other hand, textbook recipes for planned change rarely give the full scope of the human responses to change and the change agent (the fancy name for the one with the idea in the first place). Nursing students in basic and graduate programs are now learning how to plan and implement change. Those nurses who have experienced more changes can teach the students a great deal about what it is like and how the formula from the book can be made to work appropriately in real life.

Planned change that would be congruent with the basic self-determination philosophy of this book would have to be one of the community change models that give some degree of credit to the importance of the group to be altered. As mentioned before, one model is the community developmental model, in which a high value is assigned to each of the individuals in the organization or group to be changed. The change agent is responsible for developing each one of them so that participation in the change is possible—in planning for it and in carrying it out. In most cases the change agent is identified as an outsider, someone brought in because the group to be changed is incapable of producing the change independently at a rate sufficient for someone's idea of progress. This is the model on which the Peace Corps was based; it is also the model that some organizations have in mind when they bring in outside consultants.

Another model is that of community planning, in which a high value is placed on the competency of professionals, and the change is usually engineered by a planning committee or commission composed of persons acknowledged to be expert in a field related to the desired change. This is the model on which many community plans such as United Way, Community Chest, welfare organizations, and others like them have been based. It is certainly pertinent to nursing. The recent National Commission for the Study of Nursing and Nursing Education was just such a planning body of professionals. The dull, dusty, small-town streets that Sinclair Lewis described in *Main Street* have been typical of many downtown areas in towns and cities across the country. Revitalization projects have been undertaken, but the extent to which such efforts make life more comfortable, beautiful, human, and healthy has surely not been realized. One metropolitan area, Minneapolis-St. Paul has created a system of "skyways" that offers to shoppers, visitors, and workers the result of the combined knowledge of various experts in the improvement of life in this area of bitter winter winds and humid hot summers. It has often been said that "everyone talks about the weather but no one does anything about it." Not so, thanks to some creative, diligent people. It seems so obvious as not to be overlooked because surely expertise in many areas of health are required in the planning and day-to-day improvement and maintenance of such undertakings. Having not observed or been involved, we cannot describe the involvement. It does, however, provide a challenge for the future elimination of congestion, blight, and contamination by birds, animals, and humans, not to mention the addition of such comforts as air-temperature control, lighting, soft carpeting, and music.

Still another model is that of community action. This has the power focus and is based on the premise that there are individuals in a group or community who have need of services but are so removed from the power that they are unable to meet their needs. The goal is to get them a share of the power base. Many current inner-city activist groups utilize this model. The union movement, which has affected many hospitals and health care agencies, can be seen as at least partially based on this model.

None of these models seems entirely appropriate. From experience in developing change strategies the following principles affect our integration of the three models. The most valid of the models is the community development model because it places highest priority on the rights and interests of individuals, be they patients, co-workers, or others. All persons should have the right to be involved in making decisions that will affect their destiny. The change agent, however, should be subject to the change initiated; in fact, such persons should anticipate that they will be changed in the process of causing a change. In the community planning model are some useful tools. If there are professionals whose expertise has bearing on the desired change, they should be consulted, not for a prescription but for detailed facts on the issues and the possible outcomes that can be expected on the basis of current evidence. Finally, from the action model comes an awareness of power. If one allows people to share in decision making, one gives them power. Once given, power is difficult to take back. One must be prepared to work with a group of increasingly powerful individuals as one joins with others in decision making about this and future changes in the system. The approach to the various models of community change can be phrased in the form of the following questions and answers:

1. Is it ever right to plan change for others as an outsider? Rarely, if ever.
2. Is it ever valid to give more weight to the interests of so-called professionals? Only within the strict limits of their expertise.
3. Should one be bound to be affected by

the change one proposes? Whenever possible.

The community mental health movement from its beginnings was interested in the participation of individuals in programs and decision making. Of the major federal programs the National Institute of Mental Health was the first to identify citizen participation as an area for discrete programs. A special branch was created to bring together several national civic and voluntary groups to look at how they and other consumer groups could work toward improved mental health. This branch also worked toward such conferences on local and regional levels. Coordination and encouragement of volunteers in all aspects of mental health services has been promoted as well as the increased use of citizens on center boards. The use of citizens in evaluation has not received as much attention and is an area for potential change in the future.

That same community mental health movement has led to several difficulties and unanticipated problems. An initial thrust was to take advantage of new knowledge to prevent the "warehousing" of institutionalized persons in large state-run asylums. Changing laws made it more difficult to hospitalize those who were not a clear danger to the community. This ruling affects those who want to be admitted as well, and potential patients are even suspected of deliberately inflicting injury on themselves, not in a suicide attempt but as a way into treatment and out of intolerable homes and communities. Furthermore, the states have accumulated many wards of patients who although not requiring acute hospitalization, needed a place to live. Community nursing homes and domiciliaries were a natural choice, more clearly keeping people in their communities. Unfortunately state licensing and controls for nursing homes have not kept pace with the demand. Many patients who had been supposedly benefited were moved from minimally satisfactory accommodations in psychiatric facilities to life-threatening placements elsewhere. Although statistics or methods of treatment may show overall progress in community involvement, there appears to be little gain in preventing mental disorders.

Whereas people accept community process change models in some settings, their use necessitates identification of a human community to be changed. The public identifies (or fails to identify) some groups as noncommunities and thus appropriately not always able to be consulted. For example, many agree that health care for prison populations is bad or lacking, and members of such groups have requested change for a long time. A process model could work to improve health care, but only if correctional and community officials acknowledge prisoners as people deserving enough to set goals and work toward them.

One final comment on planned change is needed. There will always be unanticipated results! As nurses move into more equal status positions with other health professionals (parallel to the experiences of others in the business world), they should expect greater incidence of syndromes attributed to pressures. Perhaps an increase in ulcers, coronary attacks, and other conditions will not belong to the male executive's statistics but begin to apply to those of women also. The need to look at this is evident as nurses move into the political arena, conflict, and power struggles—it may be an unanticipated and costly consequence.

Nurses need to ask themselves if the present ills of their profession are so intolerable that they are willing to take that risk. The potentially unanticipated consequences are covered in the chart on the next page.

The heavy commitment of nursing to bureaucracies has had many unintended consequences for nurses. Among these have been the commitment to the pillars of classic bureaucratic management, chain of command, division of labor, authority/responsibility relationships, and span of control. Multiple changes and experiments in nursing practice styles today are attempts to overcome or recover from some of those unintended consequences. It is worth questioning whether or not today's crusaders for new approaches have developed the vision to anticipate the future potential or danger of their ideas.

As blacks moved into the initially white-dominated movie industry, they most often portrayed the role of cooks, scrub women, or servants of some sort. Jungle adventure films showed them as ignorant, savage, or gun-toting characters or as porters. During the industrial unrest prior to World War II, movies dealing with labor troubles rarely showed blacks. Like the general society, preserving the dignity of the black was given little attention in the roles and humor of movies. There is yet seemingly no agreement as to whether movies influence those who see them or whether they actually reflect the ideas of their viewers. Regardless of which is the more accurate, there is no question about the power and influence that the early portrayal of blacks on film had on the establishment of a precedent that would take many decades to break. Although pressure groups in the 1960s achieved a break from the servant-role stereotype, a new problem arose. Black

JOB PRESSURES ON EXECUTIVES: THE CHANGES IN 13 YEARS

The Life Extension Institute queried 2,000 business executives on job pressures affecting their living and working habits. Then it compared results with a similar survey taken in 1958. The comparison showed this:

	1958	Now
☐ **Excess tension.** Executives who complain of being under continual pressure on the job	13.3%	12.9%
☐ **Job progress.** Feel dissatisfied with job advancement	6.5%	39.5%
☐ **Recognition.** Think the boss takes credit away from them	5.6%	11.1%
☐ **Cocktails at lunch.** Regularly have one or more noonday drinks	10.0%	14.8%
☐ **Pre-dinner drink.** Regularly have a pre-dinner cocktail	36.3%	48.7%
☐ **Cigarette smoking.** Habitually smoke cigarettes	57.0%	30.3%
☐ **Decision making.** Worry about making job decisions	13.0%	32.9%
☐ **Job security.** Feel their jobs are secure	85.7%	68.9%
☐ **Sleeping.** Have no problem in getting to sleep at night	89.1%	60.7%

groups in the 1970s demand rectification of constant portrayal as mobsters, junkies, and prostitutes. No matter how competent a change agent is involved, the human animal is so complex and the human systems so much more complex that it is impossible to predict the full range of response.

Some of the unanticipated results may be positive. The change agent would then like to pretend that it was just what was intended all along. Other results are going to be negative or antagonistic. For example, many would like to avoid recognizing that an impact of equal opportunity employment campaigns has been reverse discrimination. The only healthy approach is to expect unanticipated results, be on the lookout, and be prepared to cope honestly with them as they arise. Many good developments come from bad situations, war being one example. Many technical advances, developed in times of conflict, pay off in the total community. Many people believe that the rapid advances in trauma and emergency medicine today are a direct result of the Vietnam experience.

The reaction of a group or organization is composed of the total reactions of all of the individuals who make up that group (although the total reaction is greater than the sum of the individual reactions). People are rarely neutral to a new idea when it is presented. From introspection we identify the following rationale for personal response that follows when listening to a speaker introduce a new idea. The person who reacts positively finds that the new idea was not so new after all; it is in some way related to an idea or ideas that he or she has had, and the response is a form of self-congratulation. "I was right in there with a creative one. Someone else is on the right track too. Maybe I can get support for my version now." The person who reacts negatively finds that the new idea is in opposition to his or her own idea or is "out of the clear blue," causing a response of anger. "There goes my chance. Why didn't I speak first? Where did that notion come from? Sounds like nothing anybody's ever heard of before."

What is spoken in response to a new idea usually does not sound like those previous sentences at all, since people usually respond as if they are critiquing carefully the intellectual content of the idea. The changes and potential changes evoked by the women's movement have been many. One has been the development of theoretical arguments relevant to one or another side of the issue.

Anthropological explanations correlate residence, marriage arrangements, descent systems, and other factors to the role and status of women. Although these explanations are difficult to completely discard as fact, Goldberg[12] states that male dominance is not explained by anthropologists but by biological determinants that are present even before birth. Dominance assertion, he says, is a central nervous system response to testicular secretions before birth and at puberty. Men, henceforth, seek dominance and achieve it in personal relationships with women because women are insufficiently aggressive to resist male aggression. Although constantly in competition for high status positions, women ultimately must lose in the contest because of the lower level of aggression.

It is necessary to discipline oneself severely to repress the initial enthusiasm or dislike for the real content of a concept such as that just presented, until it is possible to consider it more clearly, with intellect rather than emotions. At times this intellectual consideration leads to the same decision as the emotional reaction, but often it does not. The standard response of the American Medical Association to national health insurance sounded intellectual, with arguments about the altered doctor-patient relationship predominating and with examples cited from the British National Health Service. It would have taken someone with access to sound data, such as the difference between health insurance and a health service, to locate the flaws in the argument and deduce the emotional content it contained. The pause to consider does more; it provides the opportunity not only to see what avenues may be open for the expression of reactions but also to ensure that reactions do have an effect on the final decision. There is rarely a person who hears a new idea and is completely helpless to have some effect on its ultimate outcome; however, those opportunities are often missed through failure to stop and carefully consider before reacting.

In addition to the personal, emotional response to the idea of a change, it is possible to identify several types of behavioral responses to change, particularly the implementation of a change. Murphy[13] has labeled four such types, based on whether the change is seen as opportunity or threat and whether the person is an active or passive responder.

First, there is the passive response to change as a threat, in which the innovation is simply ignored. Perhaps it is possible to think of individuals who forget to fill out new forms or regularly neglect some newly added process as examples of those in this category.

Second, there is an active response to change as a threat, in which the person attempts to alter the innovation or preempt it. Again we can recall individuals who "do it but do it their own way," and when the methods are examined, they are clearly not accomplishing the desired goal. The movement to develop alternative health care systems has produced many forms of resistance to change. The "free clinic" movement has frequently been completely ignored by local health establishments in apparent hopes that they would simply "go away." More active forms of resistance have been attempts to fit the free clinics into the established legislative and bureaucratic molds, such as investigating them for noncompliance with state record-keeping regulations. Since a major thrust in free clinics has been the assurance of total privacy in care, it is difficult for any clinic to survive an inspection or review.

Third, there is the passive response to change seen as opportunity, in which there is commitment in policy or word. The individual agrees with the change and perhaps sends a few memoranda supporting it but fails by active participation to see that it is completely activated.

Fourth, there is active response to change seen as opportunity—and from a change agent's viewpoint this category may be the optimum. This response can be paraphrased as "full commitment of goals and resources." Not only are the memoranda sent, but the individuals who send them also expend a great deal of energy to see that actual behavior reflects the desired change. At times this response can be almost overwhelming, or it can even defeat the purpose of the change, since the committed person does so much that others have no need to participate and the change is not perpetuated in the absence of that individual.

The types rarely occur in pure form, and it is doubtful if any person always reacts in the same manner, but everyone probably falls into one of the four types more often than not. In the light of the number of changes that are occurring and the necessity for realistically living with them, each individual must be aware of his or her typical response. Particularly if an individual most often perceives change as a threat or tends to remain passive, it would be wiser for that individual to consider altering his response to change. The passive, threatened individual is the one who is least likely to have change ever go the way he wished and is the one most likely in the end to be completely overwhelmed by the changes that have occurred around him. Change always requires emotional adjustment, but when this change is slow, the adjustment is readily made with ease. The rapid planned change of today means frequently, in fact continuously, leaving a point in the present for some anticipated but assured point in the future. This is reaching into the realm of the unknown. The degree to which individuals make this adjustment with confidence is a symptom of their resilience and emotional stability.

As one looks into nature, one sees a type of change that is evolutionary, inherent in the system. Thus it seems that there is a kind of unplanned change or possibly trial-and-error change as opposed to planned change. As one looks within organizations, this becomes apparent.

This discussion may have been meaningless to the owner or manager of a handwork business or to a wooden shoe manufacturer 400 years ago. However, for an organization to be successful and progressive in today's definition of success and progress, administrators must understand the dynamics and nature of change and its effects on individuals in a society.

Mead[14] described three images or types of American schools and the types of teachers and administrators who tend to fit into these three types as follows: (1) the Little Red School House, a symbol of stability, slow change, democratic living, and "really American"; (2) the academy type, attended by children whose parents wish to maintain a heritage, that which has been valued by their ancestors for generations, along with an aspiration that their child will have it better than they had it; and (3) the city school on a built-up street, typically unattractive architecturally, in which masses of children from poor and foreign families learn the multiple expectations of a new culture. One quickly notes the state of insecurity that change produces in the large city school type, in which one may not look back and is always looking to the future, the unknown, with relative fear of it.

The teachers and/or administrators of these schools are of equal interest. The teacher and administrator of the Little Red School House is extremely close to the community in which she teaches. She is a little more intelligent, a little better educated, and more alert than others, and she marries a member of that community. Teachers in the academy symbolize the tie to the past, maintaining some of the treasured values of previous generations in the face of a busy, new, and changing world. One might say that this school is oriented to the past. The third type of school encourages the child to reject old values and even to despise the values that

are upheld in the home by parents born in a previous generation. This situation, one might say, is oriented to the future.[15]

The Little Red School House type of organization might be illustrated by a small, privately owned business, established by one with somewhat greater skill than those whom he employs. It can also be illustrated by small community police departments, health departments, and others in which the chief has been a member of the community and who is not an "expert" but rather is recognized as having somewhat greater managerial and intellectual ability than others in the organization. This organization will not be future oriented, research minded, or particularly concerned about change. It will never make headlines for achievements, but no big achievements are expected by the community or by the organization itself. In terms of Carlson's classification of executives this administrator is "place-bound," having high commitment to the community, lower commitment to his career, and a history in the social system of the organization.

The academy type of organization may be typified by those organizations in which jobs, and particularly executive jobs, are passed from father to son or to favored associates with similar commitment to a heritage, maintaining their level of status and security. Change in such an organization is slow, taking place chiefly with the passing of a generation and initiation of new ideas with the next generation of executives. One might venture that any research interests in such an organization would tend to be historical in nature.

In the large city school type of organization, change is affected rapidly. Research is of prime importance in discovering ways of attaining coveted "increased standards" of performance. Administrators in such an organization must almost learn to despise the past and instill in their employees this same quality to motivate in them a desire and feeling of being comfortable with change. With this type of organization, lag in the face of change will be at a minimum, both with regard to individual personalities and the social environment they tend to create in the community and to the cultural patterns to which they cling.

There does seem to be a rapid trend toward the large city school type of organization. Because of the various pressures of society, for example, radio and television, people see the need to change and administrators need to consider change. Consequently the Little Red School House type of organization is becoming generally extinct in the United States. The democratic climate of the Little Red School House type, the feeling of self-esteem and personal worth in the academy type, and the innovation of new and better things in the big city school type are qualities that administrators must work to maintain if their organizations are going to be considered excellent.

The innovation of new and better things, moreover, implies change—planned change. To initiate change, administrators themselves must be able and willing to set aside their emotional attachment with the past and present to move with ease toward a future with change.

Administrators, if they are willing to pay the price, can alter their personality to the extent that they are not typical of one of the three types of schoolteachers or administrators. They might see how they can effect change in themselves to the point where they can efficiently operate in different organizational settings. Therefore they might move from the Little Red School House type through various levels toward the big city school type.

One consideration which, from a practical standpoint, appears equally important is that employees become accustomed to a particular environment and must make a tremendous change when the environment, including their administrator, changes. Persons who have for many years worked in an academy type of organization will undoubtedly find it difficult to accept immediately the rapid changes expected in a big city school type of organization, where they must suddenly put aside their slow-moving heritage and progress to new frontiers through highly specialized, technical, and researched jobs. An administrator must move ahead, encouraging the employees who are ready to participate in new projects and ideas. The more rapidly these employees reach the grass roots of the organization, the sooner change will be blended throughout. The size of organizations impedes change, since it takes longer for the whole of the grass roots to be penetrated. This phenomenon, one might anticipate, will not exist if the method of how to administrate large organizations is learned.

Likert[16] discusses person-to-person patterns of organization as opposed to group patterns of organization. The Little Red School House type of organization exemplifies the person-to-person pattern. Here employees study their bosses to discover what they are interested in, what they approve and disapprove of, and what they want to hear or not hear. This tends to feed them the material they want. Likert states that a subordinate's future in an organization is often greatly influenced by how well the person senses and communicates to the boss material that fits the latter's orientation. The subordinate may be dismissed and consequently feels that acceptance of the changes is being forced by the boss.

In the large city school type of organization the group pattern of organization prevails. If the group does not approve of the change, they tend to organize and fight back. There is higher regard in such an organization for "expert opinion" so that if a specialist recommended the change, it will more likely be accepted even if it conflicts with the values of the group.

Change is not an absolute state and not static; it is, in actuality, relative and dynamic. Situations in which changes have been produced tend to return to their previous status. This indicates a desire to look back to the "known" and familiar—that environment in which one is comfortable (like the families who go back to the farm for regular weekend visits to get away from the hustle and bustle of the city). This phenomenon must be taken into account, and energy must be divided into, first, producing the change and, second, maintaining it. This argument has been used by some[17] to indicate that there is a poor prognosis for a government based on democracy because a democracy always tends toward an oligarchical state. Democracy is not something that can be ultimately achieved in a pure state.

From a philosophical point of view one might ask whether, in a democracy, administrators have the right to coerce change in the manner previously discussed. In a democracy, individuals' capacities should be encouraged to develop to the maximum. This implies continuing change. Change therefore is not always an individual's choice but rather an administrative decision. In a democracy this may be explained as change forced on individuals "for their own good." One might add that this rationale must be used with caution lest extremely undesirable changes are explained away as being for the good of the individual.

In conclusion one may question the emotional well-being, collectively, of a society such as this, which accepts the pressures of television, radio, advertising, and other means as a way after which people pattern their lives. This is carried further to the type of organizations they produce. People look at other organizations and compare them with their own; then they tend to want to do what the other organizations are doing, seeking uniformity rather than planning an organization to meet individual needs. The effectiveness of an organization certainly must be measured in terms of one's own organization, not in terms of others, yet organizational uniformity is sought.

A serious question is whether the rapid changes that are demanded by society do not cause the individual to seek for refuge, for just a little security in the face of the unknown of tomorrow. Is uniformity among modern, large organizations therefore a sort of symbol of comfort and security—Linus's security blanket?

Living with change

One of the first necessities in living with change is to find the role in relation to change that is most comfortable. The role of the change agent, the individual with the idea who attempts to plan it through and innovate it with some conscious motivation, is uncomfortable, and if one could not leave the change-agent role at times, exhaustion would result, to say the least. There is the role of the "idea person"—someone who puts concepts together in new and different ways. Some persons can produce a new suggestion or possibility at every meeting. It is difficult to entirely agree with Diderot's[18] advice that "We should speak out against foolish laws until they get reformed, and meanwhile we should obey them as they are. Anyone who takes it upon himself, on his private authority, to break a bad law, thereby authorizes everyone else to break the good ones. There is less harm to be suffered in being mad among madmen than in being sane all by oneself." After careful consideration one may decide to launch a program of planned sanity. It should be done with full knowledge that it may be forever or never before one's creativity is observed and the laws altered. It may be altogether too quickly that one is confined and limited to prevent the spread of the perceived rebellion against the social order.

There are roles for those who listen to and evaluate ideas—the sounding boards. Some people have a marvelous knack for hearing new ideas and asking just the right questions so that the idea can grow and develop into something worthwhile or can fade away before too much energy is expended. There is a role for the devil's advocate—someone who will challenge the new idea from every conceivable angle, until its flaws and weaknesses as well as its strengths have been exposed. There is a role for the mediator—someone who must facilitate the process of negotiation as the new idea is developed and altered into a form usable by the group. There must be activators—those who will test the application of the new idea to reality. Often nurses seem to be the activators of ideas which have come from elsewhere—this is part of what is being criticized when authors and speakers say that nurses do everyone else's work and have no time for their own. There probably would be less criticism if nurses were activating ideas that were their own from the beginning. Finally there is the role of the evaluator. Some individuals have the ability to look at a complex organization or group, talk to various individuals within that group, and come away with a complete picture of what is happening—who thinks what about what, which things are going well, and which things are going poorly. It is this type of feedback that is essential to the process of change, since it allows variation and alteration as the change progresses into reality and fades into an accepted part of the routine.

In addition to finding an appropriate role in regard to change nurses must all develop a time sense. This sense is not that of knowing when to introduce a change or to time it in the recipe sense (although that is useful), but a good sense of past and future. Nurses must use the past constructively. As an example, perhaps one of the greatest obstacles to the long-proposed change of nursing education to colleges and junior colleges is that nurses have not yet prepared themselves to use the past constructively, through the integration of those nurses already educated in diploma programs into this system. Just reading letters to the editor in nursing journals shows that many individuals believe there is a danger that this aspect of nursing's past and present will be destroyed rather than used constructively. Nurses must also use the future constructively. Too many individuals, when confronted with change, lose the future by pitting themselves in hopeless battles as if the future would never arrive. Partly because of training and education that emphasized quick response to requests and news media that make everything speed by in rapid motion, nurses forget the length of time needed to assimilate and respond to change. Tomorrow will come, and nurses must always leave open avenues for change in the future

and, in fact, anticipate these because people live in the present. Again a common criticism of nursing is the look backward—nurses have always done it that way so that it must be good, and so on. Nurses are not the only ones who are slow to change—it is cross cultural. The tenacious persistence of folk health myths testifies to the preference for yesterday over today in many minds. Those who fight for new programs to deal with suicide, cancer, crib deaths, and other problems will encounter this over and over in the community. The only way for individuals to avoid having an unwanted change planned over and around them is to be involved in the many places around them from which change originates. The syndrome of alienation identified nationwide in the past decade begins with noninvolvement. Without continuous involvement people can readily conclude that their efforts to affect change are useless. The comments, complaints, and periodic campaigns of the occasionally involved have less of an impact than the regular communications from persons serving on boards, committees, and councils. Involvement means energy, and people have little to spare. But much energy is wasted coping with changes after the fact.

As the reality of national health insurance approaches, one can consider how few nurses have become thoroughly familiar with the potential changes involved. The legislation is difficult to read, and the publications and news releases are slanted toward one view or another; nurses may believe that the eventual impact "at the bedside" will be negligible, yet certainly knowledge of the possible change is for nurses the only beginning step in gaining power over any aspects of the change to occur. Other groups are already deeply involved. The American Hospital Association, long a fortress that justified increasing hospital costs, is beginning to look at alternatives. Most of the earlier position of the American Hospital Association was based on the necessity of hospitalization to qualify for insurance payment. Now insurance companies have begun to pay for certain tests to be done at home, office, or clinics. Home care and halfway house care can be paid for by insurance at much less cost. If hospitalization is the preferred method of treatment, self-care units can cut costs to a fraction for those individuals who do not require the intensive care of the acutely ill. Perhaps the energy would be better spent participating in, planning, and activating the change so that it is more reflective of the collective wants of the nursing profession.

When the professionals fail to change, the public forces change on them. A recent article[19] began "Hospital administrators: Are your doctors rushed and overworked? Try a Protocol." A "protocol," developed at Harvard University and Massachusetts Institute of Technology is a systematic questionnaire administered by nurses, military medics, and minimally trained paraprofessionals. It has been developed and tested so that accurate, safe diagnosis and prescription can be done, and persons suffering from various common health conditions can receive satisfying care. The original intent was to develop a system that would save physicians time. There was initial concern that the quality of care would be lowered, but studies do not support that concern. Once a protocol is developed for a given condition, it is reviewed by a medical panel and tested on a patient sample before being put into general use. It was found that 75% to 80% of patients with respiratory and vaginal complaints who were examined by protocol-using nurses were successfully treated and sent home. It is stated that with the use of protocols almost any intelligent, thorough, warm individual even without prior medical knowledge can be effective. (High school graduates administer the diabetes protocol, for example.) The high level of patient satisfaction might be attributed to the personal attention, the type of person providing the attention; one other conjecture is that the use of protocols forces thoroughness, often lacking in physician's examinations, as well as providing support to the physician's fallible human memory.

The increasing use of computers in health care is another example. Professionals have not fostered their use; they have delayed and behaved as if the computer was a monstrous being that was shaping health care to its mold. This may be happening indeed, since when the health professionals have balked, it has been the business managers and administrators who have brought the machines in, leaving the health uses to be tacked on later instead of vice versa. As an example, one can observe that nursing care and nursing education somehow got too far apart. They were separated for the good of the nursing students to protect them from exploitation and overwork and to give them a good education; now it seems that the separation is being continued to the detriment of the patient.

One of the roles of an institution of higher learning is the discovery of new knowledge. Nurses are beginning to discover new knowledge for nursing. One of the roles of the nursing care agency is to gather information about the care given in the form of observations and nursing records. The closer that care and education are to one another, the sooner the new knowledge can be put into practice and the sooner research can be directed to those things which are of primary concern to nurses who are actually giving care. The "how" of this communication can take many forms. Among those that have been suggested are joint committees, in which persons from associated care agencies participate in each nursing school's committees. Some of the content may be incomprehensible at first, but the payoff eventually may be terrific. Another possibility is joint appointments or some sharing, such as clinical opportunities for faculty in associated agencies and opportunities for teaching by agency staff. Much of this goes on informally, so that perhaps nursing needs some method of more formally recognizing such arrangements and thus giving credit for the gain this can have for all nurses.

What does this have to do with change? Changes have originated from both educational institutions and service agencies in the last few years, and in several we have heard someone from the other side of the imaginary fence question the change, react to it, and even fight against it. If the ties of nurses were closer, the chances are greater that they would participate in each other's changes and be much more supportive to them as they are realized. Today nurses are going to hear of changes from all sides of nursing and health. We hope that this discussion of change has provided some insight into the process behind the innovations and into each reader's responses to them. More than that, we hope that the discussion will facilitate the participation of all nurses in change so that all nurses might have a share in the decision making, which by affecting nursing, affects the health care of the individuals for whom the profession of nursing exists.

References

1. Wall Street Journal, May 13, 1974.
2. Kramer, J.: A doctor who starts own health plan gets praise and injunction, Wall Street Journal, Nov. 23, 1971.
2a Tofler, A.: Future shock, New York, 1970, Random House, Inc.
3. Weinstein, F., and Platt, G. M.: The wish to be free, Berkeley, 1973, University of California Press.
4. Schulberg, H. C., and Baker, F.: The care giving system in community health programs: an application of open systems theory, Community Mental Health Journal 6:437-446, Nov./Dec., 1970.
5. Kramer, M.: Reality shock; why nurses leave nursing, St. Louis, 1974, The C. V. Mosby Co.
6. Shaffer, R. A.: More Americans turn to emergency rooms, Wall Street Journal, Oct. 5, 1971.
7. Johnson, M., and Martin, H.: Sociological analysis of the nurse role, American Journal of Nursing 58:373-377, March, 1958.
8. Henderson, H.: Information and the new movement for citizen's participation, Annals of the American Academy of Political and Social Science 412:34-43, March, 1974.
9. Cox, F. M., et al., editors: Strategies of community organization, New York, 1970, F. E. Peacock Publishers.
10. Reinkemeyer, A. M.: Nursing's need: commitment to an ideology of change, Nursing Forum 9:340-355, April, 1970.
11. Benne, W., Bennis, K., and Chin, R.: The planning of change, New York, 1961, Holt, Rinehart & Winston, Inc.
12. Goldberg, S.: The inevitability of patriarchy, New York, 1973, William Morrow Co., Inc., Publishers.
13. Murphy, J.: Theoretical issues in professional nursing, New York, 1971, Appleton-Century-Crofts.
14. Mead, M.: The school in American culture, Cambridge, 1951, Harvard University Press.
15. Carlson, R.: Executive succession and organizational change, Chicago, 1962, Midwest Administration Center.
16. Likert, R.: New patterns of management, New York, 1961, McGraw-Hill Book Co., Inc.
17. Lippitt, R., Watson, J., and Westley, B.: Dynamics of planned change, New York, 1958, Harcourt, Brace & World, Inc.
18. Diderot, D.: Supplement to Bougainville's voyage. In Rameau's nephew and other works. Translated by J. Barzun and R. H. Bowen, New York, 1956, Anchor Books, Doubleday & Co., Inc., p. 238.
19. Otten, A. L.: Politics and people: doctors' helpers, Wall Street Journal, April 4, 1974.

Faith is seeing light with your
mind when all you see with your eyes
is blackness.

AUTHOR UNKNOWN

SUMMARY

In this book we hope that we have helped some readers to further develop what we see as healthy attitudes regarding political involvement. Among these are a respect for the dignity of the individual, a respect for the rights and opinions of others, a willingness to cooperate for the common good, a belief in the power of intelligence to solve social problems, an acceptance of social responsibility, and a social and international outlook.

A framework based on a philosophy of democracy was utilized throughout. Certain assumptions or "givens" were presented within that framework. These included the following:

1. Democracy implies not only a form of government but also a way of life.

2. Democracy assumes that a person has integrity, dignity, right to opportunities, rational capacity to solve problems cooperatively with others, and a capacity for self-government.

3. A person's fullest potential can be developed in a climate of freedom. The search for freedom has been a major factor in the progress made by civilizations throughout history. An entire society benefits when its members are relatively free to develop their individual talents.

4. Human beings are creatures of self-interest. For democracy to function, however, a degree of self-interest must be curbed in favor of public interest.

5. The prime goal of democracy is the preservation and extension of human freedoms. Freedom is absolutely useless, however, unless it is coupled with a balanced sense of responsibility. Freedom seems to range from legal to political freedom and from political to genuine economic and social freedom.

Freedom

Several basic factors are necessary for health care to be optimally accessible and utilized by all members of a democratic society. The Bill of Rights must stand, with respect for the individual built uppermost into the laws of the land as opposed to laws favoring the state or crown. A broad moral code is necessary that incorporates individual responsibility based on the precept that one person's rights end where another's rights begin. Opportunity must be accessible for individual accomplishments and development of self. All citizens must have the basic education and a level of health and well-being so that they can assume the responsibilities of free citizens in a representative form of democratic society.

"Democracy desires the well-being of all men."[1] Individuals must not lack sensitivity and imagination but try to realize the experiences of all people within their scope, being convinced that they are not equal, because their circumference of experiences is different from others. This therefore is equality.

Freedom and equality have been defined in some of the following ways. Legal equality means that before the law every person is judged by the same standards. Moral equality means that individuals have equal ultimate worth and need not anticipate "violation" by others. Spiritual equality implies every person's potential spirituality, which every one earns, or in other terms every person's right to "salvation." Spiritual freedom defines a kind of inner strength, an ability to stand up under extreme adversity. One might question therefore the state of spiritual freedom in the United States today.

Equality, as the Constitution defines it, may be defined as, first stressing the ties that bind humankind and, second, recognizing what makes human beings different. People therefore respect each other so that differences, such as monetary differences, become less and less important. This is not a process of leveling but rather of allowing the individual to develop his potentialities to the fullest and then be able to look at another person's differences with respect.

Freedom does not mean license. Rather, with freedom also come discipline and self-control. In *The Paradoxes of Freedom*[2] Hook says "No one can reasonably make a demand for freedom in an unqualified sense—a freedom to do anything one pleases. For it is morally impossible to approve all freedoms. . . . There are freedoms and freedoms—and we cannot have them all. For each one we pay a price." Freedom may be interpreted as meaning a state of mind, so that a person in physical bondage may have freedom. This means that not only do people living in a democracy have freedom but also that what makes a democracy unique is its stress on individuals and their ultimate value.

Meyers[3] states that "One should be free from the threat of molestation, so as to enjoy the fruits of one's labor." In a democracy the purpose of laws is to protect the rights of the individual. Yet if law goes far enough in a democracy, it becomes an impeding influence rather than a liberating one. Benedict, Rousseau, and others speak of the danger that the more a government watches and protects a minority's equality, the less freedom actually is present.

From the agrarian days of early America to the highly accelerated industrial life of today some of the people's concepts and philosophies have been in conflict with their manner of living; thus there is what anthropologists such as Benedict[4] and Mead[5] call a relative disintegration of American culture. The question arises as to whether a democracy is applicable under industrial conditions, in which everything is specialized and people are so interdependent. This would appear to be possible only as long as individuals participate and have an interest in their destiny. When this is lost, however, minority groups rule and democracy no longer exists. If one defines freedom as a level at which individuals relate to one another, enhance one another, and participate in an exchanging relationship, we agree that this can happen in an industrialized society such as America. It is not a natural outcome, but it is entirely possible.

There is much emphasis in the United States on *success*, which immediately to most people means dollars and cents. If this is what is meant when one says that in a democracy one aims for the individual's attainment of his maximum potential, one is attaining anything but a democratic society. When individuals have achieved this *success*, they may well be hollow and have a feeling of futility. The correction of this situation is a job for all American institutions, including educators and health professionals. American society needs something to be committed to, as an adaptation to this industrial way of life from the earlier agrarian type of life. No doubt the changes will take place in terms of adaptation, but this may occur without democratic ideals and humankind will become a mass.[6]

Because some people have seen the danger of mediocrity and loss of individual identity and creativity, an overcompensation has occurred in terms of valuing strong individualism. The danger here is that the strong individualist may have a lacking of social conscience and social morality, so that destruction may result, according to Maslow.[7] Yet one must not forget that a prerequisite to morality, so defined, is freedom. If individuals harm no one but themselves by their action, this is their choice and they have liberty to do so, but only insofar as they do not endanger others. It may also be their right to be wrong, insofar as they are acting intelligently and not deliberately endangering another's freedom. Here we use *freedom* as a term implying restraint and *liberty* as implying absence of restraint.

First, in a democracy the aim is to treat individuals as "ends" and not "means." To do this, Maslow[7] points out, individuals must know themselves and must realize that they do not *need* to use people as means. Second, pathological authoritarianism is ruled out so that society grants individuals more freedom. Individuals, in terms of ends, are allowed to develop, are trusted, and thereby take more responsibility. Thus they experience more freedom. Granted, this can be a dangerous tool; however, if people practice democracy and create the proper atmosphere, they can rightly take the risk as to where such freedom leads.

Individuals as ends also implies that they are not judged in terms of their contribution to the state but rather in terms of what each may personally achieve under favorable opportunities.[8] It also means that the way in

which individuals make their living should hopefully also enrich their personality and give them a sense of satisfaction and reward.[9]

Freedom, equality, and democracy are not absolute terms. They are ideals toward which individuals aim, and as long as individuals are aiming toward these ideals it would seem that relative amounts of these qualities exist. Many lives and horrible events can testify as to what has happened throughout history when people take absolutistic stands, and often for what passed as "democracy." For this reason one wonders whether religious freedom and equality and morality are not at almost opposite ends of the continuum. Dewey and colleagues[8] say that "the idea of forcing man to be free is an old idea, but by nature it is opposed to freedom. Freedom is not something that can be handed to man as a gift from outside. . . ." It is earned and only so through the kinds of relationships that individuals have with one another. It is through this voluntary cooperation that the optimum development of the individual can be made secure and enduring.

Boundaries

It is almost impossible to provide any tidy summary or conclusion to a book such as this. The range of theories, concepts, examples, and comments has been wide. Indeed the task of the book would not be accomplished were it possible to have any sense of closure at this point. The political process is one of constant change and flux. The socialization process in nursing has all too often delivered the message that there is an ideal state to which one can conform—a state defined primarily by appearance, dexterity in tasks, and acknowledgement of organizational superiors. In fact there *are* principles to which one may wish to conform, and we have been suggesting that these include particularly the involvement of all persons in decision making when it affects their destiny. For nurses this means two things. First, they should be involved on all levels when policy is being made regarding health. Second, in achieving that end, nurses must recognize that the profession should not forget the clients of health care and their need to be a part of decision making as well.

From the study of culture groups Brown[10] has observed that when a new belief, a new tool or invention, or new custom is introduced, one of the following alternative reactions can be expected from the group:

1. It may fit into the pattern and be accepted.

2. It may clash with the existing pattern and be rejected.

3. It may be found unsuitable in its original form but capable of modification or substitution so as to make it acceptable.

4. It may conflict with deep-seated elements in the cultural pattern, and the society may disintegrate or, after a period of disintegration, manage to reorganize itself around the new trait.

As with the introduction of a new custom, invention, or belief into a culture group, so it is with a new policy that is introduced into an organization. Therefore the staff in an organization may be expected to react in any of the four ways Brown describes.

Although the settings in the two following instances are extremely different, the underlying psychological mechanisms remain the same. A tribe of African natives might completely ignore the World Health Organization's construction of sanitary privies in the area and continue their old, unsanitary customs that contaminate the soil and spread typhoid throughout their land. A professional staff, because they believe that they must show professional good manners, may go along with a change in policy but be resentful, frustrated, and generally feel exploited because decisions were made without consulting them.

Among the characteristics required of organizations is that they have boundaries, which may be defined with varying degrees of precision, along with energy, resources, coordination of effort, and channels of distribution for that effort. The boundary of an organization is defined to indicate who is within the organization and who is outside.

This may be done by means of uniforms, badges, insignia, names listed on a roster, or as in the field of public health, a directory of certified public health personnel. Membership in an organization may be voluntary, in which the boundary serves to *keep out* individuals who do not bear the marks of identity of the organization, or it may be involuntary, in which the boundary is designed to *keep* members *in* the organization. Public health agencies are an example of voluntary membership, and families, nations, prisons, and armies are examples of involuntary membership.

In public health nursing agencies an extremely apparent boundary can be drawn with uniform policies. The uniform designates to the public health nurse, to other staff in the agency, and to the public that the wearer belongs to the organization known as the health department. Some public health agencies have stringent uniform regulations, up to and including a proper pocket tab and scarf, periodically reinforced with a memorandum from the director's office, whereas other agencies permit the wearing of casual street clothes, sometimes not even excluding such daring features as sleeveless dresses and jewelry.

One might speculate as to what brings about the establishment of certain uniform or dress regulations. We might simply accept an answer that they have been long-standing or traditional with the agency. However, the beginning or establishment of the policies are of interest. Traditions or customs have their beginnings in fulfilling some human need, says Brown.[10]

Determination of uniform policies is done by the administrator of a public health nursing agency, with varying degrees of participation from the staff. As with the introduction of a new belief, new tool or intervention, or new custom in a culture group, one of the group reaction patterns may be expected that Brown describes.[10] It may be speculated that the acceptance of the new policy by the staff will be directly proportional to the amount of their participation in the formulation of policies.[11] From observations in the field of public health we are not aware of any instance in which an entire staff requested that an administrator establish a policy about uniforms. When street clothes are acceptable in an agency, in no known instance is a staff nurse prohibited from wearing a uniform if he or she wishes.

Why therefore does an agency administrator initiate uniform policies when prior to this, there have been less formal dress regulations? In other words, why does the leader decide to draw the organizational boundary with heavier, more visible markings? The verbal reasons which might be given are that the public believes that public health nurses look more "professional" in uniform, that in the long run it is less costly for public health nurses to buy uniforms than street clothes, and so on. Whether the wearing of a uniform makes one a more professional public health nurse is questionable in the same way that a certain manner of dressing is not indicative of a "good" teacher.[12] If these factors are not highly significant, what therefore brings about the change?

When "things are not going so well" in an agency, production of work declines, nurses are spending as little time as possible in the office, even to the point of recording some home visits in their cars, the agency may be described[13] as having a "closed organizational climate." The administrator perpetuates the closed organizational climate by initiating or enforcing uniform regulations, whereby all nurses are reminded that they belong in the organization and every other nurse is reminded of that individual's mark of identity. At the same time those outside the organization are told that these are marked individuals and are expected to behave in certain ways. The situation is now taking on more of the quality of an involuntary membership in that it is actually designed to *keep* individuals *in,* to require their loyalties and energies, rather than being designed to *keep* others *out,* as in the voluntary type of organizational membership.

One might speculate about other administrative decisions that would effect a sharpening of boundary demarcation. However, this one is made universally in public health agencies, and indeed in almost all health facilities, whether in terms of strictly enforced uniform regulations or varying degrees of less formal dress. It appears that strictly enforced uniform policies are introduced during a period of "closed climate" leadership and tend to relax during "open climate" leadership.[13] It may also be speculated that without open climate leadership, nursing will not move from preoccupation with the external form and boundaries of their profession, such as uniforms, to development of the content needed to survive as a vital force in health care.

Like makers of corn brooms, it is essential that nurses be able to provide evidence that they are irreplaceable by anything—other kinds of health personnel or machines. The specialized skill required to turn out good quality corn brooms[14] has not been lost to any competition by synthetics or mechanization. A recent attempt was made to develop a mechanical broom–corn harvester with funds from the government and industry, but it was abandoned. Each boom is made from broom corn fiber, which is hand sorted for length, wound, and wired so that no two are alike, and their sales tag varies accordingly. If nursing is a profession, any attempt to mechanize its membership (through uniforms or other means) should similarly fail.

Consequences

In planning change, serious consideration must be given to unanticipated consequences. It is risky to stimulate change for the sake of change. Not all change is better than no change—in fact it may be worse. An example that comes to mind is California nurses' first attempt at changing the Nurse Practice Act. Instead of accomplishing what nurses intended, it stimulated increased resistance as well as hopelessness among many nurses. Medex practitioners were prepared to augment physician manpower, but no licensure laws were passed to serve as boundaries within which they would practice. The graduates of Medex programs had difficulty in finding employment; nurses were confused and threatened, and physicians were reluctant to assume responsibility for the actions of Medex practitioners. Assuming personal risk is necessary to attain the power for change to occur, but taking foolish risks may be worse than not risking at all.

As nurses do attain power, will they be able to continue their effectiveness in caring for and serving in the best interest of the powerless? As power is attained, it is frequently accompanied by a change in life-style which more closely resembles that of members within the ranks of wealth, power, and high status. Such individuals then tend to lose their identity with the downtrodden, and they strive toward maintaining the status quo.

During the current tight economy, there are numerous applicants for most jobs, and even college graduates join the ranks of the unemployed. With increased cost of living many more persons are moonlighting to meet expenses. Pressured by inflation, layoffs in industry, and a shortage of skilled job openings, many more workers are migrating to the unskilled labor market. Jobs that previously attracted skid row residents are now filled, for example, by teachers, office workers, or truck drivers who work after hours. Help wanted advertisements are now a thing of the past for many employers; instead, posting a job opening notice or simply word of mouth obtains many more applicants than there are openings. Nurses have had a reputation of working to supplement family incomes rather than as a distinct lifelong career. The current economic changes undoubtedly are affecting nurses in various ways, including alterations in both practice and education patterns.

Any visitor to the 1974 World's Fair (Expo '74) in Spokane heard a bell ring every 10 seconds in the area of the United States pavilion. When the fair closed in November, 1974, the bell had rung more than 1.5 million times.[15] Each ring represented one new birth in the United States. Although a new birth is considered exciting, the impact that each has on the environment and the society may be somewhat less exciting and more thought provoking. The display at the fair shows this impact of each new life as follows. During an average life-span, the earth must provide the individual with 2 tons of textiles, 21,000 gallons of gasoline, 50 tons of food, and 56 million gallons of water. In return he puts back in the earth 165 tons of garbage and in the air 100 tons of air pollution. A Herculean task lies ahead in which nurses should be willing and able to assume a meaningful role in developing a harmony between man and the environment. Pollution control, environmental management, and population control must go hand in hand.

Almost every family in the United States is feeling the effects of skyrocketing consumer prices. For families on welfare it has become an extraordinary situation. An old adage frequently used is "It takes money to make money." There are those in society who for various reasons failed to make the money that would help them make more money. These people frequently find themselves on welfare assistance. There are some who have the know-how and motivation to calculate ways of making the dollars stretch to cover the costs of housing, of nutritious although inexpensive meals, and of clothing. The others join the ranks of the malnourished, depressed, and hopeless. Nurses often find more reward in helping the former type of families, but the challenge remains of finding ways of helping the latter group other than through a simple increase in income level. Income does not ensure good nutrition.

The urgency of national health insurance is supported by many facts including (1) an increase in the average personal yearly health bill by over 100% in twenty-five years, (2) lack of hospitalization insurance to cover nearly 50% of the people in income brackets at or near the subsistence level, (3) hospital expenses of hundreds of dollars a day, and (4) the poor distribution of physicians and the frequent use of foreign medical graduates.[16]

Although most people look on national health insurance as inevitable, the form in which it came about requires considerable concern. Neither the Kennedy-Mills plan to federalize all health insurance under the Social Security program nor the administration's private payroll deduction deals with the problem of cost. Compromise plans have appeared little better at solving the multiple problems. They are designed to make care available to more people, but it is contended[17] that the burden of increasing costs would still be on that 80% of the wage earners who are already subscribing and paying for some health insurance program. The solution seemingly must yet be found.

Stability or the lack of stability in government is not only a current American dilemma. It was a difficult personal dilemma for many citizens to defend Richard Nixon as the man to be President of this United States, but it was equally difficult for many to wholeheartedly support his impeachment. The controversy over the numerous conversations contained in the White House transcripts pointed to what some would call a degree of narrow-mindedness and nit-pickiness toward the executive and his assistants, made possible by technological advances. From other viewpoints, the President's years in the White House were not a total failure but produced some accomplishments. Supposedly it was Madison who once said that the American system of government was designed to work not because of noble men but despite base men. The loss of moral leadership, although it might be cause to remove the executive of other systems of government, is not automatically sufficient in the United States, where the founding fathers spelled out the requirement of "high crimes or misdemeanors" as the only cause for impeachment. Perhaps the founders were all too well aware of emotionalism and its results, therefore limiting threats to enhance a stable government. The syndrome of instability within the United States was seen paralleled across the world, with the resignation of Germany's Chancellor Willy Brandt, the inability of Prime Minister Trudeau to serve his government in spite of his charisma, the

narrow margin of support held by France's new leader, and the rarity of a majority party holding the government in Great Britain. Western governments generally seem to be in a state of crisis.

Meanwhile, one must also remember that disfavor with the President is not unique to our time. Thomas Jefferson[18] encountered some of the same during his second term of office, with the precipitating issue being an embargo he placed on foreign trade. Other issues included the treason trial of Aaron Burr, with friction because of it with Chief Justice John Marshall, a feud with fellow politicians, and details of the Lewis and Clark expedition.

The money market and currency conditions can be both economic and psychological. The uncertainty of the value of various national currency systems is partially a result of the inability to make calculations and trade with reasonable certainty that the currencies will in ten or fifteen years hold the same value in relation to others. With deteriorating value of the American dollar, psychological factors begin to play an ever-increasing role, with panic making it even harder to stabilize the economy, stave off recessions, depressions, money crises, and economic movements. People look at past experiences as they look toward the future. During the 1971 slump, many predicted decreasing world trade and ultimately a depression. Many based this on a recall of experiences from the 1930s. Current economics have puzzled many but certainly cheered few. With a recollection of this aspect of human behavior a few banks have developed a system that serves to measure mob psychology to protect their interests.

Finding new areas in which to apply their knowledge and skills, nurses may take example from what may be seemingly "far-out" approaches used by other disciplines. In 1969 the Holiday Inns of America began adding a chaplain to their payroll and began a new type of ministry—that of working with the lonely and suicidal persons who utilize their motel and hotel accommodations. The founder of the program has estimated that perhaps 1,000 potential suicides have been averted. For persons in trouble and running away a hotel or motel serves as a logical neutral place. It is a refuge for lonely people, including musicians and would-be actors, among other hopefuls or past hopefuls whose bubbles have burst. Cooper[19] writes that room service may include "3 bourbons, 2 scotch—and one chaplain." Avoiding sanctimonious lectures and drab clerical garb, he says, "Most clergymen are such duds. They come in with the starched frocked approach, and it's hard for a frightened person to relate to that. Christ is my business, and Hollywood is my beat; I try to make these people understand that I really care about them, that Christ cares about them."

The impact made by Louis Schweitzer,[20] a wealthy cigarette manufacturer known for his philanthropic, yet eccentric activities, has been described and serves as an example of how his background, creativity, and money power helped bring about changes. When irritated with radio commercials, he ordered programs be run without interruption. He bought a barber shop so that he could obtain haircuts after hours and a taxi so that he need not wait for service when he wanted it. Often he gave sums of money to persons whose lives he considered would be improved because of it. Finally he ran into an employee of Manhattan's Department of Corrections who told him of thousands of people sitting in jail because they were too poor to pay bail. A subsequent jail tour angered him so that he began an extensive reform program called "Vera" (free bail for those eligible). He argued with criminologists, negotiated with the Mayor, and after six years was able to get the free bail policy written into law (supported by former Attorney General Robert Kennedy) in the form of the Bail Reform Act. It was expanded to the issuing of summonslike traffic tickets for offenses such as disorderly conduct and petty thievery rather than making formal arrests. The Director summarizes[20] the basis of success in the program by saying: "If we had created Vera to deal with the whole administration of justice in the U.S., we would have floundered for a few years and just petered out, but we had something very specific to do."

Although those sciences that attempt to explain the past experiences of man have barely been mastered, there has been developed also a science of futurology—the attempt to predict social developments in advance. This can be combined with the movement of futurists, who attempt to engage the minds and energies of highly skilled persons not only to predict but also to plan for the future to ensure its improvement over the present. Certainly the interest of nurses in changing the future of the health care system and their place in it is not a unique, self-generated activity but a part of the total phenomenon in the culture.

Outcomes

The careful reader may have observed how many of the references are from the general press rather than scholarly works. This is particularly true in regard to examples cited. The reader should be directed toward classic works on politics, and we hope that direction is provided. However, appropriate involvement in the broad political sphere necessitates a process of constant self-education with regard to any and all issues related to health. The flow of thought should go on continuously from a headline, to memory of historical precedent, to questions of unstated options, to discussion with affected groups, and eventual translation of opinion and reaction to action.

What should be the outcomes of reading a book such as this? We will attempt not to violate our own philosophy and tell you what you should do. However, if a reader has persevered thus far, it is possible he or she will be open to suggestions or will have begun to change behavior in one of the following ways. Awareness of data sources should be heightened, and the need to take advantage of the available sources may have been stimulated. The first step in effective participatory democracy is an informed electorate. As a basic student, the reader may have had some exposure to "read the paper and bring in clippings" in a course on community health nursing. That is certainly a good beginning. One should not be afraid of ignorance. A person may read in the paper that a certain bill has passed the legislature and is going to the governor for signature. The importance of the bill to health care is so obvious that the reader assumes he or she is the guilty party who has not paid attention and hesitates to speak to anyone, despite serious reservations about the intent and provisions of the bill. However, that same reader might find, on asking questions, that no significant health professionals know anything about the measure, and it indeed had gone quickly through the legislative process, either by intent of a special interest group or because the lawmakers had failed to appreciate the consequences of their actions.

In knowing to whom one should speak at such a time, the press is again important. After one's own close work associates, a person wishing to enter political processes may not know to whom to turn. Keeping track of those health professionals serving on boards, advisory bodies, or as elected officials of health groups provides a roster of potentially powerful colleagues. One should not further downgrade one's own potential to be heard by those individuals. They sustain themselves by their responsiveness to constituencies. The knowledge that nurses expect representation and might be vocal if not attended to can have a significant impact.

Another group to whom one can always turn are those officials representing one's local area in a city, state, or national legislative body. Surveys have consistently shown that people are largely ignorant regarding such elected officials so that the reader is in good company if unable to name mayor, alderman, state senator, or United States congressman. As with those serving on boards and committees, these representatives depend on constituencies and are aware that they can ill afford to ignore the interests of their populace. They can ignore perhaps one letter or two, but regular correspondence from an informed citizen who shows evidence of being in touch with community groups can scarcely be overlooked. Given the busy life of any professional, it is obvious that one cannot write every official regarding every potentially health-related measure. Each person will probably find time to relate to one level of government broadly or to all levels regarding a narrower range of issues. A network of people who among themselves begin to encompass the whole range of electees and concerns might gradually build up.

Another potential constituency is that of one's patients. If one does a complete assessment of each new patient, one learns something about where and how that person is involved in community affairs. It is certainly not out of line to point out issues of potential significance to health. However, one must certainly do so with great care, providing all individuals with sufficient data on all aspects of the problem so that they can make up their own minds. It is always possible that their decision will be opposite or at least different from that of the nurse. If nurses are not prepared to expect or even foster such a diversity in views, they are violating again those precepts under which this book has been written.

In regard to the partisan political issues, particularly those of election campaigns, it is more difficult to comment on what directions a person might go with additional knowledge. One possibility is to become directly involved with a political party. There are those who feel an urgent need for both women in general and nurses in particular to gain elective office throughout the land. That route is not appropriate for everyone. A possible route, however, is for each nurse, during any campaign, to stimulate questions to candidates that will clarify their stands on health and health-related concerns. This serves the purpose of making the necessary data more in keeping with the philosophy expressed here, rather than proclaiming loudly, "I say vote for X because I'm a nurse and I know."

At a much more personal level each nurse should be more prepared to say "this is where I am" in regard to every health issue. Too many individuals, nurses among them, have followed battles such as that regarding a national health insurance program from a great distance, voicing concern to one another that something potentially bad is in the offing but unable to say what or how or why. In addition to following more knowledgeably the current affairs as reported one might even ask to be placed on the mailing list of one or more legislative committees or administrative bureaus, thus ensuring a steady influx of data and commentary on current issues. Such data might be used entirely for self-education or be shared with others.

On a personal level one should also be in a position to understand more clearly one's own responses and reactions to the organizational structures in which nurses move and the other persons with whom they have contact, especially those from other disciplines. If staff nurses learn about nursing and being a nurse only from within the profession, they may fail completely to understand why male hospital administrators look through them, the rules of the documentation process change around them, and patients remain unhealthy despite them. It takes a good deal more knowledge than an adaptational theory of nursing, complete with basic sciences, to prepare one for the blows the culture continues to deal women—even the professionals' manipulations of power within a bureaucratic structure like hospitals—and the failure of the society to meet the needs of all its members.

In retrospect, this summary has been prepared in a rather hindside-to manner. It is the last-mentioned personal awareness that precedes the search for data, and it is the accumulation of data that precedes useful action at any level. Hopefully the discussion here has started some readers on that long journey.

References

1. Addams, J.: Democracy and social ethics, London, 1902, MacMillan & Co., Ltd., p. 6.
2. Hook, S.: The paradoxes of freedom, Jefferson Memorial Lectures, Berkeley, 1962, University of California Press, p. 308.
3. Meyers, H. A.: Are men equal? New York, 1942, G. P. Putnam's Sons, p. 106.
4. Benedict, R.: Patterns of culture, New York, 1946, Penguin Books, Inc.
5. Mead, M.: Male and female, New York, 1949, William Morrow & Co. Inc., Publishers.
6. Whyte, H., Jr.: The organization man, New York, 1956, Simon & Schuster, Inc.
7. Maslow, A.: New knowledge in human values, New York, 1959, Harper & Row, Publishers.
8. Dewey, J., Bode, B. H., and Smith, T. V.: What is democracy? Norman, Okla., 1939, Cooperative Books.
9. Tead, O.: A case for democracy, New York, 1939, Association Press, p. 46.
10. Brown, J. A. C.: The social psychology of industry, Baltimore, 1962, Penguin Books, Inc.
11. Sprott, W. J. H.: Human groups, Baltimore, 1963, Penguin Books, Inc., p. 188.
12. Walton, J.: Administration and policy-making in education, Baltimore, 1959, Johns Hopkins University Press, p. 60.
13. Halpin, A. W., and Croft, D. B.: Organizational climate of schools, Administrator's Notebook, Chicago. March, 1963. Midwest Administration Center.
14. Groseclose, E.: This handmade item costs just $1 to $4, but who needs it, Wall Street Journal, April 23, 1974.
15. Editorial: That 10-second warning bell, The Spokesman Review, May 19, 1974.
16. Immediate action; Parade Magazine, p. 23, June 9, 1972.
17. Editorial: Surgery is not necessary, The Spokesman Review, May 19, 1974.
18. Malone, D.: Jefferson the President: second term 1805-1809, Boston, 1974, Little, Brown & Co.
19. Cooper, R.: Room service? Send 3 bourbon, 2 scotch—and one chaplain? Wall Street Journal, May 21, 1974.
20. Kivitny, J.: Vera Institute presses for judicial reform one step at a time, Wall Street Journal, July 17, 1973.

INDEX